# THE
# SmartMoney
# GUIDE TO
# LONG-TERM
# INVESTING

*How to Build Real Wealth for Retirement and Other Future Goals*

## NELLIE S. HUANG

## PETER FINCH

JOHN WILEY & SONS, INC.

Published by John Wiley & Sons, Inc., Hoboken, New Jersey.
Published simultaneously in Canada.

SmartMoney is a joint publishing venture of Dow Jones & Company, Inc., and Hearst SM Partnership, a subsidiary of The Hearst Corporation.

For general information on our other products and services, or technical support, please contact our Customer Care Department within the United States at 800-762-2974, outside the United States at 317-572-3993 or fax 317-572-4002.

Wiley also publishes its books in a variety of electronic formats. Some content that appears in print may not be available in electronic books.

*Library of Congress Cataloging-in-Publication Data:*

Huang, Nellie S.
    The SmartMoney guide to long-term investing : how to build real wealth for retirement and other future goals / Nellie S. Huang and Peter Finch.
        p.   cm.
    Includes index.
    ISBN 0-471-15203-X (cloth : alk. paper)
    1. Investments.   2. Finance, Personal.   3. Retirement income.   I. Finch, Peter, 1960–   II. SmartMoney.   III. Title.
HG4521 .H8397   2002
332.024'01—dc21                                                      2002003827

Printed in the United States of America.

10   9   8   7   6   5   4   3   2   1

# CONTENTS

v

# PART FOUR: Life in Retirement

# FOREWORD

Nothing is more valuable to an investor than time, and the more of it the better. That's why forming long-term goals is so important, and why the likelihood of realizing them is so high. Time is on your side.

No doubt you've seen charts that show the remarkable power of interest compounding over time. If not, take a look at your mortgage loan disclosure statement, if you have a mortgage. The total cost of the mortgage—the amount you are obligated to pay the bank by the end of the loan period—demonstrates the power of compounding in reverse. Bankers have known this for centuries.

The gains you will realize by investing for the long term, even at comparatively low annual interest rates, are considerable. But they will be partly offset by inflation, which even in recently tame years has been running at 1 to 2 percent per year. Money market funds give you easy access to cash and don't fluctuate much in value, but in return they barely outpace inflation, or even lag it. Unless you're already very wealthy, you need to do better. And you can do better.

Take stocks. Since the turn of the twentieth century, stocks have earned an average annualized rate of return of nearly 10 percent, far outpacing inflation and every other category of investment asset, including real estate and bonds. This despite two world wars, the Great Depression, numerous recessions, and countless crises of one sort or another. Unless history is about to change radically, this is likely to remain true in the foreseeable future.

Stocks are also the most volatile investment category, as any investor who lived through the past few years of boom and bust can tell you. But another way that time is on your side is that it helps minimize risk. You can afford even volatile swings in the value of your investments if you don't need their cash value anytime soon. How long is soon? Look at it this way: In every 20-year period since 1900, stocks outperformed every other asset class. Cut that period to 10 years, and there are only a few exceptions. In periods of less than 10 years, the risk that stocks won't outperform other assets rises considerably. Still, as long as you plan to hold stocks for a minimum of five years, the odds are very high that you will earn a positive rate of return, even if it isn't the highest possible.

Over the years I've been investing, I've learned some of these lessons the hard way. After the 1987 crash, I held on a few days, then panicked when the initial rally collapsed. I sold at exactly the time I should have been buying. Late in 1998, with the market hitting new highs, I took some profits. Then I felt foolish as the market kept soaring. That cash was burning a hole in my pocket. I ended up buying some stocks at what now seem ridiculously high prices.

Those lessons taught me how difficult it is to time the market, and over the years I have hewed to a long-term, fairly disciplined strategy similar to those outlined in this book. Technology stalwarts Intel and Applied Materials have been the stars of my portfolio, racking up incredible gains over the periods I've owned them, which now exceed 10 years. I have remained heavily weighted in stocks, and I have taken advantage of the recent steep declines to buy more. In the week after September 11, when the market plunged, I heeded my experience in 1987 and was a buyer rather than a seller. Those stocks have been some of my best recent investments.

I've become comfortable with a fairly high level of risk over the years, and the inevitable short-term gyrations of the market have little effect on my sense of well-being. Having recently turned 50, I hope to be investing for at least another 20 years. But I know from conversations with friends and family members that personal investment attitudes and goals vary tremendously, and can change over time.

So what mix of investments is right for you? Time is only one of many variables that bear on that question. If it were easy to answer, there wouldn't be an entire industry of financial advisers. But whomever you may rely on for guidance, there's only one person who can really answer the question, and that person is you. Helping you is the goal of *The SmartMoney Guide to Long-Term Investing: How to Build Real Wealth for Retirement and Other Future Goals.*

Most of us have two looming long-term financial needs: paying for our children's college educations roughly 18 years after they're born, and paying for our own retirement some time after that. An advantage of both is that they force us to think ahead and become long-term investors. If you're starting soon enough, the likelihood that you can pay for your children's education and have a decent retirement is probably far higher than you realize. And even if you're starting late, it's much better late than never. There are ways to maximize your gains even in shorter time spans.

This doesn't need to be especially difficult or unpleasant. On the contrary, I find that long-term investing keeps you alert, stimulated by current events, economic and business news, politics and economic policy, and world affairs, all of which can influence your investment strategies. And it is satisfying to make decisions and take control of your own financial future. Many others have done so, and Peter Finch and Nellie Huang have distilled the wisdom of the most succesful of them to produce this invaluable guide.

I feel we are all lucky to be living at a time of great technological progress, economic innovation, a global move toward free markets, and greater productivity. There are great challenges that remain, of course, and we have been reminded all too vividly of the potential for tragedy. Yet this is an era of great opportunity. I hope this book helps you make the most of it.

JAMES B. STEWART
Editor at Large
*SmartMoney*

# ACKNOWLEDGMENTS

The emphasis on bylines in the journalism world is, at times, unavoidable. But magazines and the articles inside them are the product of many people, from fact-checkers, reporters, and editors to the art and production departments. The same goes for this book. Though only two names are listed as its authors, in fact it is the product of many, many hands. Without the staff of *SmartMoney* past and present—whose ideas, research, and words make up much of what you are about to read—*The SmartMoney Guide to Long-Term Investing* would not have been possible.

NELLIE S. HUANG
PETER FINCH

# INTRODUCTION

**W**hat do you imagine when you picture your retirement? Jet-setting around the world? Hopping between two homes—a condo on the beach and a wintry getaway in the mountains? Or simply living the life of Riley, playing golf or tennis with your buddies as the sun sets?

Whatever your goal, we realize that it's a lot easier to dream of a glorious retirement than it is to actually *do* something about it. It's a daunting concept: Somehow you're going to save enough money to retire on while also putting aside funds for college tuition or a bigger home or even a nice vacation for your long-suffering family every once in a while. Lump in your current monthly mortgage bills, your credit card payments, and those new sneakers your youngster just has to have, and the concept of wealth building almost seems laughable.

But we're here to say that it doesn't have to be that way! The fact is, you can build the kind of wealth you'll need to pay for your long-term goals. It's going to take some time. It's going to take some discipline. But you can do it—and we're here to help.

At *SmartMoney*, we believe the secret of tackling even the most intimidating task is to break it down into discrete steps: Finish one, move on to the next, then the next . . . and before you know it you're done.

That's the approach we've taken with this book as well. In Chapter 1, we'll introduce you to the basics of stocks, bonds, and mutual funds—the building blocks of your wealth-building portfolio. In Chapter 2, you'll come across the first of several worksheets. This one lets you estimate how much you need to save for retirement each year, depending on how luxe a lifestyle you intend to lead. (Don't worry: It's not as scary an exercise as it might seem; the worksheet itself should take you no more than half an hour.) From there we'll help you set up an asset allocation strategy—an investment game plan, in other words—that works for you. We'll give you the names of some outstanding mutual funds that will deliver the kinds of investment returns you need. And we'll introduce you to plenty of real-life retirees, who have some important insights about what life after work is really like.

But that's not all. We've also got a whole section on the best ways to save for that other long-term goal—your kids' college educations—including asset allocations for that part of your portfolio as well.

Can you skip any of these steps and jump straight to what you're most interested in? Absolutely. You don't have to follow every step, for instance, to accelerate your retirement savings, as described in Chapter 6. This book is designed to work as a reference for all investors, no matter what stage of retirement planning you're in, whether it's deciding which funds belong in your 401(k) account or figuring out how to turbocharge your portfolio so you can retire early.

Either way, one thing is for sure: The investment decisions you make today will determine what kind of life you will be able to enjoy once that regular paycheck stops rolling in. Will it be in a Richard Meier–designed beach home in the Hamptons or a split-level in Levittown? Will you spend your afternoons working on your serve or arguing with the Walgreens clerk over whether your coupon for Brawny paper towels has expired?

You decide.

# PART ONE

# THE BUILDING BLOCKS OF WEALTH

# STOCKS, MUTUAL FUNDS, AND BONDS: STARTING AT THE BEGINNING

The stock market has been a scary place lately. Between the tech stock crash of 2000 and the Enron fiasco of 2002, it's enough to make you want to put your retirement savings under a mattress and forget about it.

But you've got to resist that urge with all your will, and here's why: Despite its occasionally stomach-wrenching ups and downs, the stock market is *the* place to be if you're going to build wealth over the long term.

Over the past 76 years, the stock market has grown by an average of nearly 11 percent a year, while a typical savings account accumulated just 2 percent on average every year. Nine percentage points a year is a *huge* difference. And the longer your time horizon, the bigger difference those nine percentage points will make, thanks to the beauty of compounding. After 10 years, $10,000 invested in stocks would be worth $16,204 more than the same amount invested in a savings account; after 25 years, the difference between the two portfolios would have grown to more than $120,000.

The fact is, on average nothing does better than stocks over time. Bonds will do a bit better than a savings account. But over the long term they probably won't improve the return you'll earn on stocks. For a retirement article in *SmartMoney* a couple of years ago, we studied every possible time span going back to the 1920s, testing several different mixes of U.S. stocks, bonds, and cash in a hypothetical tax-deferred account. While we found many 10-, 12-, and 14-year periods in which adding bonds or cash to your holdings resulted in higher gains than a diversified stock portfolio produced (and they were mostly periods that started in the Great Depression), we could find no period longer than 18 years where adding some bond assets improved the outcome.

This is a message *SmartMoney* has been spreading for the past decade. And, we're glad to say, our readers have benefited from it. Back in our premiere issue in April 1992, when the United States was still recovering from a recession and the debilitating savings and loan debacle, we produced an article called "The 10 Stocks for the '90s." Readers who followed our suggestions and bought those 10 stocks have since witnessed gains of better than *560 percent.* (The big winner in that portfolio was semiconductor equipment company Applied Materials, up an amazing 3,336 percent since we wrote about it.)

No, you don't want to have 100 percent of your investments in stock—particularly if you are already nearing retirement age. You want a *mix* of stocks, bonds, and cash. And in Chapter 4, we'll help you select the ideal blend for your needs with our exclusive asset allocation worksheet.

But first, allow us to walk you through the investment basics. Though some people would have you believe otherwise, don't worry: This isn't rocket science. The truth is, investing can be rather simple. Half the battle is understanding the language—some of which, we admit, comes off sounding more like mumbo jumbo than anything else. Once you get the basic concepts down, you'll find it comes pretty easily. So let's get started.

## Stocks

When you buy shares of a company's stock, you are buying a piece of that company. It's as simple as that. Buy even one share of Pfizer and you, as a shareholder, own a tiny sliver of the drug company—and you will get to share in its profits. The more shares you buy, the bigger your stake becomes.

A company's stock price reflects what investors are willing to pay for a piece of that company. Take a look at the chart in Figure 1.1. It tracks the price movement of Pfizer stock from 1997 through early 2002. You can see it had a tremendous run-up in the late 1990s, lifted in large part by blockbuster drugs like the impotency cure-all Viagra and the antidepressant

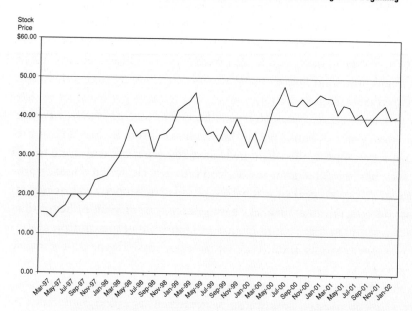

**FIGURE 1.1**　Pfizer stock, March 1997 to January 2002

Zoloft. But in the final fever pitch of the bull market in tech stocks (and as interest rates began to rise), the stock went out of favor with investors—only to rebound in mid-2000 when investors sought safer havens as the tech rally ended.

Whether it's Pfizer or any other stock, the supreme measure by which companies are valued is their earnings. Wall Street is obsessed with them. Companies report their earnings, also known as profits, four times a year, and investors pore over these numbers—expressed as earnings per share—trying to gauge a company's present health and future potential. The stock market rewards both fast earnings growth and stable earnings growth. But it has little patience for companies with declining earnings or unexplained losses. Companies that surprise Wall Street with bad quarterly reports almost always see sharp declines in their stock prices.

The worst-case scenario is that a company goes bankrupt and the value of your stock investment evaporates altogether. Happily, that's rare. More often, a company will run into short-term problems that depress the price of its stock for what seems an agonizingly long period of time.

Along with ownership, a share of stock also gives you the right to vote on management issues. Company executives work at the behest of shareholders, who are represented by an elected board of directors. By law, the goal of management is to increase the value of the corporation's equity. If it doesn't happen, you and your fellow shareholders can vote to have management removed.

How do you know when it's a good time to buy a particular stock? We recently wrote an entire book on that subject (*The SmartMoney Stock Picker's Bible*, John Wiley & Sons, 2002). But the short answer is this: What we're looking for is opportunity. We don't necessarily want stocks that are cheap (because there's often a good reason for that), but we do want them to be trading at a discount to their normal levels. This can happen during times of market distress, say, or an industry going through an inevitable down cycle, or even a company that's been beaten down but is about to turn around.

What we're talking about is closer to "value" investing than just about any other style. In case you're not familiar with the term, you should know that the investing world is divided into two broad groups: growth and value. Growth investors seek stocks that are growing earnings and sales at annual rates that beat the market, and they are willing to pay a hefty price for such a stock—generally speaking. Cisco Systems in the late 1990s was a classic growth stock. Its earnings and revenue were growing 30 to 40 percent a year, easily double what you'd find at the average company. But that came at a price. Cisco stock had a price/earnings (P/E) ratio of 50 or 60, again easily double what you'd pay for most stocks. (A price/earnings ratio is the price of the stock divided by its annual earnings per share.) For more on this and other important valuation measures, see the Glossary in the back of this book.

Value investors, on the other hand, want bargains, or stocks that trade at a discount—and that discount can be measured in a variety of ways against the market or a stock's peer group. We don't mean a low price, necessarily. A $10 stock might seem very expensive to a value investor if the company has no assets and no earnings.

We would never suggest you turn your back entirely on growth. After all, investors are never going to get excited about a company (and bid its stock price up) if they have zero hope for any earnings growth. This is why the *SmartMoney* style of investing is in effect a hybrid: To us, the ideal stock will have a low P/E ratio and a rapid rate of earnings growth. It's an investing style some call growth at a reasonable price (GARP).

But we can't stress enough the importance of that value underpinning, for study after study shows that value trumps growth over time. If you had invested $10,000 in large-company value stocks in 1974, you'd have $639,200 in 2001, according to a well-respected research outfit called the Leuthold Group. But pity the investor who put the same amount in big-name growth stocks: A $10,000 investment in 1974 would be worth just $405,500, a shortfall of nearly 37 percent.

Value wins out among small and midsize companies, too. Another influential study, conducted by, among others, Josef Lakonishok, a professor of finance at the University of Illinois at Urbana–Champaign, examined all the companies listed on the New York Stock Exchange and the American Stock Exchange between 1968 and 1990. Deep value stocks beat their growth-stock counterparts by an average of 10 percent per year over most five-year periods.

But performance isn't the only reason we like value investing. Buying cheap stocks requires a certain amount of discipline, and that can save even the most inexperienced investors from the biggest pitfall of impulse investing: themselves. All too often, investors let panic take over when the market starts to tank—they sell when they should buy—and they let greed tell them to buy when the market is climbing, which is just when they should sell.

Most would-be growth moguls wind up selling off their winners too early and hanging on to their losers too long. According to a study of discount brokerage customers conducted by University of California, Davis finance professor Terry Odean, the stocks investors sold from 1987 to 1993 went on to outperform the stocks they held by more than three percentage points a year. "People tend to get excited about growth stocks. They build up expectations, and they end up getting quite disappointed," Lakonishok says.

# Big Stocks

Market capitalization—market cap for short, or market value—is a term you'll come across a lot. This is simply the number of shares a company has outstanding in the market multiplied by the share price. If a company has 5 million shares outstanding and each one trades for $5, its "market cap" would be $25 million.

As the name suggests, large-capitalization stocks are the biggest players in the market. How big? A market value of $5 billion is generally considered the low end of this group, while behemoths like Citigroup and Exxon Mobil weigh in at more than $225 billion. Then there's General Electric, the biggest of them all, which at the beginning of 2002 had a market capitalization greater than $382 billion. (See Table 1.1.) Taken together, stocks with market values over $5 billion account for 80 percent of the market's total $12.8 trillion in value, according to the Center for Research in Security Prices. (See Table 1.1.)

These companies play an especially significant role in driving the economy. That's why everybody pays so much attention to them. The two most watched stock market indexes—the Dow Jones Industrial Average and the Standard & Poor's 500-stock index (S&P 500)—are both composed of large-cap stocks. The Dow tracks 30 of the biggest stocks. The S&P tracks 500 companies with an average market value of $21.2 billion.

The bigger you are, the harder it is to grow quickly, so large caps don't tend to expand as fast as your average technology upstart. But what they lack in flash, they make up in heft. The classic "blue chip" has steady revenue, a consistent stream of earnings, and a dividend. It also has critical mass, which means it can withstand ill economic winds better than its smaller cousins.

### TABLE 1.1   MARKET VALUE OF LARGE-CAP STOCKS*

| Company Name | Market Value as of Mid-2001 |
| --- | --- |
| 1. General Electric | $382 billion |
| 2. Microsoft | $315 billion |
| 3. Exxon Mobil | $282 billion |
| 4. Wal-Mart Stores | $277 billion |
| 5. Pfizer | $259 billion |
| 6. Citigroup | $227 billion |
| 7. AIG | $193 billion |
| 8. Intel | $192 billion |
| 9. Johnson & Johnson | $186 billion |
| 10. IBM | $169 billion |

*As of February 28, 2002.
*Source:* SmartMoney.com.

Because of their size and stability, large-cap stocks are not generally speculative in nature and appeal to a more cautious investor. That's not to say they can't run into serious trouble, but they tend to grow along predictable trend lines and, since they are well known to Wall Street analysts, their problems often come with ample warning. Big companies also tend to pay regular dividends, which act as ballast by attracting income-oriented, long-term investors. Don't be fooled: Large caps can experience jarring price swings. But there's no doubt they are less volatile than small, hot-growth stocks.

Lower risk comes with a price, however. Except during periods of rampant uncertainty, large-cap stocks tend to produce slightly lower returns than small caps (10.5 percent annually vs. 11.7 percent).

## Small Stocks

Small-capitalization stocks are fleet of foot. Or at least that's their reputation. There are plenty of small, stodgy banks and rust-belt manufacturers in the group, and there are periods when small caps don't perform so well because investors want bigger, more stable names. But companies with a market value below $1 billion can grow more quickly than bigger companies, often producing double-digit annual returns for investors.

There are several indexes that track small-cap stocks. Probably the best known is the Russell 2000, which follows 2,000 companies with an average capitalization of $530 million. Companies in Standard & Poor's small-cap index, the S&P 600, average about $524 million in market value.

Small-cap companies tend to have correspondingly small revenues. And that means many of them have just started up or are poised to expand their markets, either geographically or with new products. EPIQ Systems is a good example. The Kansas City, Kansas, software solutions provider had a market value of $264 million in early 2002. Yet, because it was so small, it was able to increase its earnings at a much faster rate than could software giant Microsoft Corporation, which had a market value of more than $300 billion.

Microsoft needs no introduction—more than 80 percent of all computer users work off its operating system, Windows. Over the five years between 1997 and 2002, its stock price gained 185 percent, fueled by earnings growth of 27 percent. Not bad for a large cap. But over the same period,

EPIQ's stock gained more than 1,264 percent as its earnings soared, on average, 44 percent per year. (See Figure 1.2.)

Of course, EPIQ was also more volatile than Microsoft. And the smaller company ought to be much more vulnerable than the mighty Microsoft during an economic downturn. But EPIQ's incredible performance over the past few years would have been a great sweetener to any diversified portfolio.

Little companies are significantly more volatile than big companies—meaning there's much more downside risk. And they don't pay dividends as often, a real detriment for investors who want some income. There are other risks as well. When the economy is uncertain, investors looking for safety and stability will often abandon small caps for blue chips. Also, because small companies have fewer shares outstanding, their price movement is necessarily more erratic. When good news hits, investors clamoring to get in will drive the price up quickly. When bad news hits, the opposite is true, and it can sometimes be difficult to get out. Because fewer Wall Street analysts cover these stocks, there's also less reliable in-

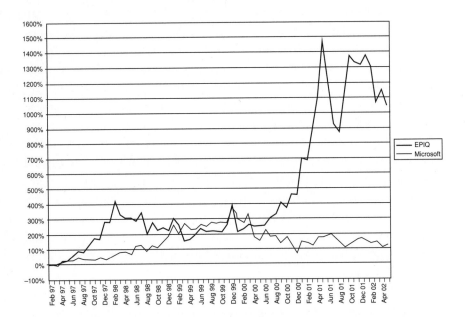

**FIGURE 1.2**    Percentage change of Microsoft versus EPIQ

formation on them. That means bad news can strike out of the blue, pounding stock prices overnight.

For all of that, however, most investors—especially young ones who have the time to make up any losses—want exposure to small caps. As we saw with EPIQ, the upside potential is simply too great to pass up.

## Foreign Stocks

At a time when the world economy has become increasingly interconnected, investors can hardly afford to ignore foreign stocks. There's too much opportunity out there and too many ways to tap it. And since the economies of the world's different regions tend to boom and bust in cycles that often offset each other, international stocks can provide excellent diversification for a portfolio heavy on U.S. equities.

Like stocks on the U.S. exchanges, foreign stocks vary in size and do not move as a single group. So you can't really say how a "Japanese stock" behaves, or how an "Italian stock" will perform. It's also true that foreign companies are subject to different rules of accounting and far less government scrutiny than U.S. investors are used to. It all adds up to this: Investing abroad is more complicated than buying stocks in the United States.

That's why most U.S. investors get international exposure either by investing in large, well-established overseas companies like Finland's Nokia or by putting their money in professionally managed mutual funds that have the expertise and resources to assemble winning portfolios from many different foreign stocks. (We'll have more on mutual funds in the next section.)

International markets are nothing if not volatile. They are highly susceptible to changes in foreign currency exchange rates, as well as shifts in regional and global economies. As the global economy slowed in 2000, for instance, stocks in most areas of the world slowed, too. But international markets are rarely that monolithic. Usually, one region is up while another is down.

A dramatic example of that sort of divergence came in 1998 during the meltdown among the Asian economies. Economic turmoil in a region that was once the world's darling taught many investors about the treachery of betting your money abroad. Japan's Nikkei index lost almost 40 percent between June 1997 and October 1998, as trading partners throughout the Pacific Rim imploded due to financial mismanagement and corruption. The ripple effects were felt worldwide, as companies with exposure to those markets lost revenues.

At the same time, however, European markets blossomed as the Continent came closer to true economic union and a rash of U.S.-style corporate restructurings began to pay dividends. One region collapsed; another made up for it. That's why it makes sense to diversify your foreign investments, or let a professional money manager do it for you.

## Tech Stocks

We live in an age when technology can change our lives seemingly overnight, and that phenomenon invariably creates rich new markets and explosive earnings growth for countless companies.

Of course, as investors learned in 2000 and 2001, there's a dark side to all that opportunity. Fearful of an economic slowdown, investors abandoned growth stocks and looked for safety in less volatile sectors like pharmaceuticals. In 2001, profitless Internet stocks like Amazon.com felt the worst impact. But even big, established technology companies like Cisco Systems and Sun Microsystems took a drubbing.

Clearly, new markets are by nature filled with danger, and that means actual earnings—or the prospects for future earnings—can fluctuate wildly. News of a personal computer (PC) sales slowdown at Christmas can cause investors to flee any number of related stocks—from PC maker Gateway to Novellus Systems, which makes the equipment that fabricates the chips that power the PCs that Gateway sells. Investors will return to the good companies once the dust has cleared. But unless you have patience and staying power, such crises can easily wipe you out.

As the tech roller-coaster ride of the past few years has demonstrated, technology stocks as a group tend to be more volatile than the broader market. Still, a selection of high-tech blue chips should be in everyone's long-term portfolio, since the volatility they do exhibit is easily offset by their superior growth over time.

# Mutual Funds

Whether you like it or not, mutual funds will probably play a big role in your retirement savings. Why? Aside from company stock, most 401(k) plans offer only funds as investment options.

But that's not the only reason to pay attention to funds. While stock picking can be fun and can boost your returns significantly (as long as you invest in great companies), the truth is, most individual investors find it difficult to build and maintain a well-diversified portfolio. To do it right, you might have to keep an eye on as many as 60 different stocks at once. Some people thrive on that sort of thing; others lack the time, interest, or experience to give a complex portfolio the attention it demands. Others may not have the money.

That's where mutual funds—pools of stocks or bonds that are managed by professional investors—come in.

At the moment there are nearly as many mutual funds out there as there are common stocks—over 9,000 at last count. Staggering, to say the least. All told, these funds comprise more than $4 trillion in assets, two times the 2002 U.S. federal budget. And unfortunately, not all of them make good investments. More than 75 percent routinely fail to beat the S&P 500 index over 10-year periods. Of course, there are times when mutual funds excel. Over the past three years through early 2002, 70 percent of equity funds have outperformed the S&P by an average of 8 percentage points a year. Over the long run, however, most mutual funds don't keep pace with the S&P 500.

Clearly you can help yourself a great deal by choosing the right funds. But to do so you'll need to learn some basics first: How do mutual funds work? What should you look out for in terms of fees and expenses? And how do you sort through the different types of funds?

Like stocks, funds come in all shapes and sizes, from Fidelity's $77 billion Magellan fund—the largest in the country—to the $1 million Oak Ridge Small Cap Equity fund. Here's how they work: Typically, a sponsor company like Fidelity or Vanguard rounds up money and pays a portfolio manager to buy securities based on a specific investing strategy. The company then sells shares in the fund to the general public. The large-cap growth fund Fidelity Magellan, for instance, invests in large companies with fast-growing earnings. But Fidelity's Small Cap Stock fund invests in smaller companies.

When you buy shares in a mutual fund, you own a small percentage of the total portfolio. Depending on the fund, you can own a piece of 20 to 500 different stocks. A $1,000 investment in Oakmark Select in late 2001, for instance, would have bought you just over 37 shares in the fund. Because the fund owns 21 stocks, your small investment would have bought you a level of diversification that would have been impossible to achieve on your own with such a small sum of money. You may have to pay a fee for the service, but a good fund offers plenty of advantages. Ideally, the pros have years of experience and are given access to piles of industry and company research. Their expertise means you don't have to keep track of dozens of stocks on your own. And unlike a bank certificate of deposit or an annuity, a mutual fund investment is completely liquid, meaning you can get in or out at any time simply by picking up the telephone.

Today there are funds geared to just about any investment objective—from funds that buy only Internet-related stocks to those that invest in Latin American utilities. In fact, Morningstar, the Chicago-based fund database firm, tracks 29 distinct kinds of equity funds—and that includes the newly hatched breed of exchange-traded funds.

For investors, this diversity provides the opportunity to tailor a portfolio of funds to meet particular objectives. Take a 55-year-old man eyeing retirement in a few years. Seeking some growth but not much risk, he may put part of his money into a steady, large-company equity fund, while protecting the bulk of his nest egg in a money-market fund with lower—but virtually guaranteed—returns. A 30-year-old woman, on the other hand, has years to make up for any short-term investment losses. So she may want to put most of her money in a more aggressive, small-company equity fund that promises more risk, but higher returns.

You don't have to understand all 29 categories to invest in funds. The truth is, there are only a few broad categories of funds that really matter to most people. And if you are investing through your retirement plan at work, you'll probably be limited to those groups, anyway. In Table 1.2 you'll find what we feel are some of the essential fund categories to know about and how they stack up next to each in terms of average return, risk, and expense ratios.

One more thing before we move on: Every fund has to publish a document called a prospectus that states clearly its strategy, or investment style.

## TABLE 1.2    ESSENTIAL FUND CATEGORIES

| Type of Fund | 10-Year Return through Early 2002 | Standard Deviation | Expense Ratio |
| --- | --- | --- | --- |
| Blend | 10.98 | 16.63 | 1.26 |
| Bond | 6.19 | 4.57 | 1.10 |
| Financial | 16.89 | 21.20 | 1.67 |
| Foreign | 5.85 | 16.34 | 1.64 |
| Growth | 10.52 | 19.33 | 1.43 |
| Index | 10.25 | 14.26 | .76 |
| Large-cap | 10.61 | 16.93 | 1.34 |
| Microcap | 12.59 | 16.87 | 2.19 |
| Mid-cap | 10.74 | 21.94 | 1.48 |
| Money market | 4.43 | .33 | .65 |
| Small-cap | 11.05 | 21.54 | 1.54 |
| Technology | 14.08 | 39.54 | 1.75 |
| Utilities | 8.81 | 13.46 | 1.44 |
| Value | 11.94 | 15.00 | 1.42 |
| World | 6.93 | 18.34 | 1.78 |

*Source:* Morningstar.com. Reprinted with permission.

Managers have been known to drift from this strategy—something you have to watch out for—but the good ones toe the line.

## Index Funds

First, what's an index? It's a grouping of stocks chosen to represent a certain market segment. The S&P 500 index, for instance, is comprised of 500 large-company stocks. The Nasdaq Composite index is heavy on technology companies. And the Dow Jones Industrial Average contains 30 large, kind of "old economy" companies. You can't watch the evening news without finding out about how one of these indexes performed in any given day in the market. They—and many others—are used by investors and together function as a barometer of the market as a whole.

An index fund, then, attempts to mimic the performance of a particular group of stocks. An S&P 500 index fund (e.g., the Vanguard 500 Index) will buy shares in the same 500 companies that comprise the S&P 500 index. Sounds boring, but it works. In mid-2000, the Vanguard 500 Index fund was the biggest fund in the world, with $107 billion in assets, largely because investors flocked to its exceptional 21.75 percent five-year annual return. By merely copying the S&P 500, it beat 93 percent of the "active" fund managers—those picking and choosing stocks instead of mirroring an index—over the same period.

Index funds have a pair of really important advantages over actively managed funds: low expenses and tax efficiency. Since the fund manager doesn't have to go out and hunt around for stocks, these funds are relatively cheap to run. The Vanguard 500 Index fund, for example, has an incredibly low annual fee of 0.18 percent of your investment. An average actively managed large-cap fund like Alliance Growth may charge six times that much. Meanwhile, low turnover limits the amount of capital gains registered by index funds, which lessens their tax liability for investors. Small wonder that many investors find that index funds are by far the easiest, most effective way to go—particularly if your goal is long-term growth without having to pay much attention to your holdings.

## Actively Managed Funds

Every fund manager approaches the market from a slightly different angle, but there are three broad archetypes when it comes to investment strategy: growth, value, and blend. Let's walk through each one now.

### Growth Funds

As their name implies, these funds tend to look for the fastest-growing companies in the market. Growth managers are willing to take more risk and even pay a premium for their stocks in an effort to build a portfolio of companies with above-average earnings momentum or price appreciation.

For example, biotech firm Chiron and the drug company Forest Laboratories are generally considered expensive stocks, because their prices have been bid high relative to their profits. But because they enjoy vibrant markets and have rapid earnings growth, top-performing managers like Richard Freeman of Smith Barney Aggressive Growth know that investors crave these supercharged growth stocks and will keep piling into them as long as the growth keeps up. But if the growth slows, watch out—the more momentum a stock has, the harder it is likely to fall if and when the news turns bad.

That's why growth funds are the most volatile of the three investment styles. It's also why expenses and turnover (which leads to greater taxes for investors) are also higher. For these reasons, only aggressive investors, or those with enough time to make up for short-term market losses, should buy shares in these funds.

## VALUE FUNDS

These funds like to invest in companies that the market has overlooked. Managers like Marty Whitman of Third Avenue Value search for stocks that have become undervalued (priced low relative to their earnings potential).

Sometimes a stock has run into a short-term problem that will eventually be fixed and forgotten. Or maybe the company is too small or obscure to attract much notice. In any event, the manager makes a judgment that there's more potential there than the market has recognized. His bet is that the price will rise as others come around to the same conclusion.

Whitman, for instance, bought passive-component manufacturer AVX in late 1998 before it was discovered by the rest of Wall Street. The stock rose 198.3 percent in 1999 and still traded at 28 times the past 12-month earnings—a steal when you consider that peer Analog Devices registered similar performance while trading at 85 times earnings.

The big risk with value funds is that the undiscovered gems they try to spot sometimes remain undiscovered. That can depress results for extended periods of time. Volatility, however, is quite low, and if you choose a good fund, the risk of lousy returns should be minimal. Also, because these fund managers tend to buy stocks and hold them until they turn around, expenses and turnover are low. Add it up, and value funds are most suitable for more conservative, tax-averse investors.

## BLEND FUNDS

These portfolios can go across the board. They might, for instance, invest in both high-growth telecom stocks and cheaply priced automotive companies. As such, they are difficult to classify in terms of risk. The Vanguard

500 Index fund invests in every company in the S&P 500 and could therefore qualify as a blend. But because it's also a large-cap fund, it tends to be steady. The Legg Mason Special Investment fund is more aggressive, with heavy weightings in technology and financials. To know whether a particular blend fund is right for your needs, you'll probably have to look at the fund's holdings.

## International Funds

When it comes to risk, some foreign funds are fairly tame; others can make your hair stand on end. Consider the experience of the summer of 1998, when the Asian economies fell like dominoes and plundered stocks in the region. Funds like Pioneer Emerging Markets and Ivy Developing Markets, with heavy exposure to Asia, got hammered. Even when foreign economies are doing reasonably well, currency fluctuations can have a negative effect on stock prices.

Of course, economic and currency risk can also swing very strongly in a positive direction. So, as always, diversification is the key to managing risk. Funds investing overseas fall into four basic categories: world, foreign, country-specific, and emerging-market. The wider the reach of the fund, the less risky it is likely to be.

### WORLD FUNDS

World funds are the most diverse of the four categories, but that's true largely because they're able to invest in any region of the world, and that includes the United States. As such, they don't actually offer as much diversification as a good foreign fund (which cannot invest in U.S. companies). A prime example: Pimco RCM Global Small Cap, which is 50 percent invested in the United States and Canada, 23 percent in Europe, 8 percent in Japan, 2.6 percent in the Pacific Rim, and the rest in smaller regions. World funds tend to be the safest international-stock investments, but that's because they typically lean on better-known U.S. stocks.

### FOREIGN FUNDS

These funds invest most of their assets outside the United States. Depending on the countries selected for investment, foreign funds can range from relatively safe to more risky. Fidelity Diversified International, for instance, has its assets spread over 35 different countries, many of which are in Europe. In early 2002, Oakmark International Small Cap, on the other hand, had significant exposure (23 percent of the portfolio) to some of the most traditionally volatile regions in the world: Japan, Hong Kong, and South Korea. It is wise to choose a fund with the best balance, or make sure the manager has done a good job of moving in and out of regions profitably.

## COUNTRY-SPECIFIC FUNDS

These funds invest in one country or region of the world. That kind of concentration makes them particularly volatile. If you pick the right country—Japan in 1999, for example—the returns can be substantial. The average Japan fund, according to Morningstar, returned a whopping 120 percent that year. But pick the wrong one, and watch out. Only the most daring investors should venture into this territory.

## EMERGING-MARKET FUNDS

Emerging-market funds are the most volatile. They invest in undeveloped regions of the world, which have enormous growth potential, but also pose significant risks—political upheaval, corruption, and currency collapse, to name just a few. Don't go near these funds with anything but money you are willing to lose. Why? Over the past five years, the average emerging-market fund is down more than 3 percent. Still, these funds do pack a punch once in a while: In 1993 and 1999 these types of funds posted better than 70 percent returns.

## SECTOR FUNDS

Sector funds do what their name implies: They invest in stocks in a particular segment—or sector—of the market. A fund like Firsthand Technology Leaders, for instance, buys only tech companies for its portfolio. Munder NetNet cuts it even finer by holding only Internet-related stocks. Fidelity has a whole stable of sector funds from Fidelity Select Insurance to Fidelity Select Wireless. The idea is to allow investors to place bets on specific industries or sectors whenever they think that industry might heat up.

While such a strategy might appear to throw diversification to the wind, it doesn't entirely. It's true that investing in a sector fund definitely focuses your exposure on a certain industry. But it can give you diversification within that industry that would be hard to achieve on your own. How? By spreading your investment across a broad representation of stocks. Fidelity Select Financial Services fund holds 122 different stocks; the Evergreen Health Care fund includes 112; and T. Rowe Price's Media & Telecommunications fund has 55.

Of course, such concentrated portfolios can produce tremendous gains or losses, depending on whether your chosen sector is in or out of favor. In 1999, Firsthand Technology Leaders soared 152.6 percent because software and semiconductor companies were hot. Real estate fund Franklin Real Estate lost 5.6 percent in the same year because the category sputtered.

Because of this specialization, any sector fund carries more risk than a generalized fund. But some sectors are clearly more volatile than others. For example, Vanguard Utilities Income fund, which invests primarily in staid electrical companies, has about one-third the volatility of PBHG Technology & Communications fund, which buys supercharged software makers.

## Charges and Fees

If there is a single drawback to investing in mutual funds, it's the corrosive effect that fees and taxes have on returns. If you aren't careful, management expenses and capital gains taxes can shave hundreds—if not thousands—of dollars from your returns over the years.

### LOADS: FRONT- AND BACK-END

A load is simply a sales charge—like the commission you pay when you buy and sell shares in a stock—that is tacked onto the price of a mutual fund to compensate the broker or financial adviser who sells it to you. Loads work in two ways: You pay them either up front when you buy your shares or later when you sell them, depending on the fund. Of the 9,543 equity funds in existence in early 2002, 5,207 (55 percent) charged a load; 4,336, or 45 percent, did not.

A front-end load is charged when you buy your shares. It typically ranges between 1 percent and 5.75 percent of your initial investment, and some funds charge you again for reinvesting your dividends in new shares of the fund. A back-end load is a fee the fund charges when you sell—or redeem—your shares. These deferred fees are essentially a tactic to keep you invested in the fund for the long term. A typical scenario would work this way: In the first year of ownership, you'd pay a charge in the range of 4 percent to 5.75 percent if you sold out of the fund. After that, the percentage declines each year until it disappears altogether after about six to eight years.

The obvious problem with a load is that it immediately trims your investment return. That might be acceptable if you believe the fund will post such superior returns that the load will pay for itself over time. But since there are plenty of quality no-load funds out there, why pay a fee if you don't have to? We never say never when it comes to paying fees, especially when it comes to some top-rate managers, but at *SmartMoney* for the most part we tend to recommend no-load funds.

## EXPENSE RATIOS

Even a no-load fund duns its shareholders for the costs of doing business. These include everything from the advisory fee paid the fund manager to administrative costs like printing and postage. These costs are expressed as an expense ratio, which is an annual percentage of the fund's average net assets under management. Published fund returns are usually calculated net of annual expenses, but you should definitely pay attention to these costs. When you get your statement at the end of the year, you can count on the costs being skimmed off the top.

There's a temptation to associate high expenses with good fund management. Some people figure it's like anything else: You get what you pay for. The fact is, however, that low-expense funds are more likely to outperform high-expense funds over the long haul. Recently, the average expense ratio for domestic equity funds was about 1.4 percent. For fixed-income funds it was about 1.1 percent. Foreign funds have higher expense ratios, averaging around 1.7 percent. There is no reason to buy funds with expense ratios higher than that.

## 12B-1 FEES

Charges known as 12b-1 fees are included in the expense ratio, but are often talked about—and listed—separately. They go to pay the fund's marketing and distribution expenses. These fees are charged in addition to a front- or back-end load, and you'll find that many no-load funds charge them, too. Note that once a 12b-1 fee rises above 0.25 percent, the fund is no longer considered a no-load. Our advice? If a 12b-1 fee puts a fund's expense ratio above the average for that class of fund, think twice before buying.

Does it sound like we're obsessing over nickles and dimes? We suggest you check out SmartMoney.com's interactive Fund Fee Analyzer to see for yourself how much a high load or expense ratio can eat into returns.

Here's an example: Say you invest $10,000 in a fund that charges 4.7 percent every time you put money in (a front-end load), and a 1.5 percent expense ratio per year (to pay management fees). Both charges are about average for the fund industry. After one year, assuming a steady 10 percent return, the fund will have made you $1,000 in profit, but after fees (about $660), your profit dwindles to $340. That means fees swallowed 66 percent of your profits in one year. After five years, that percentage diminishes to 29 percent, but after 20 years, you'll still have paid a whopping $18,522 in fees, which will diminish your overall profit of $57,143 to just $38,621.

## Share Classes

A single fund may have up to five clones—and each one carries charges and fees that are levied in slightly different ways. Ever wonder what all those As, Bs, and Cs mean that you often see after the names of some funds? Those letters indicate the different share classes of a mutual fund—the different ways charges are assessed. Although these classes are not standardized, they primarily apply to load funds and determine the various ways that investors can pay the sales charge. For example, A shares traditionally indicate a front-end load, while B shares most often indicate a back-end load. Other share classes include C shares, which usually incorporate a small back-end load and the maximum 12b-1 fee.

## Taxes

Think of a fund manager as a proxy for you as an investor. It stands to reason, then, that when he or she sells a stock for gain, it becomes a taxable event. Of course, a keen fund manager will offset that gain by a loss (i.e., by selling a losing stock), if at all possible. But if at the end of the year, the sum of all transactions adds up to an overall gain, guess who pays the tax bill? You.

These gains are paid out in the form of taxable distributions. There are a few things worse than ending the year with a fat one you weren't expecting. It's even more bitter when the gain falls into the short-term category—a big problem with fund managers who trade often. Short-term gains are taxed as regular income instead of at the lower, 20 percent tax levied on long-term capital gains.

A high turnover ratio can be a sign of a high capital gains distribution further down the line. And clearly, one way to avoid this potential problem is to be wary of managers who trade a lot. A fund with a turnover ratio of, say, 500 percent indicates that the average holding in the fund lasted less than three months. And all that trading could produce a capital gains liability for you, unless the manager is able to offset his or her gains with losses.

That said, quick trading isn't always the issue. As seen recently, funds with substantial shareholder redemptions also can produce capital gains liabilities. For example, the Credit Suisse Japan Small Company fund plunged in 2000 after triple-digit returns in 1999. As a result, an outsized proportion of investors redeemed their shares, causing the fund to sell stocks to make the payments. Remaining shareholders then had to swallow a whopping 55 percent capital gains distribution.

## Bonds

Think of a bond as an IOU. Buy one and you are in effect lending money to the issuer—whether it's the U.S. Treasury or US Airways. The issuer promises to pay you interest until the bond is due, at which point you'll get your principal back.

Bonds, with their steady stream of income, can add much-needed ballast to an otherwise volatile long-term portfolio. Here are the main types of bonds you should consider buying. We'll help you decide how much exposure to bonds you want in Chapter 4, when we discuss your ideal asset allocation.

# Buying Directly from the U.S. Treasury

If you are just starting out, you can simply buy five-year Treasury bonds, or—if you have considerable assets allocated for bonds—you can put together a so-called ladder of Treasurys. We'll show you how in a moment. Either way, your best bet for buying bonds is the government's commission-free Treasury Direct program, which allows you to bypass brokers and their fees. An application to open an account may be obtained online by linking to the Treasury Direct web site (www.treasurydirect.gov), by contacting your nearest Federal Reserve Bank, or by calling 800-722-2678.

Two-, three-, five-, and ten-year notes are available for a $1,000 minimum investment. You can set up an account online. If for some reason you need to sell the Treasurys in this account before they mature, you will have to have them transferred to a broker, who will charge at least $50 per transaction. In addition, Treasury Direct accounts of $100,000 or more face an annual $25 maintenance fee.

# Agency Bonds

Also extremely safe and liquid, but offering a slightly higher yield, are government-agency bonds issued by the likes of the Tennessee Valley Authority, the Farm Credit Financial Assistance Corporation, the Federal National Mortgage Association (FNMA), and the Government National Mortgage Association (GNMA). (These debentures should not be confused with the mortgage-backed bonds that are also issued by FNMA and GNMA; mortgage-backed securities are extremely sensitive to fluctuations in interest rates and should be avoided.)

It's hard, however, to gain any edge with these bonds over Treasurys. That's because they're generally available only through brokers and thus incur commission costs that cut into their yield. How much? The standard retail brokerage fee comes out to 0.5 percent, or, in the lingo of the bond world, 50 basis points. Even if you have $100,000 to invest and negotiate a lower commission, perhaps 20 basis points, the advantage over Treasurys will probably come to only around $50 a year.

The exception is if you have a very large portfolio and can sink perhaps $1 million into agency bonds; you might then be able to get the institutional commission rate of just 10 basis points. Or, at a more modest level, you might be able to hook up with a financial adviser who specializes in making bulk government-agency bond purchases directly from banks, lumping clients' investments together in order to build million-dollar packages of agency debentures.

## Muni Bonds

Investors with substantial income should also consider combining tax-free municipal bonds with their Treasurys. While the stated yields of munis are lower than those of Treasurys, the effective return for investors in high tax brackets is almost always better. As with Treasurys, individual muni bonds can also be laddered (a technique of diversifying your bond portfolio across dates of maturity) to limit your interest-rate exposure. But because they tend to trade in fairly large lots (usually $25,000) and because, as a precaution against default risk, investors should spread their money among a variety of different locales, building a muni portfolio requires a commitment of $100,000 at a bare minimum.

If you don't have enough now to build a muni ladder, the next best option is to look to a series of municipal-bond mutual funds. The best are Vanguard's Municipal Limited-Term Tax-Exempt and Intermediate-Term Tax-Exempt funds, which both have a minimum initial investment of $3,000. They maintain a low 0.19 percent expense ratio and are run with minimal maturity fluctuation and risk taking.

## What about Corporates?

While investors have traditionally been steered to these vehicles because they offer higher interest income than government bonds, we are dubious about endorsing them. In part, it's a question of costs eating into those higher yields. First there are the taxes: Income from corporates is fully taxed at all levels. If your state and local rates (which are not applicable to government bonds) are a mere 6 percent, that would cut the effective return of an 8 percent yield to 7.5 percent. Next come the transaction costs: both brokerage commissions and the cut taken by the bond dealers (known as the spread). All told, they can easily eat up 1 percent or more of your investment.

Perhaps most important, though, is that the best bonds are usually callable by the issuer, meaning the corporation can, at its discretion, pay off its obligation at a stated price and stop paying interest. That becomes a heads-you-win, tails-I-lose proposition for investors. If interest rates decline and the value of the bonds goes up, the corporation may call them, disrupting your expected income stream and cutting off a potential capital gain. Meanwhile, if interest rates rise, you are stuck holding a less valuable security that is yielding below-market rates.

## Up the Ladder

Diversification is as important in bond investing as it is in stock investing. It's best to spread your risk over a series of different maturities, while maintaining an average maturity of your liking in your portfolio. The best way to do that is to set up a ladder of Treasury bonds—in essence, a series of bonds with a range of maturities.

Here's how it works: You buy equal amounts of Treasurys due to mature in one year, three years, five years, seven years, and nine years. That portfolio would have an average maturity of five years (1 + 3 + 5 + 7 + 9 equals 25, divided by 5, equals 5). The next year, when the first batch comes due, you would reset the ladder by putting the money into new 10-year notes. Your portfolio would then have an average maturity of six years.

Two years later, when the next round of notes matures, you would buy more 10-years, continuing to buy new 10-years whenever a note matures. That would always keep the average maturity in the five- to six-year range.

One advantage to this scheme is that you don't need to worry about fluctuations in interest rates—especially if the ladder you construct has notes coming due each year. If rates do rise soon after you bought this year's bonds, you can take comfort in the fact that soon you will have money coming available to take advantage of the change by purchasing your new 10-years at lower prices. Similarly, if rates decline after you buy, you've managed to lock in the higher rates for that portion of your portfolio. The bottom line is, you won't get stuck one way or the other.

Treasurys for your ladder may be purchased straight from the government through the Treasury Direct program, with few fees and low minimum investments. As mentioned earlier, an application to open an account may be obtained online at the Treasury Direct web site (www.treasurydirect.gov) or by calling 800-722-2678.

A ladder may also be constructed of municipal bonds, but that would typically require a bare minimum of $100,000 in capital to gather a diversified group of issues. Trading in a muni, which you can do through most brokerage firms, also creates higher transaction costs, but if your tax rate is high enough—anything above 28 percent—the tax savings may make the costs worthwhile.

# Bond Funds

Bonds are complex—there's no doubt about it—especially if you're a novice investor with little experience in the markets. That's why a lot of people opt for bond funds when they seek to diversify their investments with some fixed-income exposure. Our view is, if you're willing to put in the effort, you're better off buying individual bonds instead of bond funds. But in the real world, a fund is sometimes worth the convenience.

Here's what you have to consider:

Like a stock mutual fund, a bond fund is managed by a professional investor who buys a portfolio of securities and makes all the decisions. Most funds buy bonds of a specific type, maturity, and risk profile—15-year corporates, for instance, or tax-free municipals—and pay out a "coupon" to investors, often monthly, rather than annually or semiannually like a regular bond.

The chief advantage of a bond fund is that it is convenient. It's also true that when it comes to buying corporate and municipal bonds, a professional manager backed by a strong research organization can make better decisions than the average individual investor. Consequently, if you want to dabble in junk bonds or shelter your income with triple-tax free New York City 30-years, you may be better off going the easy route and picking a good fund.

The disadvantage of a bond fund is that it's not a bond. It has neither a fixed yield nor a contractual obligation to give investors back their principal at some later maturity date—the two key characteristics of individual bonds. Then there are the fees and expenses that can cut into returns. Finally, because fund managers constantly trade their positions, the risk-return profile of a bond fund investment is continually changing: Unlike an actual bond, whose risk level declines the longer it is held by an investor, a fund can increase or decrease its risk exposure at the whim of the manager.

The other thing about building your own portfolio of bonds is that you can tailor it to meet your circumstances, meaning the bonds will mature precisely when you need them. A bond fund cannot deliver that sort of precision.

Our advice is this: If you lack the time or interest to manage a bond portfolio on your own, or if you want a mixed portfolio of corporates or municipals, buy a bond fund. But if you want a tailored portfolio of Treasurys to mature when your youngster goes to college—and you want to avoid the fees and added risk associated with bond funds—go ahead and take the plunge yourself.

# 2

# HOW MUCH DO YOU REALLY NEED TO SAVE?

How much money will you need in order to retire? Well, that all depends on what kind of retirement you want.

One hundred thousand dollars per year? That would do nicely, wouldn't it? If you could retire with an annual after-tax income of about $100,000, life would be pretty sweet. As long as you didn't insist on bunking down in a high-end town like Beverly Hills or Palm Beach, you could afford to do all the things we associate with the golden years: some travel, the arts, some charitable work, quality time with the grandkids.

John and Lee Jones retired seven years ago in Naples, Florida, with almost $100,000 in annual income and they are loving it. They go to the Philharmonic, play golf, and have just leased a new convertible. "This is a better lifestyle than what we had imagined," says Lee. "I never thought we'd move to Florida. Our lifestyle is relaxed, but still a little elegant."

Fair enough. But let's just say—for the sake of argument—that you wanted to aim higher than $100,000. That you weren't going to be satisfied with a merely comfortable retirement. That you wanted to retire rich—like John and Dolores James of Winter Park, Florida, with an annual income that's almost double that of the Jones family. With some $200,000 in annual retirement income, the Jameses don't stay home much now that they're retired. They're crisscrossing the globe, doing everything they didn't have time to do while they were working. "So far, we've been to Europe, Australia, and

Patagonia," John says. "I went fly-fishing in Alaska and South America. Dolores and I are really having a fun time."

No question, it takes a lot of dough to spin off that kind of income. By our estimates, a 65-year-old retiree should have $1.6 million in savings right now to count on $100,000 a year in spending money for the rest of his life. (We're assuming he—or she—would live to 90 and receive Social Security, inflation would average 3 percent a year over the rest of his life, he would average a 10 percent annual return on his investments, and he would spend his nest egg by his death.) A retiree who wants to live on $200,000 a year would need $4.7 million in today's dollars.

Think those numbers are out of your reach? Don't be so sure. If you've been taking advantage of the more aggressive choices offered by your 401(k) or other retirement plans, you probably have a decent head start. But even if you've put off saving until now, you can still get there. And we'll prove it.

Your first step is to figure out where you are financially. Worksheet 2.1 will help you calculate how much you need to save and what kind of return you must get in order to reach whichever goal you set—to retire either comfortably or really rich. Though our worksheet may look complex, you ought to be able to fill it out in about half an hour.

# How Much Will You Need?

Ah, retirement. The books you've been meaning to read. The travel. A posh second home. But can you pull it off? Can you really retire as well-off as you'd like? Complete this worksheet and find out. It will help you estimate how much you need to save—as well as what kind of investment returns you'll need—to reach your goal.

On a basic level, this worksheet can help you figure out how much you'll need to save now to cover your retirement expenses. But you can play around with your goal, too. Do you want a comfortable retirement of, say, an annual after-tax household income of $100,000, or a very wealthy, very cushy one at $200,000 after-tax a year? With this worksheet, you can play through both scenarios.

The worksheet may look about as intimidating as a Form 1040, but in truth it should take only about a half hour to complete. As you work with the tables, you can adjust the

**WORKSHEET 2.1**    How Much Will You Need?

variables to fit your lifestyle. You want to retire megarich, with an annual income of $300,000? Then plug in the numbers and find out what you need to save this year. You're on your way to the retirement you want.

One word of caution: Once you get to line 11 in Part Three and learn how much you will actually need to save each year to retire wealthy, don't despair. Remember, that number represents household savings and can also include 401(k) matching contributions or profit sharing from your employer.

### Part One: Where Do You Stand Right Now?

The first step is to figure out what you already have. In other words, if you never saved another cent, what kind of income would you still have coming to you in retirement?

The worksheet example assumes that current Social Security payments will keep up with inflation, but that by the time you retire they'll be fully taxable. (Retired couples with more than $44,000 in joint annual income now pay tax on up to 85 percent of their Social Security benefits.)

When choosing the appropriate rates of return in Tables 2.1, 2.2, 2.5, and 2.6, remember that your investment return will probably decline when you retire and start shifting some assets away from equities toward more stable bonds and cash. Also keep in mind that the growth rate of taxable investments is typically slower than that of tax-deferred investments—unless most of your equity assets are in taxable accounts and your fixed-income assets are in tax-deferred accounts.

1. Value of your current retirement savings in tax-deferred accounts—401(k), regular individual retirement account (IRA), 403(b), etc.: Enter current savings.   _____

2. Value at retirement: Multiply line 1 by the appropriate factor from Table 2.1.   _____

3. Annual income you expect from tax-deferred accounts when you retire: Multiply line 2 by the appropriate factor from Table 2.2.   _____

4. Value of your current retirement savings in taxable accounts.   _____

5. Value at retirement: Multiply line 4 by the appropriate factor from Table 2.1. (In most cases, the tax drag means choosing an annual return lower than the one you chose on line 2.)   _____

6. Annual income you can expect from taxable accounts when you retire: Multiply line 5 by the appropriate factor from Table 2.2.   _____

**WORKSHEET 2.1** *(Continued)*

## TABLE 2.1     YOUR SAVINGS GROWTH

| Years to Retirement | Yearly Return You Expect on Your Savings | | | | | |
|---|---|---|---|---|---|---|
| | **4%** | **6%** | **8%** | **10%** | **12%** | **15%** |
| 5 | 1.05 | 1.15 | 1.27 | 1.39 | 1.52 | 1.74 |
| 6 | 1.06 | 1.19 | 1.33 | 1.48 | 1.65 | 1.94 |
| 7 | 1.07 | 1.22 | 1.39 | 1.58 | 1.80 | 2.16 |
| 8 | 1.08 | 1.26 | 1.46 | 1.69 | 1.95 | 2.41 |
| 9 | 1.09 | 1.29 | 1.53 | 1.81 | 2.13 | 2.70 |
| 10 | 1.10 | 1.33 | 1.61 | 1.93 | 2.31 | 3.01 |
| 11 | 1.11 | 1.37 | 1.68 | 2.06 | 2.51 | 3.36 |
| 12 | 1.12 | 1.41 | 1.77 | 2.20 | 2.73 | 3.75 |
| 13 | 1.13 | 1.45 | 1.85 | 2.35 | 2.97 | 4.19 |
| 14 | 1.14 | 1.49 | 1.94 | 2.51 | 3.23 | 4.68 |
| 15 | 1.16 | 1.54 | 2.04 | 2.68 | 3.51 | 5.22 |
| 16 | 1.17 | 1.58 | 2.13 | 2.86 | 3.82 | 5.83 |
| 17 | 1.18 | 1.63 | 2.24 | 3.06 | 4.15 | 6.51 |
| 18 | 1.19 | 1.68 | 2.35 | 3.27 | 4.52 | 7.27 |
| 19 | 1.20 | 1.73 | 2.46 | 3.49 | 4.91 | 8.12 |
| 20 | 1.21 | 1.78 | 2.58 | 3.72 | 5.34 | 9.06 |
| 21 | 1.22 | 1.83 | 2.71 | 3.98 | 5.81 | 10.12 |
| 22 | 1.24 | 1.88 | 2.84 | 4.25 | 6.32 | 11.30 |
| 23 | 1.25 | 1.94 | 2.98 | 4.54 | 6.87 | 12.61 |
| 24 | 1.26 | 1.99 | 3.12 | 4.85 | 7.47 | 14.08 |
| 25 | 1.27 | 2.05 | 3.27 | 5.17 | 8.12 | 15.72 |
| 26 | 1.29 | 2.11 | 3.43 | 5.53 | 8.83 | 17.55 |
| 27 | 1.30 | 2.17 | 3.60 | 5.90 | 9.60 | 19.60 |
| 28 | 1.31 | 2.23 | 3.77 | 6.30 | 10.44 | 21.88 |
| 29 | 1.32 | 2.30 | 3.95 | 6.73 | 11.35 | 24.43 |
| 30 | 1.34 | 2.37 | 4.15 | 7.19 | 12.34 | 27.28 |
| 31 | 1.35 | 2.44 | 4.35 | 7.68 | 13.42 | 30.46 |
| 32 | 1.36 | 2.51 | 4.56 | 8.20 | 14.59 | 34.00 |
| 33 | 1.38 | 2.58 | 4.78 | 8.76 | 15.87 | 37.97 |
| 34 | 1.39 | 2.65 | 5.01 | 9.35 | 17.26 | 42.39 |
| 35 | 1.40 | 2.73 | 5.25 | 9.99 | 18.76 | 47.33 |
| 36 | 1.42 | 2.81 | 5.51 | 10.67 | 20.40 | 52.84 |
| 37 | 1.43 | 2.89 | 5.78 | 11.39 | 22.19 | 59.00 |
| 38 | 1.44 | 2.98 | 6.06 | 12.16 | 24.13 | 65.87 |
| 39 | 1.46 | 3.06 | 6.35 | 12.99 | 26.23 | 73.55 |
| 40 | 1.47 | 3.15 | 6.66 | 13.87 | 28.53 | 82.12 |

These multipliers adjust for 3 percent annual inflation.

**WORKSHEET 2.1**     *(Continued)*

## TABLE 2.2    INCOME FROM YOUR SAVINGS

| Years in Retirement | Yearly Return You Expect Post-Retirement | | | |
|---|---|---|---|---|
| | 4% | 6% | 8% | 10% |
| 15 | .0713 | .0809 | .0910 | .1015 |
| 20 | .0547 | .0648 | .0756 | .0870 |
| 25 | .0448 | .0553 | .0667 | .0789 |
| 30 | .0382 | .0490 | .0610 | .0739 |
| 35 | .0335 | .0446 | .0572 | .0707 |
| 40 | .0300 | .0414 | .0545 | .0686 |
| 45 | .0273 | .0390 | .0525 | .0671 |
| 50 | .0251 | .0371 | .0511 | .0661 |

Assumes 3 percent annual inflation increases in your retirement income and exhaustion of principal over the remainder of your lifetime.

7.  Value of your current savings in Roth IRAs. _____

8.  Value at retirement: Multiply line 7 by the appropriate factor from Table 2.1. (The annual return will probably exceed the choice you made on line 5.) _____

9.  Annual income you can expect from a Roth account when you retire: Multiply line 8 by an appropriate factor from Table 2.2. _____

10. Estimated Social Security income: A typical payout for your age and income level in 2001 dollars (under current Social Security rules) can be found in Table 2.3. _____

11. Spouse's estimated Social Security income. (For a nonworking spouse, take 50 percent of working spouse's benefit.) _____

12. Total Social Security income: Add lines 10 and 11. _____

13. Your pension (if any) from current job: Ask your company benefits office to project your pension for you. (Lump-sum settlements should be entered on line 15.) _____

**WORKSHEET 2.1**    *(Continued)*

## TABLE 2.3    TYPICAL SOCIAL SECURITY BENEFITS

| Age in 2001 | 2001 Income Level | | | | |
|---|---|---|---|---|---|
| | **$30,000** | **$40,000** | **$50,000** | **$60,000** | **$80,400+** |
| 35 or less | $13,440 | $16,620 | $18,252 | $19,740 | $22,788 |
| 40 | 13,332 | 16,488 | 18,168 | 19,644 | 22,644 |
| 45 | 13,212 | 16,308 | 18,072 | 19,524 | 22,452 |
| 50 | 13,104 | 16,164 | 17,988 | 19,416 | 22,236 |

Payouts stated in 2001 dollars. Benefits are those received annually at full retirement.

14. Your spouse's pension: Enter actual company estimate adjusted for inflation, or estimate it.    _____

15. Additional sources of capital: Enter the amount you or your spouse expect to realize from things such as an inheritance, a home sale, or a lump-sum pension payment or severance option. Give the current value even though you expect to receive the money in the future.    _____

16. Annual retirement income you can expect from additional sources of capital: Multiply line 15 by the appropriate factor from Table 2.2.    _____

17. Annual retirement income you and/or your spouse expect to earn from part-time work.    _____

18. Total retirement income from all sources (in 2002 dollars): Add lines 3, 6, 9, 12, 13, 14, 16, and 17.    _____

19. Reduction for the waiting period before Social Security payments start:

    (a) For age 65 retirement, enter the amount on line 12 if you are older    _____

    (b) Income reduction: Multiply line 19(a) by the appropriate factor from Table 2.2.    _____

20. Pretax income: Subtract line 19(b) from line 18. If a negative number results, continue using it.    _____

**WORKSHEET 2.1**    *(Continued)*

**Part Two: How Much Would You Like to Have?**

Now that you know what kind of retirement income you can expect from what you already have, you need to find out how much of your retirement expenses that income will cover. When filling out these items, you can be guided by your current costs, since inflation has been taken into account in the other two parts of the worksheet. Remember, though, that once you retire, new activities and advancing age will change your spending patterns. Life insurance premiums, commuting costs, and mortgage payments will shrink or disappear, while your travel and hobby expenses will rise, especially in early retirement.

### *Anticipated Monthly Expenses in Retirement*

Housing (mortgage payments, rent, and/or condo maintenance)     _____

Utilities     _____

Auto/transportation costs     _____

Food/personal care     _____

Clothing     _____

Entertainment     _____

Hobbies/subscriptions     _____

Gifts     _____

Debt repayment (other than mortgage)     _____

**Monthly Total**     _____

### *Yearly Expenses*

Annual cost of monthly spending: Multiply Total above by 12     _____

Vacation travel/memberships     _____

Health insurance premiums     _____

Medical expenses (not covered by insurance)     _____

**WORKSHEET 2.1**   *(Continued)*

Other insurance premiums (auto, home, etc.)                          _____

Home repairs, maintenance, property taxes                           _____

Emergencies/other                                                   _____

**Yearly Total**                                                    _____


**Part Three: How Much Do You Need to Save?**

Here's where we show you what you need to do to bridge the gap between the income level you're assured of already and the income that you need to generate in order to retire comfortably—and then rich. Here you may want to work three variables: Once you see how much of your retirement expenses your current income will cover, go back to line 2. Insert $100,000 to figure out how much you need to retire comfortably, then $200,000 to retire rich.

1. The income you already expect: Enter amount from Part One, line 20.                                               _____

2. After-tax spending desired: Enter Yearly Total from Part Two.     _____

3. Spending met by tax-free Roth IRA: Enter amount from Part One, line 9.                                                _____

4. Subtract line 3 from line 2.                                      _____

5. Tax rate:

   (a) Choose a tax rate from Table 2.4 that applies to the amount on line 2. Enter rate as a decimal.               _____

   (b) Tax multiple: Subtract line 5(a) from the number 1.          _____

6. Retirement income needed:

   (a) Divide line 2 by line 5(b).                                   _____

   (b) Add line 3 to line 6(a).                                      _____


**WORKSHEET 2.1**   *(Continued)*

## TABLE 2.4     THE TAX FACTOR

| Retirement Spending | Federal Tax Expense Couples | Singles | Retirement Spending | Federal Tax Expense Couples | Singles |
|---|---|---|---|---|---|
| $ 20,000 | 7% | 12% | $ 70,000 | 21% | 30% |
| 25,000 | 9 | 13 | 80,000 | 23 | 32 |
| 30,000 | 10 | 15 | 90,000 | 25 | 33 |
| 35,000 | 11 | 18 | 100,000 | 27 | 34 |
| 40,000 | 12 | 21 | 120,000 | 30 | 38 |
| 45,000 | 13 | 23 | 140,000 | 33 | 41 |
| 50,000 | 14 | 24 | 160,000 | 36 | 43 |
| 55,000 | 16 | 26 | 180,000 | 38 | 44 |
| 60,000 | 18 | 27 | 200,000 | 41 | 45 |

7. Income gap: Subtract line 1 from line 6(b). Continue to use the number, even if it's negative.　　　　——————

8. Pension preservation (skip this if your pension has a cost-of-living adjustment):

   (a) Choose a factor from one of the A columns in Table 2.5 to see how much capital you need in order to protect your pension's buying power.　　　　——————

   (b) Add lines 13 and 14 from Part One.　　　　——————

   (c) Multiply line 8(a) by 8(b).　　　　——————

9. Capital needed to fund retirement-income gap:

   (a) Choose a factor from a B column in Table 2.5 that reflects how long you'll be in retirement and how much you expect to make on your retirement wealth while you are retired.　　　　——————

   (b) Multiply line 7 by line 9(a).　　　　——————

**WORKSHEET 2.1**   *(Continued)*

## TABLE 2.5    CAPITAL NEEDED FOR RETIREMENT

Use Column A to find out how much capital you need to preserve your pension's buying power. Use Column B to find out how much capital you need to cover your retirement-income gap. Use the Social Security table to find out how much capital you need to cover the years between 55 and the first year you can get a full Social Security payout.

| | **Yearly Return You Expect Post-Retirement** | | | | | | | |
|---|---|---|---|---|---|---|---|---|
| **Years in** | **4%** | | **6%** | | **8%** | | **10%** | |
| **Retirement** | **A** | **B** | **A** | **B** | **A** | **B** | **A** | **B** |
| 15 | 2.47 | 14.03 | 2.07 | 12.37 | 1.75 | 10.99 | 1.49 | 9.86 |
| 20 | 4.14 | 18.28 | 3.28 | 15.44 | 2.63 | 13.23 | 2.13 | 11.50 |
| 25 | 6.07 | 22.32 | 4.55 | 18.10 | 3.47 | 15.00 | 2.69 | 12.68 |
| 30 | 8.19 | 26.17 | 5.81 | 20.40 | 4.23 | 16.39 | 3.16 | 13.53 |
| 35 | 10.43 | 29.84 | 7.03 | 22.40 | 4.90 | 17.49 | 3.53 | 14.14 |
| 40 | 12.75 | 33.34 | 8.18 | 24.13 | 5.48 | 18.36 | 3.82 | 14.58 |
| 45 | 15.12 | 36.67 | 9.24 | 25.63 | 5.96 | 19.04 | 4.05 | 14.90 |
| 50 | 17.50 | 39.85 | 10.22 | 26.92 | 6.37 | 19.58 | 4.22 | 15.13 |

| | **Social Security Supplemental Capital** | | | |
|---|---|---|---|---|
| **If You Are . . .** | **4%** | **6%** | **8%** | **10%** |
| Older than 42 | 9.58 | 8.82 | 8.15 | 7.57 |
| 42 or younger | 11.39 | 10.30 | 9.37 | 8.58 |

All calculations assume 3 percent inflation and annuitization.

10. Total capital needed: Add lines 8(c) and 9(b). A negative number here means you have sufficient resources to fund your retirement.                                   _____

11. What you should save this year: Multiply line 10 by the appropriate factor from Table 2.6.                                   _____

*Note:* The amount you need to save each year will increase. That's because the worksheet assumes your income will rise at least at the inflation rate, if not more. Save this worksheet and do it again in 12 months—or visit www.smartmoney.com for an electronic version—to make sure you stay on track.

**WORKSHEET 2.1**    *(Continued)*

## TABLE 2.6    ANNUAL SAVINGS NEEDED

| Years to Retirement | Yearly Return You Expect on Your Savings | | | | | |
|---|---|---|---|---|---|---|
| | 4% | 6% | 8% | 10% | 12% | 15% |
| 5 | .196 | .189 | .182 | .175 | .168 | .159 |
| 6 | .163 | .155 | .148 | .141 | .134 | .124 |
| 7 | .139 | .131 | .123 | .116 | .110 | .100 |
| 8 | .121 | .113 | .105 | .098 | .092 | .082 |
| 9 | .107 | .099 | .091 | .084 | .078 | .069 |
| 10 | .096 | .088 | .080 | .073 | .067 | .058 |
| 11 | .087 | .078 | .071 | .064 | .058 | .049 |
| 12 | .079 | .071 | .063 | .057 | .050 | .042 |
| 13 | .073 | .064 | .057 | .050 | .044 | .037 |
| 14 | .067 | .059 | .052 | .045 | .039 | .032 |
| 15 | .062 | .054 | .047 | .040 | .035 | .028 |
| 16 | .058 | .050 | .043 | .036 | .031 | .024 |
| 17 | .054 | .046 | .039 | .033 | .028 | .021 |
| 18 | .051 | .043 | .036 | .030 | .025 | .019 |
| 19 | .048 | .040 | .033 | .027 | .022 | .016 |
| 20 | .046 | .038 | .031 | .025 | .020 | .014 |
| 21 | .043 | .035 | .028 | .023 | .018 | .013 |
| 22 | .041 | .033 | .026 | .021 | .016 | .011 |
| 23 | .039 | .031 | .025 | .019 | .015 | .010 |
| 24 | .037 | .029 | .023 | .018 | .014 | .009 |
| 25 | .036 | .028 | .021 | .016 | .012 | .009 |
| 26 | .034 | .026 | .020 | .015 | .011 | .007 |
| 27 | .033 | .025 | .019 | .014 | .010 | .006 |
| 28 | .031 | .024 | .018 | .013 | .009 | .006 |
| 29 | .030 | .022 | .016 | .012 | .008 | .005 |
| 30 | .029 | .021 | .015 | .011 | .008 | .004 |
| 31 | .028 | .020 | .015 | .010 | .007 | .004 |
| 32 | .027 | .019 | .014 | .009 | .006 | .004 |
| 33 | .026 | .018 | .013 | .009 | .006 | .003 |
| 34 | .025 | .018 | .012 | .008 | .005 | .003 |
| 35 | .024 | .017 | .011 | .008 | .005 | .003 |
| 36 | .023 | .016 | .011 | .007 | .005 | .002 |
| 37 | .023 | .015 | .010 | .007 | .004 | .002 |
| 38 | .022 | .015 | .010 | .006 | .004 | .002 |
| 39 | .021 | .014 | .009 | .006 | .003 | .002 |
| 40 | .021 | .014 | .009 | .005 | .003 | .001 |

All calculations assume 3 percent inflation and yearly increases in income.

**WORKSHEET 2.1**    *(Continued)*

Your next step is to read on. In this chapter we will walk you through the steps you should be taking now—whether you're in your 20s, 30s, 40s, 50s, or 60s—to boost your chances of retiring the way you want. These moves aren't based on idle theory; they're from real people who are either well on their way to a rich retirement or are already there.

We're not going to give you much in the way of specific investing ideas just yet. There will plenty of time for that in Chapters 4 and 5, as we help you sort out the ideal asset allocation for your long-term goals. But first we want to ground you in the fundamentals of investing for the long term.

Two bits of advice before you begin: First, don't panic if you discover that you need to save $17,800 each year for 30 years just to retire comfortably. Remember that this sum represents savings from you and your spouse together—and that you can include both your contributions to your 401(k)s to reach it. Second, you may think you can live frugally as a retiree, but chances are you're going to want more money than you expect. Trust us. You'll want to take that European vacation, so you might as well start thinking big right now.

Steve Walden knows what we're talking about. He retired almost two years ago in Flat Rock, North Carolina, but didn't anticipate a number of expenses that have turned out to be important. Now, to pick one example, he finds himself writing a check for $1,000 to the local country club each month. Not having to drag himself out of bed for work every morning, he's always popping in at the club. "There are the New Year's Eve parties, the Christmas parties, the prime rib nights," says Walden. "I hate to miss out on anything."

## 20s

You're one lucky soul. Because you're beginning to squirrel away retirement money so early—with 40 years or more to go before you retire—that $200,000 annual income is all but yours. Yes, it's going to take some discipline. No, it won't always be easy. But starting now gives you an enormous jump on the game.

Let's say you are 25 years old and you've saved exactly nothing. By our calculations, you can set aside $8,500 a year and—assuming you can earn 10 percent annual returns—you should have no trouble hitting the

$100,000 income mark by the time you're 65. You'd prefer the deluxe retirement instead? Try saving $24,500 a year and you should hit the megarich $200,000 level.

Granted, these seem like huge sums of money on a 20-something's salary. But there are three things you need to keep in mind: First, even if you can't cough up the entire $24,500 this year, you *can* make it up in future years, as long as your salary increases faster than inflation. Second, this does include any matching contributions you get in your company's 401(k) or profit sharing plan. And finally: You're young, so you can choose a more aggressive mix of investments that could potentially deliver far greater returns than 10 percent a year. Think technology stocks and small caps.

Joseph Gregory, 24, won't retire until 2043, but he started investing about $25 a month when he was 18. Loading up on big-name stocks such as Motorola, he has built a portfolio worth some $20,000. Through his job as a product specialist at ECI Telecom, a digital telecommunications company in Herndon, Virginia, Gregory chips in 15 percent of his salary to his 401(k), most of which is invested in the Fidelity Aggressive Growth fund. It delivered a 21.7 percent annual return in the late 1990s, making Gregory one happy man. He's determined to retire with at least $200,000 in annual income and dodge the retirement anxieties that his parents have. "They still have a lot of debt," he says. "I don't want to be in that position."

At this stage, there's no doubt what sort of account your savings should go into. You've got to start with your company's 401(k), of course, since you get that match—and the money grows tax-deferred. Try to contribute enough to obtain the largest match your company offers. You say your company is a dud when it comes to matching funds? Then consider changing jobs. Seriously. Though it seems like a drastic move to make based purely on your retirement plans, the gains can be enormous. Matt Gegen, a 25-year-old accountant in St. Louis, is pondering leaving his company, which matches only up to 2 percent of his salary. His goal: Sun Microsystems, which matches up to some 4 percent and chips in a fair amount of stock options to boot. "If I went to Sun, my 401(k) would be worth $800,000 to $2 million more, simply because of the match," he says.

If you have money left over for savings after contributing to your 401(k), you'll definitely want to open a Roth individual retirement account (IRA), available from most brokerages, banks, and fund companies. To be fully eligible for a Roth, single filers need to have an adjusted gross income of less than $110,000 a year in 2002, or if they're married, $160,000 (the figure changes each year). You can put up to $3,000 into the account annually and, most important, you will owe *no tax* when taking the money out at retirement. You'll also have a nice windfall if you begin making contributions now, while you're young. Invest $3,000 each year for 30 years and, assuming 10 percent annual growth (and not accounting for inflation), you'll have $519,823. Do it for 40 years and you'll wind up with $1,398,652.

## 30s

The spending demands that hit during your 30s can derail even the best of retirement strategies. The mortgage, the kids, and their college funds all threaten to lay waste to those 401(k) funds that were supposed to last a lifetime. And if you didn't start saving in your 20s, here's another strain for you: To retire with a yearly income of $100,000, you'll need to start putting away $17,800 a year by age 35; to hit $200,000, make that $51,000 a year.

This is where you have to start getting creative. Many determined retirement savers, for instance, pad their income with investment property. This has worked wonders for Irwin Sherry. The former Hewlett-Packard salesman contributed to his 401(k) and stock-purchase plans throughout his career, but when he was 30 he and his wife bought a duplex in Beverly Hills for $80,000. They lived in one unit and rented out the other. Today the property is worth 10 times what they paid for it, and the Sherrys have since acquired five other properties, most of which are in Los Angeles. Irwin recently retired from Hewlett-Packard at age 61, and he and his wife are living off the rental income from these properties. The best part: They've yet to touch any of their retirement savings.

The important thing is that an extra chunk of cash, no matter how small, can really build into something big if you put it away now, while you're in your 30s. Selwyn and Helen Rose of Wilmington, Delaware, are now living on $200,000 a year in annual retirement income, thanks in part to an income that once seemed insignificant: the $10,000 salary Helen earned as a part-time dental hygienist in the 1970s and early 1980s. While the family lived primarily off the $35,000 salary that Selwyn earned then as a researcher at chemical company Himont, she was able to put much of her income into an IRA that's now worth some $325,000.

Even as you move into your late 30s, you'll want to keep close to 100 percent of your retirement savings in stocks or stock funds to take advantage of the superior growth that equities generally produce over time. A typical asset allocation for someone in his or her 30s would look like this: 60 percent large U.S. stocks, 20 percent international stocks, and the remainder divided among mid-caps and small caps. Our easy-to-use worksheet in Chapter 4 will help you set up a more precise allocation plan for your needs. Since your goals may change—you might decide to take more risks, for instance, to play catch-up—you should reexamine your asset allocation at least every few years.

## 40s

So you've fallen a little behind on your retirement savings? You can still catch up, although you'll have to take some risks to pull it off. In his mid-40s, Bill Ward was running the radio division of Golden West Broadcasters, Gene Autry's media company. After convincing Autry to buy an FM station in Los Angeles, Ward agreed to give up any future raises in exchange for an ownership stake in the station. The deal paid off—the station sold for $113 million in the late 1990s, making Ward a millionaire. "After 40 years of busting my butt, it was about time," he says.

You may have to feel some pain to get back on track, but it may be easier than you think. One way to catch up: Take your old spending habits and shatter them to pieces. Wayne and Scottie Andre of Indianapolis had mastered the art of belt-tightening by their middle years. Wayne worked for 26 years at Eli Lilly, most recently as a business systems analyst, contributing regularly to his 401(k) plan and investing half his income in stocks such as Microsoft and Dell Computer. Meanwhile, he and Scottie (who ran a day-care facility out of their house) opted to postpone any luxuries until retirement. "We tried to live well below our means for years," the 50-something Wayne says, taking vacations only if they could drive to their destination, playing golf on public courses, and shopping for the kids' clothes at garage sales.

Now retired, they have a portfolio worth roughly $5 million. Like many retirees who are unaccustomed to their new fortune, the Andres are just now figuring out how they want to spend it. They're planning a two-week trip to

Europe (taking along the kids and their spouses), and after that, Wayne says, "I'm going to play all the great golf courses in the country."

Once you're comfortable that you're saving enough, concentrate on chipping away at your mortgage through extra payments—especially if you're thinking of retiring early. "It's largely psychological," says Nancy Nelson, a financial planner in Olympia, Washington. "But it's hard to put a price tag on living in a paid-for home. Those additional payments can be comparatively small—even $25 a month can make a huge difference."

If you're way behind on your retirement savings, real estate isn't your best investment. You'll likely get much better returns in the stock market. "A 90 percent stock allocation would be appropriate for someone [in their 40s] who's behind on saving as long as they can tolerate the risk," says Ron Roge, a financial planner in Bohemia, New York. "You need a 10-year [investment] horizon to be heavily invested in stocks in order to protect yourself from the market's volatility." Forty-something savers who aren't playing catch-up should start moving roughly 15 percent of their money into diversified bond funds such as the Vanguard Total Bond Market Index fund to preserve their savings and maintain steady growth.

## 50s

You can almost see yourself sitting on a quiet beach with nothing in view but your sprawling retirement estate. Almost. The question is, can you get there from here?

If you need a boost, start with your pension. Old-fashioned pensions are less common these days, but if you're fortunate enough to have one, you may be able to boost its annual payout significantly by putting aside your dreams of an early retirement and working a few extra years. It's crucial that you know what the minimum retirement qualifications are for your pension, because leaving just a couple of years early can cost you thousands of dollars. With one of Utah's state pensions, for example, a person making $100,000 a year could get $60,000 a year if he or she retired at 65 after working 30 years. If that same person retired at 58, he would receive only $32,658.

Larry Foote, a former manager with the Minnesota Department of Transportation, hadn't done much about saving for his retirement until he attended an investing seminar in 1990, when he was 59. He came home and worked the numbers, and was shocked to realize that he and his wife had saved only about half of what they needed to cover their expenses. Foote was able to make up the difference by saving aggressively and ultimately delaying his retirement six years, until he was 65. The move boosted his annual pension payout 47 percent, to $28,000. The Footes have used the extra cash to travel extensively through Europe and Alaska, and took a cruise around Cape Horn. "My only regret," says Foote, "is that I didn't pay attention to what we were doing [in terms of our retirement] for the last 20 years."

Another way to generate a sizable chunk of cash, which you can then invest, is to downsize your home. A change in the tax law in 1997 allows you to take up to $500,000 in capital gains tax-free. Before the law changed, one way to avoid the tax hit was to roll the capital into the purchase of another home. Now that people have more options, some are investing the windfall for their retirement.

After Michael Arrata's company—KPC Medical Management, a chain of clinics—filed for bankruptcy, he decided to sell his house overlooking the Pacific Ocean in Palos Verdes, California, and use the capital gains to help fund his retirement. Although Arrata, a 70-year-old obstetrician/gynecologist, could have retired on what he had saved, he knew he didn't have enough to maintain his lifestyle, which included a second home in Palm Springs and traveling to such exotic locales as Thailand and Egypt. "It's kind of difficult going through it," he says of the downsizing. "But it's definitely worth it." Arrata hopes to get at least $350,000 in capital gains to invest—but may end up with even more.

As you near retirement age, having a diverse portfolio of investments becomes more and more important. This is especially true for anyone whose company has used stock as part or all of its matching 401(k) contribution. You can easily have 30 percent or more of your portfolio in just one stock. When Willie Hamer retired in 2000, United Parcel Service (UPS) stock made up a staggering 90 percent of his portfolio. The Hamers began to sell small portions at a time, starting with 20 percent, and to move the money into municipal bonds.

At this point, you ought to have at least 20 percent of your portfolio in bonds—that is, unless you absolutely need a 10 percent or greater return from your holdings. If that's the case, you will probably want to keep 90 percent of your portfolio in both growth and value stocks as long as you're not retiring for 10 years. Just understand that there's a good chance a market correction will come along and deal your retirement plans a severe blow.

You say that you've got plenty of cash already and you want to retire *early?* Bully for you! Here's one last thing to keep in mind: Your employer may give you the option of leaving your 401(k) with the company or rolling it over into an IRA. If you can wait until you're $59^1/_2$ before tapping this money, then take the IRA rollover. With the money in an IRA, you'll likely have many more investment options than you could ever get in a 401(k). However, if you will need the money before age $59^1/_2$, consider leaving it in the company plan. The reason: Take a distribution from your IRA at age 55 and you could pay a 10 percent penalty. You'll avoid that fine with your 401(k), provided you've left your company.

## 60s

The great day is close—very close. Go ahead, let yourself fantasize about how you're going to spend all that wonderful cash: a new Mercedes, that trip to South America, a palatial home in Boca Raton.

Okay, that's enough. You can't overdo it on the daydreaming just yet, because you've got some work to do: It's time to pull out your retirement statements from all of your accounts and figure out how and when you're going to get all that money. The most important thing when you retire is to hold off dipping into your tax-deferred savings—IRAs, 401(k)s, and the like—until federal law says you have to, at age $70^1/_2$. That will let you dodge the tax collector for the longest time possible as well as keep the majority of your retirement income growing.

Be sure to use money from your after-tax accounts first to cover big purchases. For instance, you want to avoid taking a single hefty distribution from your IRA or 401(k) to buy that new $18,000 Harley Davidson. That's because cash coming out of an IRA or 401(k) could be taxed as income, meaning that you'd have to take out $25,720 pretax to afford the $18,000 hog if you were in the 30 percent federal income tax bracket. If you used money in your taxable accounts instead and drew it from investments where you had a capital gain, you'd pay the lower 20 percent capital gains tax—or even the lower 18 percent tax, as long as you held the securities for more than five years and you acquired them on or after January 1, 2001.

Whatever you do, though, don't take a penny from your Roth IRA until you've completely run through all your other savings. "There's nothing better than a Roth IRA," says Nelson. "It's literally tax-free, and [your heirs] will be allowed to drag out receiving their distributions over a lifetime."

How should your investments be allocated in your 60s? Someone, somewhere will undoubtedly tell you to move all your assets into bonds. Don't believe it. The right asset allocation for you depends on your age, your risk tolerance, and how much you need your portfolio to grow. (Again, see Chapter 4, "Your Ideal Asset Allocation," for more specifics.) So it's not unusual for retirees—and near retirees—to have 70 percent of their holdings in growth and value stocks, especially if their portfolio needs a little extra oomph. Yes, there's going to be some volatility if you invest that way, but you also need your portfolio to keep growing strongly if it's going to fund your retirement expenses for another 25 to 30 years.

Okay, so you may not want to be that aggressive. If you have more than enough cash to retire loaded and spend freely, you may want to move more—say, 35 to 45 percent—of your assets into bonds. The money will grow steadily and provide you with enough income so you can maintain a posh lifestyle.

Ideally, you want to be as well-off as the Hamers, who admit they are having a little trouble figuring out how to spend up to $250,000 of their retirement income each year. Willie is starting to look for a new Mercedes, and Karen is beginning to collect art. "Our daughter got married last year, and we told her to spend whatever she wanted," says Karen. "But she bought her dress off the rack. She had been working since she was 15 and pinching her pennies. She's not been able yet to make the switch [to spending freely]." Perhaps an all-expenses-paid five-star honeymoon might bring her around.

# 3

# YOUR RETIREMENT ACCOUNTS

The next time you and your colleagues are standing around the water-cooler complaining about your boss, swapping tales about how you're overworked and underpaid, trying to top one another with examples of how you're being exploited, keep this one thought in mind: Your employer may be making you rich.

Got a 401(k) plan at the office? Is there employer matching? Are you contributing the maximum amount you're allowed each month? Then all this should add up to a very comfortable retirement, one that you'd be hard-pressed to match if you were doing it all on your own and thus couldn't benefit from the extraordinary tax breaks that come with one of these company-sponsored retirement plans. Take a look at Sidebar 3.4, which shows the growing power of just $100 a month in savings over the past 20 years if it had been invested in a typical 401(k) plan.

Taking into account the power of tax-free compounding and the typical 50 percent employer match, you would have $184,000 by now—more than you would have earned in a typical individual retirement account, and much more than you could have hoped to gain by investing that money with a high-flying fund manager. That manager would have had to nearly double the performance of the stock market over those 20 years to do the same job your employer has just done for you.

So remember that the next time you see your boss walking by your cubicle and you find yourself fighting the urge to sound off.

Of course, having a 401(k) plan at work is only half the battle. Investing in it as aggressively as possible is just as important, and that's often easier said than done. Too many things can put you behind schedule, especially

## SIDEBAR 3.1

# How Did the 401(k) Plan Get Started?

It all began as an arcane paragraph added to Section 401 of the Internal Revenue Code in 1978. Designed as an antidiscrimination rule, paragraph "k" basically said that companies wanting to set up a tax-deferred savings plan—something that at the time was used mostly to shelter executives' incomes—could do so only if they could show that more than the highest-paid third of employees would benefit.

In 1980, when paragraph "k" took effect, benefits consultant R. Theodore Benna saw it not so much as a restriction for executives but more as a way to entice lower-paid employees to contribute to tax-deferred savings plans. Why not, he wondered, set up a regular savings program with paycheck deductions that would protect top management's plans and attract the rest of the workforce as well?

The idea, which Benna convinced his then employer to test, caught fire in the mid-1980s, when new accounting rules required companies to report pension-plan payouts as future liabilities on their income statements. Embracing a new kind of retirement vehicle was a perfect way around this change.

early in your career, when you're likely to move from job to job, each time moving up the corporate ladder perhaps, but never staying in any one place long enough to be vested in the company plan. Or perhaps the temptation of all that money sitting in a retirement account becomes a bit too much to resist when you change jobs and suddenly have access to it. It's all too common for someone to cash out a 401(k), rather than rolling it over into an IRA or a new employer's plan. "Young people aren't as focused on retirement," says Paul Yakoboski, then an analyst at the Employee Benefits Research Institute. "They see the cash and they think about paying bills, taking vacations before starting a new job, or buying a car." And even when you do settle down, other things—like that down payment on a house or tuition bills for your kids—can drain off the money you know you should be setting aside for retirement.

So if you're like a lot of people, you now find yourself in your mid- to late 40s or even older, realizing that you are nowhere near where you need to be with your retirement investing.

It's panic time.

Don't worry—it's not as bad as you may think. Even if you get a late start, aggressive, intelligent investing can get you back on track within a few years. The key is that 401(k) plan. Our advice is simple: Max out. Put in as much as your employer allows you to each year.

What's next? Yes, there is a "next" step. As we discussed back in Chapter 2, chances are you'll need to save more money than your 401(k) allows if you plan on financing a luxury retirement life. Where do you allot the rest of your retirement-savings dollars—Roth IRA, traditional IRA, or variable annuity? Why not just open a regular trading account instead? Or what about tax-free municipal bonds or small-cap mutual funds? (For a primer on all the different kinds of retirement accounts, turn to the end of the chapter and read Sidebar 3.7, "The ABCs of Retirement Accounts.")

We looked at more than 100 different scenarios—and tested them against market data covering the past 30 years—to help you make the most of all the tax-advantaged options that employers and the government make available in this post-pension, Social Security–challenged world we live in now.

# Six-Step Strategy for Retirement Savers

## Step 1: Maximize Your 401(k) Contributions

First, join your 401(k) plan and max out on the contributions that will earn a company match.

Why is the match so important? Think of it this way: What other investment gives you the equivalent of a 25 percent, 50 percent—or in almost one-fifth of the 401(k) plans in a study by the firm KPMG—100 percent return on the first day? There is no other such investment.

Of course, it would be nice if we could all contribute as much as we want to a 401(k) and have our company match all our contributions. But

## SIDEBAR 3.2 Did You Know That . . .

- The average limit for employee pretax contributions to a 401(k) is 14 percent.
- A good plan will allow employees to make after-tax contributions. But less than one quarter of all plans do.
- A 100 percent match is best—but only 19 percent of all employers match dollar for dollar (that's up from 12 percent in 1994). Some 35 percent of all employers provide a 50 percent match.
- Only 2 percent of all companies match contributions of 10 percent of compensation or more.
- A cash match is best, because it offers the most flexibility. Unfortunately, 45 percent of plans match with company stock or other assets.
- How soon do you vest? Immediately is the best answer, but only about 33 percent of all plans have immediate vesting.
- Nearly two-thirds of plans offer daily trading among investment options. If yours doesn't, it's way behind.
- More than 90 percent of all plans offer hardship withdrawals. A little less than that offer loans for any reason.

*Source:* Hewitt Associates.

that's just not the real world. Some companies don't have a defined contribution plan, and others that do have plans don't match your personal contributions.

Even if you have a 401(k)—or a 403(b) plan in the case of a nonprofit—with a 100 percent match, federal rules limit how much you can contribute. Those limits become a real nuisance if you started saving for retirement late in life and need to sock away as much as you can in the next few years. The same is true if you're young and want to make a big push for early retirement. If you want to save more than $11,000 a year (in 2002), you won't be able to put all that money into a 401(k). So what do you do if your employer doesn't match your contributions or if the amount your company will match is limited to less than what you need to save? There are several alternatives; the right one for you depends in part on your income level and on the tax laws, which we'll get to in the following steps.

# What the New 401(k) Rules *Really* Mean for You

SIDEBAR 3.3

Politics aside, there's one thing George W. Bush's tax act has done for all of us: let us save more in our 401(k) than we ever could before.

There is, however, one sticking point. Chances are you won't be able to take full advantage of these new rules immediately. For starters, most of them are phased in; for instance, many don't kick in completely until 2006. But more important, companies aren't required to actually implement these new rules—immediately or ever, in part or in full.

"This is entirely voluntary," says David Wray, president of the Profit Sharing/401(k) Council of America. "However, the companies will want to do it. But they will do it on their own time frame." Wray estimates that most large companies—the likes of General Electric and Microsoft—will have implemented the new rules in their programs by the middle of 2002. "The real question is the smaller companies," he adds, because of the complex record keeping involved.

Even so, there's considerable excitement over these new rules. Here's the lowdown on what they really mean for you.

**Increased Contribution Limits**

You can save more—pretax, after-tax, and through your company matches—eventually.

In 2001, you could contribute a pretax maximum of $10,500 a year. But by 2006, you'll be able to save up to $15,000 in pretax contributions. This increase will be phased in over the next few years, in $1,000 increments, starting in 2002. (So it goes that the pretax maximum will be $11,000 in 2002; $12,000 in 2003; and so on until 2006, when the maximum will hit $15,000.) After 2006, the contribution limits will increase in $500 increments to factor in inflation.

Now, the rub is that the Feds say you can save up to $11,000 in 2002, but your company plan may not let you. Employers, says Martha Priddy Patterson, a director at Deloitte & Touche, "can set any limits they want."

Actually, it's not as arbitrary as it sounds. Companies have limits to comply with, too. Until 2001, employers could deduct from their taxes the amount of 401(k) contributions made in any given year (whether it came from them or from the employees) but only up to 15 percent of total compensation (the total sum it spent on salaries in any given year). Above that, the companies had to fork over a hefty excise tax. But with the 2001 tax act, there is no excise tax and the tax deductible limit jumps to 25 percent—another reason for your company to be more generous.

Technically speaking, you should be able to contribute more after-tax, too. And your company ought to contribute more to your 401(k) as well. This is because the new tax bill also increased the limits on the total annual contributions to 401(k)s, for both your contributions and your employer's combined. The limit used to be either 25 percent of your compensation or $35,000 a year—whichever was less. Now it's 100 percent of your compensation or $40,000, whichever is less. Say you make $60,000 a year. Under the old limits the most you could have in total plan contributions—pretax, after-tax, and company contributions combined—would have been $15,000 (25 percent of $60,000). Under the new rules, the total contributions to your plan could be up to $40,000. That's a big difference. Of course, this is just the federal guideline. Your company plan can set its own maximum, which may be lower than the federal limit.

Will anyone—say in a dual-income family—ever be able to save 100 percent of salary in a 401(k)? Probably not. "No employer is going to permit that," says Patterson. There's FICA and Medicare withholding to think of, for starters. "But I can see people—double-income families working on their savings—going up to 50 or 60 percent."

## Here Come the "Catch-up" Contributions

Trying to make up for lost time? If you're 50 or older and feel like you're lagging behind in your retirement savings, you can make annual, pretax "catch-up" contributions—on top of your other savings—to your 401(k) (assuming your plan allows it). The limit on catch-up contributions will be phased in from 2002 to 2006 ($1,000 each year), until it hits $5,000 in 2006.

## Lower-Income Individuals Get a Tax Credit

The new tax law allows lower-income wage earners to receive a tax credit of up to 50 percent of $2,000 annually for contributions to IRAs and qualified retirement plans such as 401(k)s, 403(b)s, and 457 plans. Like all tax credits, there's a schedule based on adjusted gross income:

| Joint Return | Head of Household | All Others | Credit Percentage |
| --- | --- | --- | --- |
| $30,000 or less | $22,500 or less | $15,000 or less | 50% |
| $30,001 to $32,500 | $22,501 to $24,375 | $15,001 to $16,250 | 20% |
| $32,501 to $50,000 | $24,376 to $37,500 | $16,251 to $25,000 | 10% |

Just because you make over $25,000 each year doesn't mean you're out of luck. If you fork over enough of your pretax pay into a qualified retirement plan, you may be able to bring your adjusted gross income down enough to qualify for the credit. The bad news with this one: It's effective only for the tax years 2002 through

2006. The good news: It's a federal tax credit, so your employer can't mess things up by choosing not to offer it.

### Faster Vesting Schedules

The new tax law didn't go as far as eliminating these irritating vesting schedules—which basically make you wait a few years before you can claim any of the money your company has contributed to your 401(k). But it did shorten them: Before the 2001 tax law, employer-provided benefits generally had to vest according to either of two vesting schedules. Either "cliff" vesting, in which the employee's interest becomes 100 percent upon the completion of five years of service; or "graded" vesting, in which the employer-provided benefits vest in 20 percent increments, beginning with the completion of three years of service and ending with the completion of seven years. Under the new tax law, employer matching contributions that are not immediately available to you must vest either on a three-year cliff schedule or on a six-year graded vesting schedule at the rate of 20 percent after two years of service and an additional 20 percent for each following year through the sixth year.

### Looser Rules about Rollovers

Believe it or not, it used to be that you could only roll over a 401(k) into another company's 401(k) plan or an IRA. You couldn't, say, roll it over into a 403(b) plan or even an annuity. And vice versa. A 403(b) could be rolled over only into another 403(b) or an IRA. Now you can roll over distributions from any qualified plan—403(b), IRA, 401(k), 457 plan—into any other kind of plan, effective beginning 2002.

After-tax contributions are a different story. Before the new tax law, after-tax contributions to employer retirement plans could not be rolled over to another company plan or an IRA. Now they can be rolled over into another company's plan or an IRA—along with the pretax and matching contributions—as long as you keep the after-tax portion in a separate account. The reason: These separate amounts will be taxed differently when you withdraw them in retirement.

## Step 2: Open a Roth IRA

Once you've chipped in to your 401(k) plan, stick your next retirement savings dollars in a Roth IRA—which you can do if you earn less than $110,000 (adjusted gross income; less than $160,000 if you're married). That's a better option than putting it in the 401(k) without a match. You can't deduct any of your Roth IRA contributions on your tax return, but all the gains on your account will be tax-free when you withdraw them—which will outweigh any immediate benefit you'd ever get from a tax deduction. With the pretax money you've got sitting in your 401(k), you'll eventually owe taxes at your income tax rate. That could lop a quarter to a third off your gains.

Keep putting your excess savings into the Roth until you've hit the limit you're allowed to contribute to it each year—it's $3,000 in 2002 to 2004; $4,000 from 2005 to 2007; and $5,000 in 2008. Thereafter, the contribution limit will be adjusted for inflation in $500 increments.

# Your 401(k) versus Roth IRA and Other Investments

**SIDEBAR 3.4**

There are a lot of places you can put your retirement money, but—based on our analysis of the stock market over the past two decades—none compares with an employer-matched 401(k) plan. If you had invested $100 a month for the past 20 years in your 401(k), it would have outdistanced any other investment vehicle. (All returns were assumed to have matched the S&P 500. All figures assume that deferred taxes were paid the day you retired and tax savings were reinvested. Typical commissions and fees are included.)

| | |
|---|---|
| 401(k) plan with 50% employer match | $184,074 |
| Roth IRA | $147,287 |
| Regular IRA | $133.237 |
| Nondeductible IRA | $108,966 |
| Your own large-cap portfolio | $108,259 |
| Taxable no-load mutual fund | $100,820 |
| Variable annuity (large-cap subaccount) | $97,013 |
| Taxable fully loaded mutual fund | $91,488 |

## Step 3: Maximize Your Nonmatched 401(k) Contributions

Next, go back to the 401(k) and max out on your nonmatched contribution limit.

The reason for this is simple: Pretax dollars go into your 401(k). That means you save, depending on your income tax bracket, probably 27 to 35 cents on every dollar (and that doesn't even include city and state taxes) as it compounds over time. It's true that eventually you'll owe income taxes on the money and the gains that have accrued when you start drawing on your 401(k). But at least this money will be growing tax-deferred until then.

# The Best Way to Roll Over Your 401(k)

**SIDEBAR 3.5**

So you've handed in your resignation, you've boxed up those pictures of your adorable offspring, and you're getting ready to burn rubber out of the company parking lot for the last time.

It's a great feeling. But before you go, here's a question you might not have thought about much: What are you going to do with the money you've got stashed in your 401(k)? Will you take it with you and invest it somewhere else, or will you leave it behind to keep growing in your current plan?

Here's what we suggest.

Roll over the money into an individual retirement account. Why? Because it will give you the flexibility to invest your savings wherever you see fit. "With a typical 401(k) plan, you have five to seven investment choices," says Richard Moran, a financial planner at Financial Network Investment Corporation in Rolling Hills, California. "With an IRA, they're countless."

Some people mistakenly think they're not eligible to roll over their 401(k)s into IRAs because their income levels are too high. Big mistake. They're confusing regular IRAs (the kind where you can put in $3,000 every year and deduct the contribution on your tax return) with rollover IRAs. You can roll over *any* amount from a qualified retirement plan into an IRA, no matter what your income. It will grow tax-deferred until you start taking it out.

Any mutual fund company will be more than happy to set up an IRA for you. So, too, will discount brokers such as TD Waterhouse, Muriel Siebert, and Charles Schwab. The advantages of using a broker are: (1) you'll be able to choose from a far wider variety of mutual funds, and (2) you can also buy and sell individual stocks, bonds, and even options through your account (though we wouldn't advise the latter).

The fees in most discount-brokerage IRAs are no different from what you'd pay in a 401(k) plan. For example, Waterhouse—a firm that continually wins top ratings in our annual broker survey—has no start-up or administrative fees for IRAs. The only time you'll pay a fee is when you make a trade.

If you do roll over your 401(k) into an IRA, keep it in a separate account from any other IRA or simplified employee pension (SEP) money you might already have, financial advisers suggest. (In other words, don't roll the 401(k) money into an existing IRA or SEP account.) The reason: If you decide at some later point to move the 401(k) money into the retirement plan at your new company—because your employer comes out with a great new program you just can't resist, say—you'll have an accounting nightmare on your hands. That's because any *non*-401(k) money in the IRA will have to be separated out, along with interest and dividends, before you can move it along. Trust us; it's a mess.

Is there any advantage to skipping an IRA and rolling your 401(k) directly into your new company's plan? Absolutely. You'll have all your retirement money in one account, for one advantage. A lot of companies these days will let you borrow against your 401(k), which is something you can't do with an IRA. And you'll have an extra layer of protection if your finances take a turn for the worse: In 1992 the Supreme Court decided that 401(k)s are exempt from creditors suing for assets in a bankruptcy. Some states afford IRAs the same protection, though not all of them do.

The important thing, whether you're putting the money into an IRA or into your new company's retirement plan, is to do what's called a direct rollover. Your benefits department will make out a check directly to the brokerage company or the 401(k) plan where you're putting the money. If you do an indirect rollover—where you receive the check in your name and then deposit it in the fund's account—your old employer has to take out 20 percent for tax purposes. Yes, you'll get the money back as an income tax refund, but who wants to deal with that? (In case you're tempted to just keep the cash and not roll it over, consider this: You'll owe income taxes on the money if you don't roll it over within 60 days, and you will be slapped with a 10 percent penalty—and you won't get a penny of it back.)

How about simply leaving your money behind in your old company plan? There's not necessarily anything wrong with that, assuming you're happy with the investment choices. The biggest disadvantage is that the money is in the hands of your *ex*-employer. Is that really who you want lording it over your retirement money, now that you've left the company? Clearly, the rollover option is better.

## Step 4: Open a Nondeductible IRA

If you can't open a Roth because of your income level, the next best place for your savings after you've maxed out with your company plan—both the matched and unmatched portions—is a nondeductible IRA.

Again, there's a cap on annual contributions: $3,000 for single filers from 2002 to 2004 ($6,000 for married couples); $4,000 from 2005 to 2007; and $5,000 in 2008. After 20 years, the tax-deferred compounding on an average stock market investment will give you 5 to 15 percent more to spend during retirement than the same investment in a taxable account would.

One last word: One of the greatest selling points about an IRA is that the contributions you make to it are tax-deductible. But if you are contributing to your 401(k), then the money you put away every year in your IRA is *not* tax-deductible—unless your income falls within a certain range. In general, you can take up to $3,000 (in 2002 and 2003) in deductible IRA contributions a year, as long as you have at least $3,000 in earned income.

# IRA Participation

- Of the 89 percent of all single workers eligible to make tax-deductible IRA contributions, only 5 percent contribute.
- Of the 56 percent of dual-earner married couples eligible to make deductible IRA contributions, only 10 percent choose to do so.
- Among the 82 percent of eligible single-earner married couples, 9 percent make IRA contributions.

*Source:* Employee Benefits Research Institute.

But if you're an active participant in an employer-sponsored retirement plan like a 401(k), here's the deal: For single taxpayers, the maximum IRA deduction ($3,000 in 2002) starts to shrink when your adjusted gross income (AGI) hits $34,000—and if your AGI is over $44,000, the deduction is $0. For married couples, the range is $54,000 to $64,000. Every year the AGI range will be raised a little:

*Singles*
$34,000 to $44,000 in 2002
$40,000 to $50,000 in 2003
$45,000 to $55,000 in 2004
$50,000 to $60,000 in 2005 and thereafter

*Married Couples*
$54,000 to $64,000 in 2002
$60,000 to $70,000 in 2003
$65,000 to $75,000 in 2004
$70,000 to $80,000 in 2005
$75,000 to $85,000 in 2006
$80,000 to $100,000 in 2007 and thereafter

## Step 5: Invest in Stocks

Open a regular brokerage account and invest in individual stocks or stock mutual funds.

When you've exhausted all the options described so far, in most cases you should turn to a taxable investment, especially if you plan to put the money in stocks of any type: small-cap, mid-cap, large-cap, or foreign. The key to choosing taxable investments for your retirement savings is to keep your expenses down and get the most benefit from the 20 percent long-term capital gains rate. (If you aren't retiring for a while, you may qualify for the new 18 percent rate, which is open to anyone in the 27 percent income tax bracket and above who has held a security for more than five years. But this rate doesn't kick in until 2006 and applies only to securities acquired on or after January 1, 2001.) To qualify for the 20 percent rate means holding your stocks for at least 12 months—longer, if possible—and choosing mutual funds with a low annual turnover (the rate at which the fund manager buys and sells holdings). Since the law requires that mutual funds' gains from selling stocks be distributed to fund investors, the higher the turnover rate, the greater the amount of your return each year that will be subject to taxation—and that amount may be taxed at higher rates.

## Step 6: Forget Variable Annuities

Where do variable annuities, those retirement investments so beloved by financial advisers and insurance salespeople, enter into all this? (Surely you've gotten one of those sales-pitch phone calls by now.)

Forget them. Their exceptionally high expenses often counteract the tax-deferred aspects of those contracts. Variable annuities make sense only for a fixed-income asset such as bonds or cash, *and* only if you are saving for at least 12 years. In that case, the gains from compounding your interest free of income tax eventually outweigh the drag created by higher fees. The exact number of years necessary to come out ahead depends on your tax bracket and the income yield of your investments.

# The ABCs of Retirement Accounts

When it comes to retirement savings, your first line of attack should be tax-advantaged accounts like an IRA, your 401(k), 403(b), or Roth IRA. But to the uninitiated, the names of these various accounts—much less how they differ from one another—sound more like traffic violations in police-speak.

For those *not* in the know, or for anyone who needs a refresher, here's a primer on retirement accounts. How much can you sock away every year in each one? How is each account taxed upon distribution? And most important (because this is what sets retirement accounts apart from regular ones), what kinds of tax breaks come with each one? One last thing: Since all these are retirement accounts, there's one rule that applies to all of them. If you withdraw money from an account prematurely—before the age of $59\frac{1}{2}$—you'll likely pay income taxes on the sum plus a 10 percent penalty. Penalty-free early withdrawals are allowed in some cases. For instance, Roth IRA funds can be used for education expenses.

## 401(k) Plan

Named after a section in the U.S. tax code, the first 401(k) was launched in 1981. Now, some 20-plus years later, more than 42 million Americans participate in one. This type of retirement-savings plan is sponsored by your employer, but you do most of the funding, with contributions that are siphoned from your salary before taxes have been deducted. That's the first bonus these accounts present: You save (or rather keep), depending on your marginal tax rate, 27 to 38 cents for every dollar you contribute to the plan, and lower your adjusted gross income (or possibly federal tax rate) at the same time. But the biggest bonus, which makes participating in a 401(k) almost a no-brainer, is that many employers will match your contributions up to a set limit. And you can borrow against your account in case of emergencies. Finally, you manage how the money is invested (which is why these accounts are often described as "self-directed"), allocating the funds among a selection of stock, bond, and cash investment funds chosen by your employer, and in some cases company stock. Investment gains aren't taxed until the money is withdrawn.

*Who qualifies:* Either your company offers a plan like this or it doesn't. If it does, every employee is eligible, but the timing of when you can start contributing money—and get matching contributions from your employer—depends on the rules for your company plan (often it hinges on how long you have worked there). At most companies, you can enroll immediately in your 401(k) on your first day of employment. But some companies make you wait a year or even more. At many companies, too, there is a waiting period, called a vesting period, before you can consider the money the company has contributed to your account as yours. In other words, if you leave your employer before you vest, then you forfeit any of the matching money your company has chipped in. (The money *you* have contributed is yours to take with you, of course.)

*Yearly contribution limit:* In 2002, the maximum contribution limit is $11,000. (Over the following four years, that limit will rise $1,000 a year to $15,000 in 2006.) But this amount may vary, depending on how much you earn a year and the rules of your company plan.

*Tax benefits:* Pretax money goes into 401(k) accounts. Investment gains aren't taxed until the money is withdrawn.

*Distribution:* Any withdrawals (assuming you have retired) will be taxed as income.

### 403(b) and 457 Plans

There are two other retirement plans that work like the 401(k): the 403(b) plan and the 457 plan. The 403(b)—often called the 401(k) for nonprofits—is a retirement-savings plan for employees of colleges, hospitals, school districts, and nonprofit organizations. The plan is funded by employees with contributions that are deducted from pretax pay. Employees manage the money themselves, selecting from fixed and variable annuities, and from mutual funds. Investment gains aren't taxed until withdrawn, but once withdrawn the money is taxed as income.

A 457 plan is a tax-deferred savings account for employees of a state or local government. Under Section 457 of the Internal Revenue Code, you may defer each year a maximum of 100 percent of compensation or $11,000 (in 2002), whichever is less. This is pretax pay, and the money, once withdrawn during retirement, is taxed as income. In addition, in most cases, you can't tap into the money unless you are no longer an employee or you have an unforeseeable emergency.

### Individual Retirement Account (IRA)

This is the granddaddy of tax-deferred retirement plans. In some cases—for people whose income falls under a certain amount ($34,000 for singles, $54,000 for married couples to get the full deduction) or who aren't participants in an employer-sponsored retirement plan—annual IRA contributions are tax-deductible (then they're often called "deductible IRAs"). Otherwise, IRA contributions are nondeductible (and these accounts are called "nondeductible IRAs"). A single person can contribute up to $3,000 and a married couple up to $6,000 annually. The contributions grow tax-deferred until withdrawn. (By contrast, contributions to Roth IRAs—see below—grow tax-free and stay tax-free even after withdrawal.)

*Who qualifies:* Everyone who has earned income (of at least $3,000) that year.

*Yearly contribution limit:* $3,000 for single filers; $6,000 for married couples. (This limit will increase to $4,000 in 2005 and to $5,000 in 2008.) If you're 50 or older, the 2001 tax law also permits so-called "catch-up" contributions. The limits on these will be $500 (in addition to the $3,000) between 2002 and 2005; $1,000 in 2006 and thereafter.

*Tax benefits:* You can deduct your full contribution on your federal tax form—as long as you don't participate in an employer-sponsored retirement plan, and as long as your income falls under $34,000 for single filers and $54,000 for joint filers. Investment gains are tax-deferred until you withdraw money from that account.

*Distribution:* Taxed as income.

There are two other kinds of IRAs: Savings incentive match plan for employees (SIMPLE IRAs) and simplified employee pensions (SEPs).

You'll find only SIMPLE IRAs at mom-and-pop type of business or companies with fewer than 100 employees that don't otherwise offer a retirement plan. Think of it as a combination IRA you'd open on your own and a 401(k) plan that an employer would offer you. Both you and your employer make contributions, all of which grow tax-deferred until withdrawal. At that time you'll pay taxes on the money as ordinary income. There is of course a cap on contributions: $7,000 (in 2002) for employees, plus your employer's contribution. A SEP (simplified employee pension) is a tax-deferred retirement plan for self-employed and small business owners.

**Keogh Plan**

This is another retirement plan for the self-employed, but the difference is you can make significantly higher contributions—25 percent of your self-employed income or $40,000, whichever is less. There are two main types of Keogh plans—a profit sharing plan and a money purchase plan. With the money purchase plan, the annual contribution is fixed—you must make the same percentage of salary contribution every year. With profit sharing plans, contributions can change each year, depending on how well the business did, for example. Like most retirement plans, contributions and earnings grow tax-deferred until withdrawal, presumably at the time of retirement. At that time they are taxed as ordinary income.

*Who qualifies:* Anyone who is self-employed.

*Yearly contribution limit:* For both money-purchase plan and profit-sharing Keoghs, contributions are limited to the lesser of $40,000 or 25 percent of your self-employment income.

*Tax benefits:* You can deduct the entire amount of your Keogh contributions from your income each year.

*Distribution:* Withdrawals are taxed as ordinary income.

## Roth IRA

This is a new twist on an IRA and was established a few years ago with the Taxpayer Relief Act of 1997. The difference between a regular IRA and a Roth IRA: Your contributions are nondeductible—you can't write them off on your tax return, unlike with an IRA—but withdrawals, subject to certain rules, are tax-free. Translation: Once the money is in there, it can grow and grow and grow and you'll never pay a penny in taxes on it. The distinction makes a big difference at the end of the road when you start taking distributions. Let's say you save $3,000 a year for 30 years and earn a 10 percent return. At the start of your retirement, both a Roth IRA account and a traditional IRA account will total $519,823. But as you begin to take distributions, assuming you're still earning a 7 percent rate of return on your investments, taxes (assuming a 27 percent federal and a 10 percent state rate) will eat away more than $78,000 from the traditional IRA. The Roth, on the other hand, won't lose a penny to taxes.

*Who qualifies:* Those with an adjusted gross income below $110,000 for single filers; $160,000 for joint filers. Anyone who makes over that amount is out of luck and will have to open an IRA.

*Yearly contribution limit:* $3,000 for single filers; $6,000 for married couples. (This limit will increase to $4,000 in 2005, and $5,000 in 2008.) If you're 50 or older, the 2001 tax law also permits so-called "catch-up" contributions. The limits on these will be $500 (in addition to the $3,000) between 2002 and 2005; $1,000 in 2006 and thereafter.

*Tax benefits:* Contributions and earnings grow tax-free, and withdrawals—whether it's principal or investment gains—aren't taxed at all.

*Distribution:* Money withdrawn is tax-free.

### Roth 401(k) and 403(b) Plans

Don't get too excited—yet. These accounts won't be available until 2006. But be ready to sign up when the time comes. It is what it sounds like: You can designate after-tax contributions as "qualified Roth contributions." When you withdraw these contributions (and the earnings), they will not be subject to tax, as long as (1) those particular distributions have been accounted for separately; (2) the account is at least five years old; and (3) you are $59\frac{1}{2}$ or older; or in the event of death or disability. These distributions also may be rolled over from a designated Roth account and into another designated Roth account or into a Roth IRA.

# PART TWO

# YOUR
# RETIREMENT
# SAVINGS

# 4

# YOUR IDEAL
# ASSET ALLOCATION

We'd all like to fund our entire retirement on the spectacular gains of a single well-chosen stock. During the late 1990s, stories of genius-like ordinary investors who happened to make $1 million on Dell Computer or Cisco Systems flowed freely. But the reality is, that never—or very rarely—happens.

At *SmartMoney*, we like to think it doesn't happen for good reason. Betting the farm on a single stock—or a single anything, even a money-market account or Treasury bills (T-Bills)—more often leads to shattered dreams than it does lottery-like riches. Let's say you go "safe" and plunk your entire nest egg in a money-market account. At a measly 4 percent (if that) annual growth rate, you'll never make enough money to fund your golden years. You may not even keep pace with inflation.

This is where asset allocation comes in—a structured program to balance your long-term investments among various types of stocks (or mutual funds), bonds, and cash.

Why asset allocation, you ask?

When it comes to risk and reward, different asset classes—stocks, bonds, or cash—behave differently over time. Stocks offer a high return—about 11 percent a year on average, historically—but they also carry the highest risk of losses. Just look at what happened to the S&P 500 index in recent years (it dropped 10 percent in 2000 and 13 percent in 2001). Intermediate-term bonds, meanwhile, have returned about 8 percent historically over the past 30 years. But they're considerably more stable than stocks. Finally, money-market returns are puny—historically less than 4 percent on average and in 2002 less than 2 percent—but the upside is you'll never lose your initial investment. Bottom line: The greater the risk, the higher the return.

Whether your goal is to preserve the money you've saved so far, grow it as fast as you can, or something in between, an asset allocation strategy allows you to achieve what you want with the optimal blend of risk and reward. Getting ready to retire and you don't want to risk a sudden downdraft in the market? Or are you just normally risk-averse? A portfolio of mostly bonds and fewer stocks is more appropriate for you. You have 30 or more years to retirement and you're gunning for growth? Go for mostly stocks.

You already allocate your assets in some form or another—by accident or by design—by dividing what you own into various investment categories: real estate, cash, stocks, and mutual funds. Put simply, asset allocation embodies the time-honored adage, "Don't put all your eggs in one basket." (See Figure 4.1.) But very few people, at any moment, can say what percentage of their total assets is devoted to any particular investment. And even fewer have any idea how to approach the task of asset allocation.

Yet it can make a huge difference. Study after study has shown that portfolios invested in different kinds of assets perform better and are less

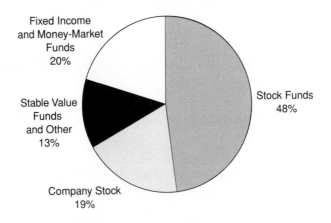

**FIGURE 4.1**   Average 401(k) Allocation
*Source:* Profit Sharing/401(k) Council of America.

risky than portfolios that are heavily weighted toward one type of asset. Some research, in fact, suggests that your investment results depend more on how your assets are allocated among stocks, bonds, and cash than on the actual investments you choose.

Say you had 54 percent of your money in one-month T-bills (the equivalent of cash), 18 percent in long bonds, 18 percent in the large-cap stocks of the S&P 500, and the remaining 9 percent in small-cap stocks. Over the years 1972 to 1999, you would have averaged a 9.4 percent return with a standard deviation of 3.9 (that's a measure of volatility; the higher the number, the greater the volatility).

But what if you scaled back the T-bills in your portfolio to just 20 percent of your portfolio and invested 12 percent of your portfolio in bonds? With 50 percent of your money in small caps and 18 percent in large caps, your average annual return over those 24 years sprouts to 12.6 percent and your best six months grows to a remarkable 43 percent. Your volatility rises, too, but over that amount of time, you can certainly afford to wait out the declines.

In some cases, you don't have to sacrifice higher returns for increased volatility; a well-diversified portfolio can actually lower your volatility and fetch a better return at the same time. When we asked the well-regarded researchers at Ibbotson Associates to put together some diversified portfolios (for illustration purposes only), we found that with some combinations you can actually lift your return and lower your volatility at the same time. (See Table 4.1.)

What's the right mix for you? It depends on a number of factors, including your age, the size of your portfolio, how much risk you're willing to take on, your tax bracket, and your outlook on the economy, among others.

Many retirement books offer general guidelines for asset allocation depending largely on your age. The younger you are and the more money you have, the more you can afford the short-term volatility of stocks. But as you age, or if your spending needs increase, the more you'll need to protect your principal by shifting money toward bonds and cash.

But "general" is the operative word when it comes to these guidelines. Most often, the advice for anyone under 30 goes something like this: 90 percent equities; 10 percent cash. As you get older, the mix gets slightly more complicated. Over 50 years old, and you start getting into bonds and safer kinds of equities: 30 percent growth and income; 30 percent utilities;

## TABLE 4.1   HIGHER RETURN–AND LOWER VOLATILITY, TOO

| Portfolio | Allocation | Average Annual Return | Standard Deviation |
| --- | --- | --- | --- |
| **Portfolio One** | | 11.58% | 11.17% |
| Large-cap stocks | 60% | | |
| Intermediate-term bonds | 15% | | |
| Long-term bonds | 15% | | |
| Cash | 10% | | |
| **Portfolio Two** | | 11.92% | 10.58% |
| Large-cap stocks | 37% | | |
| Foreign stocks | 15% | | |
| Long-term bonds | 15% | | |
| Intermediate-term bonds | 15% | | |
| Cash | 10% | | |
| Small-cap stocks | 8% | | |

*Source:* Ibbotson Associates.

30 percent high-yield bonds; 10 percent cash. Frankly, we don't think that's enough information.

What those guidelines don't help you with is how much of your stock portfolio should be allocated to international stocks or small-company stocks or blue chips. Does it matter? You bet.

If you had invested all of your money in the S&P 500 (basically a portfolio of just blue-chip stocks) 30 years ago you would have earned 13.21 percent. See Table 4.2, "Returns of Stock Market Investments." A portfolio of small-cap stocks performed better—14.71 percent a year from 1971 to 2000—but it was also significantly more volatile. Meanwhile, say you'd put all of your money in international stocks over the past 30 years. You'd have less money than if you had invested in large-cap blue-chip stocks, and your portfolio would have suffered a lot of bumps along the way. Slice and dice your money into all three kinds of stocks, however, and look at the result: a better return than the all-blue-chip or all-international portfolio (but not the all-small-cap), but with far less volatility.

Which brings us to the SmartMoney One asset allocation program. (We

## TABLE 4.2     RETURNS OF STOCK MARKET INVESTMENTS

| $10,000 INVESTED IN ... Portfolio | Return After 30 Years | Standard Deviation* | Money After 30 Years |
|---|---|---|---|
| 100% Blue-chip stocks | 13.21 | 16.45 | $413,565 |
| 100% Small-cap stocks | 14.71 | 22.15 | $613,816 |
| 100% International stocks | 13.06 | 21.75 | $397,438 |
| Mixed portfolio: | 13.75 | 15.82 | $477,026 |
|   70% Blue-chip stocks | | | |
|   15% Small-cap stocks | | | |
|   15% International stocks | | | |

*Standard deviation is a measure of volatility.
*Source:* Ibbotson Associates.

call it that because we consider it the *one* asset allocation program you'll ever need.) If our worksheet later in this chapter looks a little daunting, don't worry. You should be able to complete it in 15 minutes or less—and when you're done you will have a very good idea of how to spread your assets among large, small, and international stocks (as well as bonds and cash). What's more, it is customized to your goals and personality—not the needs of some hypothetical *über* investor—because it incorporates variables that are particular to you: age, income, net worth, your risk tolerance, and your expectations about the future.

The allocation we're designing here is for your wealth-building portfolio. By that we mean the money that you've set aside for your long-term savings, including your retirement accounts. However, money that you have already earmarked for shorter-term goals, such as a dream vacation or a down payment on a new house, should not be included. Keep in mind, too, that this is a *guide* to asset allocation, not a hard-and-fast plan. The mix you derive after running through the worksheet isn't meant to be carved in stone. The more experience you get investing, the more you'll be able to fine-tune your investments to fit your needs, investment style, and risk tolerance.

What's more, a good asset allocation plan should be rebalanced every year. Uneven price movements in your investments can upset the balance of your portfolio over time. In addition, your circumstances can change—you grow older every year, your tax bracket jumps up (and hopefully not down), or your outlook on the future of the economy changes. So be sure to check in every year and redo the worksheet. This will add a vital measure of discipline to your investing as well: It will prod you to take the appropriate amount of risk when you're feeling overly cautious and will rein you in during those times when the sky seems to be the limit.

Say you do the worksheet and your ideal allocation calls for 10 percent cash, 15 percent bonds, and 75 percent stocks—with the stock portion split three ways among large-company, small-company, and international equities. As the year progresses, your large-cap stocks soar for a 20 percent gain, but your small caps decline and everything else stays about the same. At the end of the year, you'd have a choice of ways to restore the balance. You could use new money to buy more small-company stocks on the cheap, as well as new portions of bonds and cash. Or you could sell some of the more expensive large-company winners. Buy low, sell high. It's fundamental to sound investing.

# The SmartMoney Allocation Principles

The SmartMoney One program starts with how old you are. In Worksheet 4.1, you first assign yourself a score based on your age; then you make adjustments to your score depending on your answers to eight different questions about your financial situation. Certain answers will increase your stock or bond allocations. Other answers will lead to neutral or negative adjustments, reducing your exposure to market volatility.

## Age

The longer you have to save and invest, the more risk you can take on, and thus the less you need to cut back your exposure to equities. That's why your age—rather, how much time you have before you hit retirement—is arguably the most important factor in how you allocate your investments.

A 30-year-old with 30 or more years of investing returns to look forward to can take on a little market volatility; there's still time to make up any losses later. Of course, we're not saying that 50-year-olds can't be aggressive when it comes to equities. Wealth building is still important. But so is

# The SmartMoney One Worksheet

**PART A** To fill out the SmartMoney One asset allocation worksheet, you will first need to answer the following questions about your financial situation and your investment outlook. We suggest you highlight or circle the entire row (columns A through D) of the response that best fits. Then, when the worksheet requires you to make adjustments to your allocations based on this table (lines 2, 4, 11, and 18), it will be easier to find the required score from the appropriate column. *Note:* You will not know the correct response to the last question (Interest-Rate Exposure) until you fill in line 7 of Part B. (NA = Not applicable.)

| | A | B | C | D |
|---|---|---|---|---|
| **Portfolio Size** | | | | |
| What is the value of your investment portfolio? | | | | |
| Less than $50,000 | 3 | 0 | 0 | 0 |
| Between $50,000 and $250,000 | −1 | 15 | 4 | 4 |
| Greater than $250,000 | −3 | 20 | 6 | 10 |
| **Yearly Savings** | | | | |
| How much do you save a year? | | | | |
| Less than $2,000 | 2 | NA | 0 | 0 |
| Between $2,000 and $10,000 | −1 | NA | 2 | 2 |
| Over $10,000 | −2 | NA | 8 | 6 |
| **Spending Needs** | | | | |
| What portion of your investments do you plan to spend (for education, home, etc.) over the next 10 years? | | | | |
| 0 to 30 percent | −3 | NA | 15 | 10 |
| 31 to 60 percent | 2 | NA | 5 | 4 |
| 61 to 100 percent | 7 | NA | 0 | 0 |
| **Investment Income** | | | | |
| How much income do you need to generate from your investments? | | | | |
| Less than 1 percent | NA | 10 | 10 | NA |
| Between 1 and 4 percent | NA | 15 | 4 | NA |
| More than 4 percent | NA | 25 | 0 | NA |
| **Federal Tax Bracket** | | | | |
| What is your marginal federal tax rate? | | | | |
| 15 percent | 0 | NA | 0 | NA |
| 27 percent | −1 | NA | 2 | NA |
| 30 percent or greater | −4 | NA | 6 | NA |
| **Volatility Tolerance** | | | | |
| How much volatility can you live with? | | | | |
| As little as possible | 2 | 5 | 0 | 0 |
| A moderate amount | −1 | 10 | 5 | 3 |
| A lot | −5 | 15 | 14 | 6 |
| **Economic Outlook** | | | | |
| What is your reading on the U.S. economy over the next 12 months? | | | | |
| Weak | 2 | 20 | 0 | 10 |
| Average | −5 | 10 | 6 | 0 |
| Strong | −8 | 0 | 10 | −10 |
| **Interest-Rate Exposure** | | | | |
| To make sure you are not overly exposed to interest-rate risk, you will adjust your small-cap and foreign allocations for the size of your bond holdings. When you get to line 7 of Part B, note if the bond allocation is . . . | | | | |
| Less than 15 percent | NA | NA | 0 | 0 |
| Between 15 and 35 percent | NA | NA | 6 | 10 |
| Greater than 35 percent | NA | NA | 10 | 20 |

**WORKSHEET 4.1**   The SmartMoney One Worksheet

**PART B**

**1. Enter your age.** _____
(If you are younger than 25, enter 25; if you are older than 80, enter 80. If you are filling out the worksheet as a couple, average your ages.)

**2. FIXED INCOME:** Choose the score in column A from Part A.
   a. **Portfolio Size** _____
   b. **Yearly Savings** _____
   c. **Spending Needs** _____
   d. **Federal Tax Bracket** _____
   e. **Volatility Tolerance** _____
   f. **Economic Outlook** _____

**3.** Add lines 1 and 2a through 2f. (If result is greater than 100, enter 100.) _____

**4. BONDS:** Choose the score in column B from Part A.
   a. **Portfolio Size** _____
   b. **Investment Income** _____
   c. **Volatility Tolerance** _____
   d. **Economic Outlook** _____

**5.** Add lines 4a through 4d. _____

**6.** Divide line 5 by 100. _____

**7.** Multiply line 3 by line 6. _This is your Bond allocation._ _____%

**8.** Subtract line 7 from line 3. _This is your Cash allocation._ _____%

**9. STOCKS:** Subtract line 3 from 100. _____

**10.** Subtract your age from 70. (If answer is less than zero, enter zero.) _____

**11. SMALL CAPS:** Choose the score in column C from Part A.
   a. **Portfolio Size** _____
   b. **Yearly Savings** _____
   c. **Spending Needs** _____
   d. **Investment Income** _____
   e. **Federal Tax Bracket** _____
   f. **Volatility Tolerance** _____
   g. **Economic Outlook** _____
   h. **Interest-Rate Exposure** _____

**12.** Add lines 10 and 11a through 11h. _____

**13.** Divide line 12 by 200. _____

**14.** Multiply line 9 by line 13. _This is your Small-Cap allocation._ _____%

**15. FOREIGN STOCKS:** Enter 40. Then, if you are younger than 60, skip to line 18. Otherwise continue with the next two lines. _____

**16.** Subtract 60 from your age. _____

**17.** Subtract line 16 from line 15. Use this result on line 19. _____

**18.** Choose the score in column D from Part A.
   a. **Portfolio Size** _____
   b. **Yearly Savings** _____
   c. **Spending Needs** _____
   d. **Volatility Tolerance** _____
   e. **Economic Outlook** _____
   f. **Interest-Rate Exposure** _____

**19.** Add either the amount in line 15 or line 17 to the sum of lines 18a through 18f. (If the result is negative, enter zero.) _____

**20.** Divide line 19 by 200. _____

**21.** Multiply line 9 by line 20. _This is your Foreign Stock allocation._ _____%

**22.** Add line 14 and line 21. _____

**23.** Subtract line 22 from line 9. _This is your Large-Cap allocation._ _____%

**24. YOUR INVESTMENT MIX:** Enter the total value of your portfolio. $_____

**25. ALLOCATION AMOUNTS:**
   a. Multiply line 24 by percent on line 8.
      **Cash** $_____
   b. Multiply line 24 by percent on line 7.
      **Bonds** $_____
   c. Multiply line 24 by percent on line 23.
      **Large-cap U.S. stocks** $_____
   d. Multiply line 24 by percent on line 14.
      **Small-cap U.S. stocks** $_____
   e. Multiply line 24 by percent on line 21.
      **Foreign stocks** $_____

**WORKSHEET 4.1**   _(Continued)_

**How Long Should You Plan on Your Money Lasting?**

What could be worse than strategically saving and planning for your retirement, only to have your funds run out? We suggest you ignore the statistics on average life expectancy. They will lead you to adopt a plan that will leave you with a 50 percent chance of outliving your money—an even greater chance if medical science keeps lengthening people's lives. Use the ages listed in Table 4.3 instead. You'll have much less chance of your retirement funds running out.

**How Much Can You Spend Each Year?**

To see how much income you can safely extract from your retirement portfolio each year, divide the current value of your investments by $1,000 and multiply the result by the appropriate dollar amount in Table 4.4. Thus, someone expecting to live 20 more years in a world of 2 percent inflation could withdraw $33,485 each year from a portfolio worth $500,000 if it earned 7 percent a year after taxes (500 × $66.97 = $33,485). If inflation rose to 4 percent, the retiree could safely spend only $27,550.

## TABLE 4.3    LIFE EXPECTANCY– 20 PERCENT CHANCE

| At Age . . . | You Have at Least a 20 Percent Chance of Living . . . | |
| --- | --- | --- |
| | **(Female)** | **(Male)** |
| 54 | 37 more years | 33 more years |
| 55 | 35 | 31 |
| 56 | 33 | 29 |
| 58 | 31 | 28 |
| 60 | 29 | 26 |
| 62 | 28 | 24 |
| 64 | 26 | 22 |
| 66 | 24 | 20 |
| 68 | 22 | 19 |
| 70 | 20 | 17 |
| 72 | 19 | 16 |
| 76 | 17 | 14 |

*Source:* National Center for Health Statistics.

**WORKSHEET 4.1**    *(Continued)*

## TABLE 4.4   RETIREMENT SPENDING MULTIPLIER

| Years Remaining after Retirement | Your Expected Inflation Rate | Average Annual After-Tax Investment Growth | | | | |
|---|---|---|---|---|---|---|
| | | 5% | 6% | 7% | 8% | 9% |
| 10 | 2% | $81.03 | $86.07 | $91.23 | $96.50 | $101.85 |
| | 3 | 76.01 | 80.88 | 85.87 | 90.98 | 96.19 |
| | 4 | 71.22 | 75.92 | 80.74 | 85.68 | 90.73 |
| 15 | 2 | 64.94 | 70.31 | 75.86 | 81.56 | 87.39 |
| | 3 | 59.66 | 64.79 | 70.10 | 75.59 | 81.22 |
| | 4 | 54.68 | 59.56 | 64.64 | 69.89 | 75.32 |
| 20 | 2 | 55.42 | 61.09 | 66.97 | 73.06 | 79.31 |
| | 3 | 49.90 | 55.26 | 60.86 | 66.68 | 72.70 |
| | 4 | 44.76 | 49.80 | 55.10 | 60.64 | 66.40 |
| 25 | 2 | 49.19 | 55.12 | 61.32 | 67.75 | 74.37 |
| | 3 | 43.45 | 49.02 | 54.88 | 61.01 | 67.37 |
| | 4 | 38.16 | 43.35 | 48.85 | 54.65 | 60.71 |
| 30 | 2 | 44.82 | 51.01 | 57.50 | 64.25 | 71.19 |
| | 3 | 38.88 | 44.65 | 50.76 | 57.18 | 63.85 |
| | 4 | 33.46 | 38.78 | 44.48 | 50.52 | 56.86 |
| 35 | 2 | 41.63 | 48.05 | 54.81 | 61.84 | 69.08 |
| | 3 | 35.49 | 41.45 | 47.79 | 54.58 | 61.43 |
| | 4 | 29.95 | 35.38 | 41.27 | 47.54 | 54.15 |
| 40 | 2 | 39.21 | 45.86 | 52.87 | 60.15 | 67.63 |
| | 3 | 32.89 | 39.02 | 45.59 | 52.52 | 59.72 |
| | 4 | 27.22 | 32.78 | 38.84 | 45.33 | 52.18 |
| 45 | 2 | 37.33 | 44.19 | 51.43 | 58.94 | 66.63 |
| | 3 | 30.84 | 37.14 | 43.92 | 51.07 | 58.49 |
| | 4 | 25.04 | 30.72 | 36.95 | 43.65 | 50.72 |

*Note:* These figures include a five-year safety cushion in case you live longer than you expect or the initial years of your retirement coincide with a major bear market. They also assume that you increase your withdrawals in step with the inflation rate.

**WORKSHEET 4.1**   *(Continued)*

wealth preservation. This is particularly true as you begin to set aside big chunks of your savings for retirement. The less time you have to let your investments run freely, the more stock market fluctuations will make an impact on your final results. The SmartMoney One program takes all this into account and methodically shrinks your stock allocation as you get older.

## Portfolio Size

One of the sad truths about investing is that size matters. Simply put, the less money you have, the more you need to exercise caution and the harder it is to completely diversify your holdings. All told, it's a financial catch-22. (Take heart, however, for there's a general rule for rich people, too: The more money you have, the more capital preservation looms as a primary concern.)

If you have savings that even approach $50,000, you're ahead of most of your fellow Americans. (Check out Figure 4.2, "Are You on Track?") Unfortunately, though, with less than $50,000 even a little misstep at this point

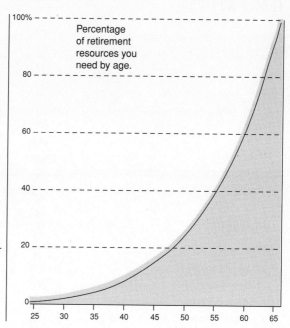

Few of us will build our retirement wealth in a nice smooth textbook curve, but it's useful to know what one looks like. Here, we took a hypothetical household that starts saving at age 25 by putting aside a little more than 10 percent of its income each year in retirement accounts. We assume this household's income increases 5 percent in real terms until age 55. Finally, we assumed 7.5 percent average real returns. (Real returns for large-cap stocks have averaged 7.7 percent annually since 1925. For small-cap stocks, the rate is 9.0 percent.) The chart shows the growth of the household's wealth as a percentage of the final nest egg value.

**FIGURE 4.2** Are You On Track?
*Source: SmartMoney.*

can make a big difference in your portfolio, because you still do not have much of an extra cushion to break your fall.

Scoring in this section of the question will ensure that more of your money goes toward the safest asset: cash. Among the other assets, bonds and large caps will be favored for their lower volatility. See Table 4.5 "Volatility of Different Assets."

With $50,000 to $250,000, you ought to feel reasonably comfortable; you have enough assets to diversify over a wide variety of investments. However hard it was to build up your nest egg, your good fortune means you can afford to risk some of these assets. At the same time we're not going to ignore the need to preserve capital; a big loss can still drag down your lifestyle even if the days when it would wipe out your savings are behind you.

If you have more than $250,000, that's sufficient to get all the diversity you need and take on as much risk as is appropriate for your age. Our point system takes all of this into account.

## Yearly Savings

The more money you save each year, the more risk you can take on in your allocation. The reason: A steady flow of new savings every year gives you a chance to make up for losses if part of your portfolio takes a hit. It's also a lot easier—and cheaper—to adjust your allocations. You can simply apply the new money where needed to restore balances, rather than selling part of

### TABLE 4.5    VOLATILITY OF DIFFERENT ASSETS

| Asset Class | 30-Year Average Annual Return | Standard Deviation |
| --- | --- | --- |
| Large-cap stocks | 13.21 | 16.45 |
| Small-cap stocks | 14.71 | 22.15 |
| International stocks | 13.06 | 21.75 |
| Long-term bonds | 9.23 | 12.30 |
| Intermediate-term bonds | 8.54 | 6.82 |
| T-bills (30-day) | 6.67 | 2.65 |

your holdings and using the proceeds to buy more of other holdings—a round trip that often involves commissions, fees, or tax liability. This is why the SmartMoney One program hikes your equity position if you maintain a steady stream of new savings.

## Spending Needs

Generally speaking, most allocation models tend to be more aggressive for young investors (a larger part of your portfolio goes into equities) and more conservative for older ones (more bonds). Our asset allocation model is no different (as we mentioned earlier, it starts with your age). But your spending plans can reverse that pattern. Let's say you must dip into your nest egg in your 30s or 40s because you need the money to buy a house or even pay for a big vacation. If you need the money within 10 years, there is no guarantee that the market will recover from any setback it experiences. So the more you plan to spend in the foreseeable future, the more you need to shift into large caps from small caps and foreign stocks—and generally, the more you need to move out of equities. This section of the worksheet lets you take into account any big purchases you plan to make that might eat into your retirement savings and if so makes your allocation more conservative.

## Investment Income

This is a here-and-now question: Do you currently need any income from your investments? If you're just getting started and you have a small portfolio, your investments probably won't generate much income, anyway. (So the answer would be no.) Ditto for those who are still earning a regular paycheck—chances are you don't need to supplement your wages with income from your investments.

Still, there are some who need the extra money, whether they're retired or not. That's why, for those who do need income from current investments, this program boosts the bond portion of your allocation further if you need more than 4 percent in annual income from your holdings. It will also put more money in large caps—the ones most likely to have substantial dividends.

# Federal Tax Bracket

This seems like a straightforward question, and in many ways it is—just pick the appropriate tax rate and circle that line. There is, however, one important caveat. If most of your wealth is in tax-advantaged retirement accounts such as 401(k)s and IRAs, your current tax bracket is of little concern. Gains on assets in the account are not taxed until the money is withdrawn when you're retired. If most of your investments are in such accounts, we suggest you choose the 15 percent response to complete this question. If your investments are evenly split between taxable and nontaxable accounts, choose the 27 percent. Tax-deferred accounts aside, in general the higher your tax bracket, the more you want to avoid distributions such as dividends and bond coupons while your investment grows. Otherwise taxes will bleed your total return. So, regardless of your age, we decrease your bond allocations and large-cap allocations in favor of small caps when your tax rates are high. Most small-cap appreciation gets assessed at the low 20 percent capital gains rate (or 18 percent if you've held the securities for longer than five years and you acquired them after January 1, 2001), because you don't get much in the way of income-producing dividends from these stocks.

# Volatility Tolerance

In the most rational of worlds, concern over volatility would be confined to those of us with short investment horizons. But this question recognizes that there is a substantial emotional component to any successful investment program. We know lots of perfectly sane, intelligent people who simply cannot stomach even a small decline in their stocks, let alone the occasional free fall.

Only you can measure your true tolerance of price fluctuations, and you have to be honest. Some people like to think they are risk tolerant, even like to boast about it, and yet are actually risk averse. If you have never owned a stock that has plunged—if you didn't live through the October 1987 crash, the bear market of 1973–1974, or even the tech free fall in 2000 and 2001—you don't know what losing money in the market feels like. Until you do, you shouldn't assume that you have a strong appetite for risk.

Here are some questions to ask yourself: Have you ever panicked and sold a stock that was going down? Do you tend to buy stocks only after your friends and acquaintances have already bought in? Do you look at stock tables only on days when the market is up? Are you uncomfortable admitting to friends that your stocks have experienced declines? Do you agonize over interest rate swings? Do you worry about the value of your home, even though you have no intention of selling? If the answer to any of these questions is yes, you may not be able to live with volatility as easily as you think. Stick to either the medium or low answer. Those responses will put less of your assets in stocks and bonds, transferring them to super-safe cash.

## Economic Outlook

What's your outlook on the U.S. economy? Put simply, this is a measure of how optimistic you are now about the future of the American economy. Where is it headed? Are you optimistic or pessimistic? We don't mean over the next quarter or two. Trying to make that kind of short-term prediction will destabilize most portfolios very quickly. Think instead in terms of where we are in the business cycle: Are we nearer to the beginning, the middle, or the end of the current expansion?

Generally speaking, the more optimistic you are, the more heavily weighted you should be in U.S. stocks, because the stock market rises with corporate earnings and national income. In contrast, if you're a pessimist you don't need the extra risk of stocks. But you might want to increase your bond allocation. That's because when the economy slows, interest rates usually fall and bond prices rise. Pessimism should also lead you to increase your overseas equity portion, because the timing of recessions in different global regions seldom coincides.

So what's the bottom line for our recommendations? If your outlook for the economy is strong or average—roughly equivalent to the beginning and middle of economic expansion—then the scoring will indicate a stronger mix of cash and small stocks. The stepped-up mix of cash in good economic times may surprise you, especially if you are younger than 45 or so and fixed income makes up only a small part of your investments. Even though bonds typically have higher yields than T-bills or money-market funds, they offer almost no protection against rising prices or rising interest rates. Since strong economies are much more likely to spur price and interest rate hikes, sacrificing a little yield gives you better protection against loss of capital.

## Interest-Rate Exposure

This can be answered only after you've worked through question 7 on Part B of the worksheet. Here, what we're trying to do is make sure that if you end up requiring a lot of bonds in your mix, you don't load up with large-cap stocks. That's because bonds, which pay interest, and large-cap stocks, which tend to pay dividends, have similar reactions to changes in interest rates. (As rates go up, the interest payments and dividend payouts seem less attractive.) Therefore, even though small caps and foreign stocks are more volatile than the other assets in this model, in combination with bonds they can help reduce your interest-rate risk.

# 5

# GETTING THERE: THE BEST STOCK AND BOND FUNDS FOR YOUR NEEDS

I f you want, you can let investing become a full-time job in itself: checking the stock market obsessively, constantly monitoring your investments online, reading every last research report your brokerage firm sends you. But for most of us, one full-time job is quite enough, thank you. We'd just as soon devote a small portion of our portfolios to individual stocks and let mutual funds handle the bulk of the work.

In this chapter we'll introduce you to 31 truly top-notch mutual funds you can drop right into the asset allocation you worked out in Chapter 4—large-cap, small-cap, international, and bond funds, and some domestic hybrids (funds that invest in both stocks and bonds).

How did we settle on this bunch of funds? Through a combination of careful research and one-on-one interviews.

First, with the help of mutual fund database company Morningstar, we went looking for consistency. We wanted funds that had outpaced the market and the average funds in their peer groups for the past five-, three-, and one-year periods (ending in December 2001). To get at those funds, we applied what's known as a "screen" that allowed us to eliminate all but the most consistent performers.

On top of that, we analyzed each fund based on two key characteristics—growth and volatility. For the first, we compared each portfolio against its peers, dividing them into four broad groups: domestic equity, international equity, taxable bond, and municipal bond. We looked at the number of rolling 12-month periods (48 in all) that funds returned more than 10 percent—and we also took into account by how wide a margin. To measure the funds' short-term volatilities, we looked at each fund's rolling *three-month* returns. How often did the fund turn in a negative return in each three-month period (58 in all) over the past five years, and how big was the shortfall? Our system penalized funds with frequent and large short-term losses.

The last step: culling through our final funds. We focused on funds that had been able to score in the top quartile in each screen, as well as post a top-quartile five-year annualized return. Then we picked apart short-term performance of each fund. If the fund tended toward choppy performance, down one year and up the next, we avoided it. Likewise, if the fund didn't have a good explanation for a down year, we were skeptical. And a manager with less than three years' tenure automatically got the boot. We want *experienced* investors at the head of our retirement portfolio. In the end, there were only 16 equity funds that passed our test, plus 2 hybrid and 13 bond funds.

## Large-Cap Funds

### Smith Barney Aggressive Growth
800-451-2010/SHRAX/(A shares); SAGBX (B shares)

Richard Freeman gives his rival managers nightmares. The manager of Smith Barney Aggressive Growth is like the killer in a B horror movie, moving at an eerily slow pace but always managing to track his quarry down. His fund has about 40 core holdings at any one time, and he moves in and out of stocks at a snail's pace. "We don't feel the necessity to sell something just because everyone else is," Freeman says. "If earnings continue to come through, the stock will come back."

Works for us. His fund, on average, has gained more than 21 percent a year for the past three years, the best in Morningstar's large-cap growth category. It's also the top performer—and one of the most tax-efficient—when you look at 5-year and 10-year performance.

This alone sets Freeman apart from rivals. But so does his approach. Rather than buying behemoths, he concentrates on small and midsize companies that he can own for years as they grow into large caps. Some—Intel is one—have been in the fund since it opened in 1983. His average cost per share for that chip maker, which recently traded at $31? An amazing 88 cents.

Freeman looks for companies that have sustainable earnings growth, sound balance sheets, and experienced managers. He shies away from companies that are trading at more than 1.2 times their P/E-to-growth rate. In tough economic times, he adds, "Own as many companies as you can that can at least meet their earnings estimates."

## Clipper Fund
### 800-432-2504/CFIMX

The team at Clipper Fund is obsessed with price, refusing to buy companies that are trading at more than 70 percent of their real value. They are finicky, holding only 15 to 35 stocks, and are quite willing to let cash build up until they find attractive buys. Tight portfolios usually lead to more risk, but Clipper is actually less volatile than the broader market and its peers. The team—composed of James Gipson, Bruce Veaco, Michael Sandler, and Peter Quinn—has had just one losing year in the past seven: 1999, when it was down 2 percent.

You won't find any tech stocks in this fund—they're too tough to value, says Veaco. At this writing, there weren't any health care names, either, though they were looking at drug stocks. Long-term winners Fannie Mae and Freddie Mac still have upside, Veaco insists, because the mortgage financiers have been taking market share from banks and savings-and-loan associations.

## Thompson Plumb Growth
### 800-999-0887/THPGX

John Thompson, manager of Thompson Plumb Growth, invests like a classic contrarian. "We try to rotate into sectors when they look depressed and then rotate out before they overheat," says Thompson, who looks for reasonably priced growing companies. In early 2002, for instance, he was stocking up on companies in the ravaged telecom sector, including Qwest Communications. When he bought Qwest at the end of 2001, he concluded that Wall Street wasn't giving the company enough credit for its local phone service. "The Street has a tendency to get too bearish on an asset when it's down," he says.

Another one of Thompson's axioms: Potential buys must have steady earnings. It's a rule that drew him to Concord EFS, which clears credit card purchases. When Thompson went to a Concord presentation at an investment conference in early 2000, there were only nine other people in the room. Later that afternoon, Thompson had to squeeze into the same auditorium to hear Internet highflier Ariba make its pitch. He left after five minutes. "I couldn't understand their business model," he admits. He went on to buy more Concord, which gained 118 percent in the 15 months he owned it. Ariba, on the other hand, has plunged 95 percent since its 2000 peak.

### Ameristock
800-394-5064/AMSTX

Want a lot of action and excitement from your portfolio manager? Don't look to Ameristock's Nicholas Gerber. He's a trading sloth, changing his picks at a quarter of the rate of the average equity manager. During the wild market swings of 2000, Gerber unloaded just one of the portfolio's 45 holdings—Philip Morris—because he was no longer convinced it was still a "blue-chip stock." "We're not like a shark," he says. "We're not forever moving forward because if we stop we'll die. We're rather fond of inactivity."

Gerber's infrequent trading helps to keep this fund's expenses far lower than most, but it's his ability to pick steadily growing yet underappreciated stocks that makes Ameristock a standout. Since it opened in the mid-1990s, the fund has finished in the top 20 percent of its large-cap value peer group every year but one. Over the past five years, it has returned about 17 percent a year, 6 percentage points better than the S&P.

Because of the fund's strict value orientation, Gerber and comanager Andrew Ngim spent 1999 on the sidelines as tech stocks rallied. That was the year the fund fell behind its peer group. But as tech stocks got crushed in 2000, Ameristock was almost perfectly positioned, with huge stakes in financials such as Washington Mutual and PNC Financial Services, both of which gained more than 70 percent. All told, the fund climbed 21 percent in 2000 and was up 1 percent in 2001, thrashing the S&P 500 in both years by 30 and 13 percentage points, respectively. "Sometimes our strategy and style don't work," says Gerber. "But we tend to do well when investors change their minds and realize they would rather own companies with earnings."

So how do Gerber and Ngim go about finding these great stocks? They start their search by raking through the nation's largest companies—those with at least $15 billion in market cap—looking for the ones with consistent growth in sales, earnings, and free cash flow. They're *not* looking for the fastest-growing companies. "Ten to 15 percent is good enough for us," Gerber says. "We don't think 25 percent is realistic in the long term." To really catch the managers' eyes, a company has to be trading at a price/earnings ratio that makes it attractive when compared to its competitors and with stocks already in the fund.

## Heritage Capital Appreciation
800-421-4184/HRCPX (A shares); HRCCX (C shares)

Herb Ehlers, who heads up a 20-person management team, has been running this fund since 1985. In the world of revolving-door fund managers, that's an eternity. But that may be one secret behind this fund's consistent record. The fund ranks among the top of all large blend funds for the past three, five, and ten years. Its five-year record—16.5 percent—beats the broader market by more than 6 percentage points.

The core of the managers' stock picking strategy is a "buy the business" kind of attitude. "The emphasis is on buying high-quality growth businesses at attractive valuations," says Mike McKee, a research analyst with the fund. They stick to dominant companies with established brand names, and they focus more on cash flow than they do on earnings. "We like subscriber-based businesses," says McKee, referring to, for example, the recurring revenue that a business like cable companies enjoys. So the New York Times Company, a longtime holding, fits those paramaters well. It dominates the nation's newspaper business, it has a strong subscriber-based business model, and it has a high return on invested capital. "It is going to have an indefinite product life cycle, an enduring competitive advantage," says McKee. Once the managers get into a stock, they stay; the fund has a low turnover ratio of about 30 percent historically. The fund has owned Time and Warner (premergers) since the 1980s.

It's a concentrated fund (about 40 stocks make up the portfolio), and that can enhance upside (and downside) returns. The latter happened in the third quarter of 2001. Three of the fund's holdings got slammed post-9/11:

Harrah's Entertainment, Cendant, and Sabre Holdings. In addition, Viacom, the fund's biggest holding, slumped due to advertising slowdowns, and wireless tower operator Crown Castle International is suffering from a telecom-spending crunch. Even so, many of the fund's holdings rebounded in the fourth quarter of 2001. The result: It finished the year down 8 percent, but it beat the S&P 500, which declined nearly 12 percent.

### Calamos Growth
800-582-6959/CVGRX (A shares); CVGCX (C shares)

By giving investors exposure to quickly growing sectors, the Calamos Growth fund has racked up a 26 percent gain in the past five years. One of the steadiest earners in Morningstar's mid-cap growth group, the fund did well in the late 1990s, thanks to its heavy tech weighting—but father-and-son managers John Calamos Sr. and John Calamos Jr. knew when the party had ended. By the time of the March 2000 meltdown, they had cut their tech weighting in half. Once a decision is made, these two don't waste time, making trades in days, as opposed to weeks or months.

The feverish activity is the result of Calamos' battery of computer models, which quickly assess a company's attractiveness. If a company has accelerating sales, earnings, and return on capital, the managers buy, taking a small position while they dig into the company's financial statement. "We've found that we're better off moving first, if it passes the critical screens," says Calamos Sr. "The markets are so fast-moving now, and information flow is so fast, that if you identify an attractive stock—one that, say, has new management or great sales numbers—a lot of other people are identifying it at the same time." If a company looks as if it can deliver 20 percent annual growth three years out, it's a keeper. The firm's analysis led them to H&R Block in late 2000. In 2001, the stock jumped 120 percent.

## Small-Cap Funds

### Aegis Value
800-528-3780/AVALX

Scott Barbee was just 27 back in 1997, a recent graduate of Wharton's MBA program, when he was recruited to run the small-cap Aegis Value fund, which launched the next year. It turned out that small value stocks were just about to take a dive. "It was really a bizarre time," says Barbee. "We were faced with a difficult decision: Do we stay with our criteria—or make a deal with the devil to keep clients?"

Barbee decided to dodge the devil, and the results have been, well, heavenly. Aegis had a blistering 2001, running up a 42.7 percent gain—54 percentage points better than the S&P 500. It's no wonder that Aegis' assets have risen to over $100 million from $10 million in 1999, as investors have flocked to the small fund.

What kinds of companies does Barbee buy? An Aegis holding must have no more than $1 billion in market capitalization and must trade at either less than book value or less than seven times earnings. Next, Barbee looks for major events—say, a management change or industry consolidation—to help spur the price forward. In late 1999, the fund acquired a stake in Standard Commercial, a tobacco processor and wholesaler to industry giants like Philip Morris. The stock was trading at just $3, pulled down, according to Barbee, by the lawsuits facing the tobacco industry. After the settlements, Standard's share price rose to as much as $18 before Barbee cut back.

## Buffalo Small Cap
800-492-8332/BUSFX

This fund follows the crowd. Managers Kent Gasaway, Tom Laming, and Bob Male use 18 long-term trends to identify stocks with stellar three- to five-year growth prospects. One major theme: "The 55-to-64 age group is growing four or five times faster than the overall U.S. population," says Laming.

Once they identify companies taking advantage of the trends, they look for profitability, a clean balance sheet, and undervalued shares. The macro- and microeconomic views led the team to bookstore chain Borders Group, which appeals to the managers on a couple of different levels. The fast growing 44-to-54 age group reads the most books, Male says, and the company has a strong free cash flow and little debt. Buffalo started buying in bulk after September 11, 2001, when Borders stock sank to $15. It soon ran up into the mid-20s. Meanwhile, the children of baby boomers are growing weary of the Gap, says Gasaway, and are now shopping at Abercrombie & Fitch and American Eagle Outfitters. And as usual, Buffalo Small Cap was there early on.

### Wasatch Core Growth
800-551-1700/WGROX

There's a chance this fund may be closed to new investors when you read this. But it has closed and then reopened in the past (it usually stops taking in money when its assets hit the $1 billion mark or so), so we've included it in this chapter because we think it bears watching.

Sam Stewart is the lead manager of the fund, and he's been at the helm since 1986. But the success of this fund—a 22 percent five-year record, which ranks in the top 2 percent of all growth funds—rests with the team of managers behind it. For whenever they catch a whiff of an interesting small company, four of five of them will meet with management trying to uncover any weakness. For weeks, or even months, Stewart and his cohorts keep probing and prodding, trying to assess the executives' leadership skills, experience, and strategy.

Using historical financial data and the information pulled from interviews, Stewart's team builds models to estimate each company's future growth and reliability. Yet it's the visits and calls, insists Stewart, that bring the most critical information to the surface. After 25 years of running his own investment shop, he says, "You start to get a feeling as to whether the executives are straight shooters. Are they making sense? Does their strategy? Does their story add up?" And the interviews don't stop once a company is in the portfolio. Since few Wall Street analysts cover the small companies the Wasatch fund buys, Stewart and his team continue to hound the executives, making sure they're on track. Doing so has helped them dodge more than a few bullets.

But it's the timeliness of their picks—like Rent-A-Center, one of the fund's largest holdings, which shot up 95 percent from 2000 to late 2001—that makes the fund one of the best among its small-cap blend peers. It has gained about 18 percent annually for 10 years, beating the S&P 500 and 9 out of 10 of its rivals. Keep an eye on Wasatch Micro Cap (WMICX), too. The fund won high marks in our screen for consistent, strong returns and low volatility. It was closed to investors at this writing, but could reopen later.

### Fremont U.S. Micro-Cap
800-548-4539/FUSMX

Of all the small-cap funds we've profiled here, this may be the most volatile. That's because manager Robert Kern focuses on micro-cap companies—smaller than small—with market values from $10 million to $700 million. The fund sports a median market cap of just over $300 million. (Most small-cap funds will venture higher, using $1 billion as their top measure, with a median market cap averaging over $900 million.) Sure, this is a volatile area, but investors have been duly compensated for the risks: Kern has returned 19 percent a year for the past five years, whomping the S&P 500.

Kern, who has been picking small-cap stocks for more than 30 years, concentrates on the four areas of the market where he finds the most innovative companies; technology, health care, consumer products, and service companies. Then Kern starts digging. Taking advantage of the fact that few other big-time investors come calling, he quizzes management. "He's got a much higher, layers-deep kind of focus" than most investors, says Jim Clark, the former chief financial officer of Internet-services company Netopia, one of Kern's holdings. "He transcends the fundamental overview."

### Royce Low-Priced Stock
800-221-4268/RYLPX

This fund falls in the small-cap category, but that's more by default: It focuses on stocks selling below $20, which usually means small companies. So it goes that the fund's median market cap is $470 million, one of the smallest medians of all the small-cap funds highlighted here (aside from Fremont U.S. Micro-Cap).

Of course, it's worth noting that a low price can also raise the volatility level, as even a $1 movement—either way—can mean huge results. But manager Whitney George has proven himself a star stock picker: The Royce Low-Priced Stock fund has posted returns of better than 19 percent in five of the past six years. Its five-year record, 19.7 percent, ranks in the top 6 percent of all funds (and its three-year record is equally strong). And by sticking to companies with strong balance sheets and that are trading cheaply, George has managed to stem the risk level of the fund (he also limits individual positions to 2 percent of assets). According to Morningstar, the fund has a risk ratio of 0.84, compared to the average small-cap fund's 1.26. And George isn't a frenetic trader. The fund has a 56 percent turnover ratio, below average for small-cap stock funds. Typically he hangs onto a stock for three to five years.

# International Funds

### William Blair International Growth
800-742-7272/WBIGX

In times of trouble at home, many investors look for safe harbor overseas. Problem is, good managers in this category are even tougher to find. W. George Greig, who runs William Blair International Growth, is one of them. Even though his fund lost 14 percent in 2001, it was still in the top 11th percentile of all international funds. Greig isn't afraid to wade into some of the less stable markets in the world. In early 2002, he had 19 percent of the fund's assets in countries such as Indonesia and South Africa. This latitude "gives us the broadest range of exposure to good-quality companies that we can get," he says. "It's a fund for all seasons." He's not restricted to companies of a particular size, and the fund is spread across the market-cap spectrum.

Greig considers only companies with proven managers that can deliver high returns on equity, strong cash flow, and consistent profits. In 1999, a year in which his fund rose nearly 100 percent, Greig bet the farm on tech. However, unlike some more adventurous investors, he got nervous about high valuations at the end of the year. He moved into far less sexy stocks, such as household products maker Reckitt Benckiser. (It has since climbed 50 percent.) Early in 2002, he was tiptoeing back into tech. Greig added to positions in Taiwan Semiconductor Manufacturing and Samsung, feeling that the demand in consumer electronics would boost business for both holdings. Companies like these will benefit from U.S. demand, and "we're seeing a real strong awakening, in a sense, of the consumer outside the United States."

### Tweedy, Browne Global Value
800-432-4789/TBGVX

Most funds look mediocre compared to Tweedy Browne Global Value: The fund has a healthy 13 percent five-year record that ranks in the top 3 percent of all foreign funds, according to Morningstar. How do they do it? Managers Chris Browne, Will Browne, and John Spears—who have been running the fund as a team since it opened in 1993—are old-school value players. Global Value's average price-to-earnings ratio is 21.0, lower than the 25.5 P/E of its average peer.

"It's all very simple," says Will Browne, explaining how this fund picks stocks. "We figure out how much a business is worth, just as we would a piece of real estate. If the shares are trading at a discount to that value, then we consider buying it." The managers use value measures such as price/book and price/earnings, and indicators like insider buying. Finding good bargains is one of the reasons the company started an overseas fund in the first place. "We were not lured by diversification," says Browne. "We were looking for undervalued stocks."

When these managers approach a company, they try not to think like fund managers. "We think like we're the owners of the company," says Will Browne. "We ask ourselves, 'What do we believe the company as a whole is worth?' It's got nothing to do with markets or industries or anything else." Indeed, the managers almost make it their business to chart their own path through the world's markets. The fund has steered clear of undue volatility in recent years because of its low exposure to technology stocks (a slim 1.6 percent of the portfolio at year-end 2001). And it often falls upon stocks that its rivals don't. It is one of the few funds to own Mexican bottler PanAmerican Beverages and publishing firm Trinity Mirror, for instance. What's more, the managers like to hold on to stocks for a long time, so the fund typically has a turnover ratio in only the 16 percent range. The average foreign fund sports a turnover ratio of 97 percent, according to Morningstar.

## Artisan International
### 800-344-1770/ARTIX

As far as funds go, this isn't the most diversified international fund. It doesn't follow the weightings of a general foreign index, like the Morgan Stanley Capital International (MSCI) Europe, Australasia, Far East (EAFE) index, where 66 percent is in Europe and 26 percent is in Asia.

But that's precisely what you want if you bet on Artisan International and its manager Mark Yockey. A consummate stock picker, Yockey has been able to rack up his 13 percent five-year record through shrewd market moves. For instance, the fund has a slim 1.1 percent weighting in tech stocks—because Yockey dumped many of his telecom and tech names in 2000. (And he unloaded his shares in two telecom stocks in 2001, NTT DoCoMo and China Mobile, shortly before those stocks nose-dived.) Instead, he loaded up on financial services companies like the United Kingdom's Lloyds TSB Group and the Swiss banking giant UBS AG.

All told, the fund has proven itself during a bad market. It lost 16 percent in 2001, but that was far better than other funds, which averaged a 22 percent loss, and it outpaced the MSCI EAFE index by nearly 7 percentage points. That said, there is a little volatility with this fund, but its upside—and its relative consistency at delivering it—more than makes up for its downside. From 1998 through 2001, the fund's annual return ranked in the top quartile of its peer group three out of four times.

### UMB Scout WorldWide
800-996-2862/UMBWX

The biggest drawback to some international funds is volatility. Looking at their year-to-year returns can turn you off easily. But there are several things about UMB Scout WorldWide that keep volatility to a minimum. First, the fund is well-diversified by country: In late 2001, 48 percent of the portfolio was invested in Europe (evenly divided among the United Kingdom, and France; 12 percent in Japan; 6 percent in the Pacific Rim; and a smattering in Latin America.) Second, it is well represented in nearly every sector: For example, industrials get the biggest portion, with 22 percent of the fund; but there's 10 percent of the fund in durables and 8 percent in staples. Third, manager James Moffett keeps individual stock positions to less than 3 percent of the fund.

All told, the fund has produced a relatively smooth ride over time (it finished in the top quartile in six out of the seven years from 1995 to 2001), and what a ride it has been. From 1997 through 2001, the fund averaged an 8.4 percent annual return, better than 90 percent of its peers.

### Nations International Value
800-321-7854/NIVLX (A shares); NVICX (C shares)

Normally, a new manager at the helm would drive us away from recommending a fund. But Chris Richey, who replaced Jeff Busby in late 2001, has managed institutional accounts for Brandes Investment Partners, which manages this Bank of America/Nations fund. On top of that, the fund is in fact run by a team of managers that has been there from the beginning (the fund was launched in late 1995), and it is carefully supervised by the Brandes investment committee.

This fund is a fine combination of safety and risk. The managers use a classic value approach to stock picking, which helps to keep volatility at bay. When they find a company they like, they view it as a small piece of business that's for sale. Is it going for a price that falls below its intrinsic value? If the answer is yes, they'll snap up shares and hold them for an average of three to five years. The strategy has, so far, churned out chart-topping returns. From 1997 through 2001, the fund chalked up a 13 percent return, better than 97 percent of all foreign funds.

## Bond Funds

Go ahead. Admit it: You don't really get what's going on with bonds. That's understandable. The simple truth is that these kinds of investments—as dowdy as the term "fixed-income" may seem—are much trickier than they let on. They are supposed to soften capital losses when stocks on occasion exercise their ineluctable right to head south. They provide the balance, a sort of ballast against the stock market's swirling currents. But truth be told, they can be a little bumpy, too. Consider that in early 1994, when relentlessly rising interest rates took their toll on everything fixed-income, no fewer than 115 bond mutual funds lost at least 10 percent of their value. It was, by some measures, the worst year ever for bonds.

Yes, that was a bit of an aberration. In recent years, with the stock market in retreat, bonds have done what they traditionally do: They've offered relatively healthy returns. In the middle of 2001, Treasury bonds gained some 11 percent as the Federal Reserve cut interest rates. But the fact is, some bonds are a lot safer than others.

# Four Common Mistakes of Bond Investors

**SIDEBAR 5.1**

1. **Confusing interest rate with yield to maturity.** The total return you can expect on a bond is called the yield to maturity. It takes into account the amount of interest a bond pays during its lifetime and the amount you will get once the bond matures. Note that this is different from the current yield on a bond,

which essentially is the amount of the coupon, or interest, the bond is paying in relation to its price. Calculating the coupon rate of a bond is simple. Let's say you bought a 10-year bond for $1,000 paying 8 percent in interest. You'll make $80 a year on the bond, which boils down to an 8 percent coupon ($80/$1,000). So far, it's straightforward. But say you bought the same bond for just $800. You'll still get the $80 coupon, but the effective rate, or current yield, is 10 percent. When the price of a bond goes up, the yield goes down; and vice versa. Now for the complicated stuff. Remember yield to maturity takes into account not only the coupon payments, but also the value of the bond when you sell. It's a difficult number to calculate, but if that $1,000 bond drops in value to $800, the yield to maturity is 10.14 percent. If the bond increases in value to $1,200, the yield to maturity drops to 6.48 percent. To see how a change in the bond's price can affect the yield go to *SmartMoney*'s bond calculator at www.smartmoney.com.

2. **Betting on the wrong horse.** Because of the higher yields on long-term Treasurys, many investors consider them the best buy-and-hold investments. Not true: According to Ibbotson Associates, 5-year Treasury and 20-year bonds have equal returns over the long haul, and in some years (1996, 1999, and 2001, for instance) 5-year Treasurys have outperformed long-term bonds.

3. **Not bypassing the middleman.** Some of the best fixed-income investments are Treasurys that are held to maturity—but only if you buy them directly from the government and not through your broker, who tacks on fees that will eat into your returns.

4. **Not being skeptical enough.** A bond's principal and the interest it pays often are secured by an issuer's other assets or by insurance that bond issuers buy, but they're not guaranteed—not the way the Federal Deposit Insurance Corporation stands behind bank deposits. And defaults do happen: According to Standard & Poor's, 0.6 percent of investment-grade corporate bonds defaulted.

Our view is that most bond portfolios should have a mix of aggressive and more conservative holdings. Stan Carnes, a Salomon Smith Barney bond strategist, agrees. He suggests paying as much attention to diversification within the fixed-income portion of your portfolio as you would with equities. He recommends a mix of investments: some risk-free government debt as well as corporate debt, which pays a higher yield. A portfolio composed in equal parts of corporate debt and essentially risk-free government bonds would have returned about 6.8 percent through late 2001. Over the past 10 years, it would have returned 7.9 percent, according to Ibbotson Associates.

Worksheet 5.1 will help you arrive at the best mix of conservative and aggressive debt for your own portfolio. As we said back in Chapter 1, you can certainly buy bonds on your own—and there are genuine advantages to doing it that way—but plenty of people use mutual funds to round out their bond portfolios. Here are the bond funds we like best.

# The Bond Allocation Worksheet

While the SmartMoney One asset allocation worksheet in Chapter 4 tells you roughly how much money to put into bonds, this worksheet helps you decide how much of that stake should be in low-risk income-oriented bonds and how much can go toward more aggressive, profit-seeking investments.

This worksheet is structured around when you plan to retire: As you approach that time, the amount of risk you take should decline. (If you're already retired, calculate the speculative portion of your bond investments differently, risking only those assets you don't need to generate income for expenses.)

The first question in the worksheet applies directly to how far from retirement you are. Your score for each of the next four questions will be adjusted depending on your stage of life:

*Current income:* Even people who are bringing home a paycheck may need investment income from time to time to supplement wages. Our scoring will increase the relative safety of a bond portfolio for investors looking to this source.

*Big-ticket spending:* Many investors plan to tap their principal to pay for a new home or their child's college education. They must be sure that the principal is there when they need it.

**WORKSHEET 5.1**    The Bond Allocation Worksheet

*Risk tolerance:* This question measures how comfortable you are with market volatility. If you don't have to sell, periodic market declines shouldn't concern you. But for many of us, temporary paper losses can be as gut-wrenching as the real thing.

*Market outlook:* You should add to the safe portion of your bond holdings if you are pessimistic about interest rates (i.e., you think they are likely to rise).

The total of all five scores gives the percentage of your bond portfolio that should be devoted to safe income. The remainder of your bond assets can be invested aggressively.

| | Years to Retirement | | | |
| --- | --- | --- | --- | --- |
| | More Than 25 Years | Between 7 Years and 25 Years | Less Than 7 Years | Your Score |
| 1. Start by choosing the applicable column and entering the score from this line. | 50 | 60 | 70 | _____ |
| 2. Do you need current income from your investments? | | | | |
| • If no, enter zero. | 0 | 0 | 0 | |
| • If yes, and your stocks yield more than 3 percent on average. | +5 | 0 | 0 | |
| • If yes, and your stocks yield between 1 percent and 3 percent on average. | +10 | +5 | 0 | |
| • If yes, and your stocks yield less than 1 percent. | +20 | +10 | +5 | _____ |
| 3. Do you plan to spend more than 10 percent of your total principal? | | | | |
| • Not until retirement. | −10 | −10 | NA | |
| • Not for 7 years or more. | −5 | −5 | NA | |
| • Once or twice in the next 7 years. | +5 | +5 | 0 | |
| • Several times in the next 7 years. | +10 | +10 | +15 | |
| • At least once a year. | +20 | +20 | +20 | _____ |
| (If you chose "At least once a year," skip question 4.) | | | | |
| 4. What is your market risk tolerance? | | | | |
| • You can't stand to see your portfolio devalued by more than 5 percent a year even if you aren't planning to use the money immediately. | +15 | +20 | +5 | |
| • You can stand 5 percent, but not 10 percent. | +5 | +10 | 0 | |

**WORKSHEET 5.1**    *(Continued)*

| | Years to Retirement | | | |
| | More Than 25 Years | Between 7 Years and 25 Years | Less Than 7 Years | Your Score |
|---|---|---|---|---|
| • You can stand 10 percent, but not 20 percent. | −5 | −10 | −5 | |
| • You can stand a setback of more than 20 percent. | −10 | −10 | −10 | _____ |
| 5. What is your market outlook? | | | | |
| • You are optimistic about the stock market and pessimistic about interest rates (you think rates will rise). | +30 | +15 | +5 | |
| • You are optimistic about the stock market and optimistic about rates. | −10 | −5 | −5 | |
| • You are pessimistic about stocks and pessimistic about rates. | +10 | +5 | +5 | |
| • You are pessimistic about stocks and optimistic about rates. | −25 | −20 | −10 | _____ |
| 6. Sum up your entries, including the starting number. (If greater than 100, enter 100.) | | | | |
| • This is the percentage you should invest for safety. | | | | _____ |
| 7. Subtract line 6 from 100. | | | | |
| • This is the percentage you can invest more aggressively. | | | | _____ |

**WORKSHEET 5.1**  *(Continued)*

# Conservative Bond Funds

What if you could beat money-market rates by 1 percent or more while adding only a slim margin of risk? That's exactly what Pimco has managed to do with **Pimco Short-Term** bond fund (PSHDX; available without a load from fund supermarkets, 888-877-4626) since its inception in 1987. In 2001, the fund, now managed by Paul McCulley, posted a 5.3 percent return, compared with the 4.0 percent average for money-market funds.

Pimco's Bill Gross, who oversees the firm's bond strategy, has a simple approach to bonds right now: Invest in maturities of less than three years from a broad range of sources, avoiding ratings lower than AA (a high enough grade to ward off the risk of default even in recessionary times). The fund holds mostly short-term corporate debt and has a record of beating its benchmark, the Salomon Smith Barney three-month Treasury bill index, in one-, five-, and ten-year periods.

Another option is the **Pimco Low Duration** bond fund (PLDDX), managed by Gross; it returned 7.7 percent in 2001. Its low volatility is perfect for investors looking for stability, which it gets by investing heavily in so-called agency debt, issued by quasi-governmental agencies such as the Federal Home Loan Bank Board. Gross calls agency debt the "Tylenol PM" of fixed-income investments because it helps investors sleep at night. The Short-Term bond fund can be used as a money-market alternative, while the Low Duration bond fund is better for money you plan to keep in place for one to three years.

If you're looking for a short-term bond fund with dirt-cheap expenses—an important consideration with investments that will not give you double-digit returns even in the best years—consider the **Vanguard Short-Term Treasury** fund (VFISX, 800-662-7447). It gained 7.8 percent in 2001; in 2000 it returned 8.8 percent.

## HIGH-QUALITY CORPORATE BOND FUNDS

To juice your returns even more and give you some diversification away from the mortgage markets, salt your portfolio with some high-quality corporate bonds. The good news about corporates is that worry over the economy has forced companies to pay higher interest rates in order to attract investors. In early 2002, the combined one- to five-year AA and AAA credit was paying a healthy 0.75 percent over Treasurys.

Of course, the worries that have increased the spread between corporates and Treasurys have some foundation. Bonds issued by blue-chip corporations don't have the same implied guarantees against default, but keeping credit quality above AA has historically been a fairly conservative strategy. Another positive: Corporate bonds may well appreciate substantially when the economy improves and default risks fade. (You can check out credit ratings at www.moodys.com.)

As for funds, you could do worse than to start with Pimco. The firm uses proprietary computer models, which crunch 3 trillion calculations daily, essentially what-if scenarios that allow Pimco managers to see what impact any minute change in the yield curve, interest rates or economic vitality will have on each bond holding and each fund's performance.

The result? Consistent market-beating returns. Pimco has 18 bond funds with three-year records. Amazingly, of those 12 are in the top 20 percent of their respective Morningstar categories. On average, those funds have gained 9.2 percent annualized through 2001, which beats even the S&P.

We think your best bet is the **Pimco Total Return** fund (PTTDX, 888-877-4626), which is managed by Bill Gross. The institutional share class of this fund has been around for 15 years, and it holds the record for best performance over the past 10 years, thanks to prescient sector bets. As of early 2002 the fund had a 12-month yield of 4.9 percent. It returned nearly 10 percent in 2001 and is heavily weighted in corporate AAA bonds. An alternative is the lower-fee **Fremont Bond** fund (FBDFX, 800-548-4539), also managed by Gross, which sports a similarly impressive performance record, ranking in the top 2 percent for the five-year period by investing heavily in agency debt.

If you simply want a bond index fund (a great way to get diversification quickly), our favorite is the low-fee **Vanguard Total Bond Market Index** fund (VBMFX, 800-662-7447), which tries to match the Lehman Brothers Aggregate Bond index. From 1997 through 2001, it beat more than 90 percent of its peers with a 7.3 percent annualized return.

## TAX-FREE MUNICIPAL BONDS

What about tax-free municipal bonds? Investors in high tax brackets are always tempted to invest in munis, and right now both Fidelity and Vanguard offer low-fee muni funds with strong track records. **Fidelity Spartan Municipal Income fund** (FHIGX, 800-3443-3548) has a 6 percent annualized five-year record and an expense ratio of just 0.42 percent. (This fund requires a $10,000 minimum investment.) The **Vanguard Long-Term Tax-Exempt** fund (VWLTX, 800-662-7447) requires only $3,000 to start and has a slim, slim 0.19 expense ratio. Plus it has consistently ranked in the top decile for the past ten-, five-, and three-year periods. Its five-year record: 5.7 percent.

## More Aggressive Bond Funds

In general, we believe investors should look to the stock market for capital appreciation, not the bond market. But there are times when the outlook for the bond market is particularly bright—when interest rates appear to be cresting and the economy seems to be slowing. (To wit: While the S&P 500 shed more than 13 percent in 2001, investment-grade bonds gained 8 percent.) This argues for moving some of an investor's speculative position into bonds.

Zero-coupon bonds will give an investor the swiftest, biggest profit from falling interest rates. Issued by the government, these bonds are sold at deep discounts and pay no interest until they mature. For example, a 25-year zero with a 5.9 percent yield and a maturity value of $10,000 could be had in late March 2002 for about $2,214 (excluding commission). If over the course of the next year long-term interest rates were to fall by 1 percentage point, the bond's market value would improve by 37 percent, including both capital appreciation and accruing interest. On the downside, a 1 percentage point rise in rates over a year would hammer the bond's value by 15 percent. (To make matters worse, holders of zeros are obliged to pay taxes each year on the accrued but unpaid interest.) Long-term zeros are for investors who are convinced that interest rates are falling, who can keep a daily watch over them, and who don't mind selling in a heartbeat if the interest-rate outlook changes.

One easy way to buy zeros is through the **American Century Target Maturities** funds (800-345-2021). American Century offers six no-load funds, each with a minimum initial investment of $2,500, that aim to match as closely as possible the return of individual zeros maturing in the years 2005, 2010, 2015, 2020, 2025, and 2030. You can even construct your own ladder of speculative zeros at minimal cost.

### CORPORATE-BOND FUNDS

While *SmartMoney* generally prefers actual bonds to bond funds, corporate funds are different: they offer investors the expertise of fund managers in choosing bonds, executing trades, and managing to call risk (i.e., reinvesting the proceeds if a company calls its bonds). Unlike zeros, they have a substantial income element that cushions their risk. **Stein Roe Intermediate Bond** fund (SRBFX, 800-338-2550) has an average A credit quality, and in the past five years it has returned an annualized 7.3 percent. Its three-year record beats the Pimco Total Return fund—also a good fund in this category although its average credit quality, at AA, is higher than Stein Roe's—by more than half a percentage point. Over the past 15-, 10-, 5-, and 3-year periods, in fact, this fund has consistently returned over 7 percent on an annualized basis. Then there's **USAA Income** fund (USAIX, 800-382-8722), which sports a 7.2 percent five-year annualized return. A little more than 21 percent of the fund is invested in BBB-rated bonds, but the rest of the fund is invested in AAA (61 percent) or AA (5 percent) and A (13 percent) bonds.

## High-Yield (Junk) Bond Funds

Bond gurus are willing to take on the additional risk of junk bonds when they foresee stable economic growth (even in less robust periods), especially when the stock market isn't going to make double-digit leaps and bounds. In 2001 and 2002, that's what made the 11 to 12 percent yield on the average junk bond highly appealing. For junk bond exposure, check out **Strong Short-Term High Yield** fund (STHBX, 800-368-1030). Managers Jeff Koch and Thomas Price take less risk than most of their rivals, while still consistently performing near the top of their class. During 2000, the managers sidestepped defaults and credit downgrades. While competitors got chewed up, this fund gained 5 percent, beating the average junk bond fund by nearly 13 percentage points. And from 1999 through 2001 the fund gained about 3.4 percent annually, making it tops among its peers. "We're not bottom feeders," says Koch. He looks for improving fundamentals and management teams with experience and a plan to increase revenue and cash flow. **T. Rowe Price High-Yield** fund (PRHYX, 800-638-5660) is another (relatively) low-volatility fund that's worth a look. Backed up by the firm's strong bond research team, manager Mark Vaselkiv has an impressive long-term record.

## Convertibles

To give your fixed-income portfolio a little more spark, consider convertible bonds, which typically pay yields nearly as high as corporate bonds but can be converted into company stock. When the stock market is down, these instruments trade like bonds, but if there's a stock rally they can take off, enjoying most of the underlying stock's appreciation. The **Calamos Convertible** fund (CCVIX, 800-823-7386) outpaced the S&P 500 from 1997 through 2001, with an average gain of 13 percent. And as stocks plunged during 2001 more than 12 percent, this fund dipped just 4 percent.

Managers John Calamos Sr. and Nick Calamos, who each have more than 18 years' experience, built that record by finding undervalued companies that are increasing return on capital and aren't choked with debt. (The fund has a 4.75 percent sales charge, so buy it only for the long run.) The same caveat, but maybe even more rosy reviews, go for **Calamos Convertible Growth & Income** fund (CVTRX). This fund has an even better five-year record, 17 percent, partly because it looks in the small- to mid-cap company range in addition to large caps. That would tend to make it more volatile, but in a volatility screen that we performed with the help of Morningstar, Calamos Convertible Growth & Income held up better than any other convertible fund in the database company's universe over the five years ending December 31, 2001.

## SIDEBAR 5.2

# Uh-Oh: What to Do If You're Getting a Late Start on Saving

There has always been something better to spend your money on: a new house, the kids' school bills, a once-in-a-lifetime travel opportunity. But now that you've hit your mid-40s and 50s and you realize you've got basically nothing put away, saving for retirement has suddenly become a priority.

Is it too late to get started? No—just don't squander the time you have left. The key step, obviously, is to set aside every dollar you can. Increasing the amount of your annual savings by one-quarter, to, say, 10 percent of your income from 8 percent, actually pays higher dividends over a 15-year time frame than increasing your rate of investment return by one-quarter, to 10 percent from 8 percent.

But beyond that, what should you do with the money you're hoarding? Focus on aggressive investments that could help you make up for lost time? Buy into a variable annuity, to shelter more of your savings from taxes? The answers, as it turns out, aren't what you would expect.

Just when you most need to shoot the moon—to find that hot mutual fund or stock that's going to double your money in a year or two—it's actually the worst time to try taking a flier. That's because you can't afford to lose what little you have. Let's say that in 2000, a 55-year-old man with just $25,000 in retirement savings put the whole thing into technology-sector fund Firsthand Technology Value, enticed by its 190 percent one-year return in 1999. Since then the fund has lost nearly 50 percent. That means the now 57-year-old man would have only about $12,500. Even if he managed to engineer a 20 percent gain next year, he'd still be below his starting point—with only eight years left before retirement instead of 10. Obviously, you can't afford to go backward like that when you're starting late.

Still, that doesn't mean you shouldn't be aggressive—more aggressive in fact than someone who has been saving for decades. You just have to be careful about managing that risk. And the only way to do that is through diversification. To start out, buy a hybrid mutual fund that holds both stocks and bonds, such as Oakmark Equity & Income I, Transamerica Premier Balanced fund, or Dodge & Cox Balanced (more on these funds later). That way, you have exposure to two asset classes that don't always move in tandem. It's the easiest way to do that if you don't have a lot of money to commit to several funds at once. These funds typically have at least 25 percent of their assets in fixed-income securities. In 2000, the average balanced fund was up 1.93 percent; the average diversified U.S. stock fund was down 1.5 percent. In 2001, the average balanced fund was down 4.4 percentage points; the average U.S. stock fund, down 10.8 percent. Once you've got a nest egg of $20,000 or more, *then* begin adding funds of other types.

Here are two rules to follow:

1.  Never have more than 20 percent of your portfolio in any single asset class (small-company growth, large-company growth, equity income, international stocks, fixed income, or cash).

2.  Never have more than 5 percent of your portfolio in any single security or fund.

This kind of spread-out portfolio may be more complicated to keep track of, but it will free you to push the outer edges of each asset in a way that would be much riskier otherwise. For instance, while a 50-year-old with sizable savings might have the bulk of his or her wealth in blue-chip stocks and his or her international exposure in industrialized economies like Japan and Europe, a late starter the same age could hold small-cap funds as well as blue chips, and emerging-market funds as well as major-market international funds.

Will these tactics allow you to have the same retirement as you would had you started at age 30? Probably not. Still, it will help maximize your gains while limiting the damage from any down years.

### Where to Keep It

It's no grand revelation to suggest that late starters make the maximum allowable IRA and 401(k) deferrals. The pretax and tax-deferred nature of these accounts effectively increases your savings rate (not to mention any matching dollars your employer may provide). But if you're focused on catching up, you'll likely end up reaching the limit for these accounts—$3,000 a year for IRAs and $11,000 a year for 401(k)s in 2002. So what do you do with any additional money you want to put aside?

One of the hottest options these days is buying variable annuities. These are essentially mutual fund accounts with a life-insurance wrapper: They include a modest death benefit. The insurance component frees the account to grow tax-free in the IRS's eyes, which makes annuities seem quite enticing.

But there's the rub. The death benefit adds an expense, so if you're buying a variable annuity for investment purposes as opposed to insurance, you need to measure whether the tax advantage outweighs the cost of the insurance. It's a balance the annuity will almost always lose, unless you are getting very high returns or have many years to let the annuity run.

Let's say, for instance, that an annuity charges a 1.3 percent fee for insurance (average for the group, according to Morningstar) and returns 8 percent a year (also about average, over the past 10 years). According to a study by investment adviser Lynn Hopewell, it would take about 15 years before the annuity's tax-free compounding catches up to the returns of an identical investment in a taxable mutual fund (assuming a 35 percent combined marginal federal and state tax rate).

And even this comparison is understated. That's because it assumes that the mutual fund's full gains would be taxable as income every year, whereas that is rarely the case. That would extend the break-even point even further. (Not to mention the effect of a sales charge, which most variable annuities also levy.)

So where should you go? For investments that have a substantial income component, use up the $3,000 annual limit for nondeductible IRAs: These take only after-tax dollars, and you won't have to pay taxes on your gains until you make withdrawals. But don't despair. If a mutual fund has only nominal distributions each year, you may actually be better off in a regular taxable investment than a retirement account. Why? The money you take out of a 401(k) or an IRA (or for that matter, a variable annuity) is taxed as income, meaning you could end up paying 30 percent or more in taxes at the time of withdrawal. In a regular account, of course, capital gains are taxed at just 20 percent (or 18 percent after 2006 for investments held for more than five years).

Here are six great domestic hybrid funds to get you started. We found them with the same criteria that we used for our core retirement funds in the main part of this chapter.

## Oakmark Equity & Income
800-625-6275/OAKBX

Shrewd stock and bond picking is what makes this domestic hybrid fund a standout. Managers Clyde McGregor and Edward Studzinski—in step with the rest of the Oakmark family—employ a strict value approach to picking stocks, targeting cash-rich companies that sell at discounts to their intrinsic values. J.C. Penney, a company that's going through a successful restructuring and posting strong same-store sales, is one such stock; it gained nearly 100 percent in 2001. On the bond side (35 percent of the fund), they hold at least 25 percent in Treasurys. In early 2001, they moved into inflation-indexed Treasury bonds, a well-timed move given the market's growing expectations for inflation.

### Transamerica Premier Balanced
800-892-7587/TBAIX

This fund isn't like most domestic hybrid funds. On the equity side—which is a relatively hefty 64 percent of the fund—lead manager Gary Rolle will sometimes pay up for growth stocks, and tech companies (like Intel) made up 18 percent of the fund in early 2002. On the fixed-income side, manager Heidi Hu keeps much of the assets in corporates—a more aggressive choice than, say, Treasurys. Even so, the mix has brought about a low-volatility fund with extraordinary results. Its five-year record, 15.0 percent, ranks among the top 2 percent of all funds (and the top 1 percent of all domestic hybrid funds).

### Dodge & Cox Balanced
800-621-3979/DODBX

A team of portfolio managers (eight on the equity side; 10 on the fixed-income side) all pitch in on this 70-plus-year-old fund, choosing the right mix of both stocks and bonds. The 60 percent of the portfolio devoted to equities in early 2002 was split among large-company stocks like Golden West Financial, FedEx, Dow Chemical, and Bank One. On the fixed-income side, the managers scout for intermediate-term government and corporate bonds that are outperforming Treasurys. The mix keeps volatility very low, yet with a 12.8 percent five-year record the Dodge & Cox Balanced fund consistently ranks among the top-returning balanced funds.

### Vanguard Balanced Index
800-871-3879/VBINX

This fund delivers a broad portfolio of stocks and bonds at very little cost. The stock portion of this Vanguard fund (59 percent of the fund) tracks the broad-based Wilshire 5000 stock index. On the bond side, the fund tracks the Lehman Brothers Aggregate

Bond index, which covers almost all taxable fixed-income securities. Plus, investors pay only a low 0.22 percent in expenses. It has a 9 percent five-year record, which ranks in the top 23 percent of all domestic hybrid funds.

### Columbia Balanced
800-547-1707/CBALX

The Columbia Balanced fund's stock weighting can run as low as 35 percent, but typically falls between 53 and 63 percent. Lead stock manager Guy Pope starts with a macroeconomic approach that helps him identify sectors and themes that will be emphasized or avoided. Then a team of seven analysts uses those selections to pick large-cap stocks. Bond managers Leonard Aplet and Jeffrey Rippey keep the rest of the fund in a mixture of government securities, corporate bonds, mortgages, and asset-backed securities.

### T. Rowe Price Tax-Efficient Balanced
800-541-8803/PRTEX

If you're concerned about high taxes (and who isn't?), take a look at this T. Rowe Price fund. Half the fund is invested in municipal bonds from 20 to 30 states, most of which are investment-grade. Hugh McGuirk has been the fund's bond manager only since April 2000, but he has previously produced solid returns on two state-specific muni bond funds. The rest of the fund is mostly in large-cap stocks picked by Don Peters and in cash.

SIDEBAR 5.2

# 6

# GETTING THERE FAST: HOW TO "ACCELERATE" YOUR PORTFOLIO

The perfect retirement always used to be described as "comfortable." But nowadays that seems almost quaint and old-fashioned. Sure, we'd all like to be comfortable when we retire. For many of us, though, the operative word when it comes to retirement is "early"—as in long before we turn 65.

Will you be able to retire early? That depends on how much you save, of course, and how much you earn on those savings. For most of us, it would take several years of exceptional investment performance to make early retirement a reality. Think of it as turbocharging your portfolio.

What specific investments should you be focusing on to boost your returns? And equally important, how do you get those hefty returns without taking the kinds of risks that could wipe out everything you've saved for? The key is to adopt an aggressive but still diversified asset allocation program. By spreading out your investments in a number of different areas, you ensure that no single investment choice can ruin you if it goes awry.

Unfortunately, mutual funds alone are probably not going to give your portfolio the lift it needs. Most people will require the kind of outsize gains that typically come with a few well-timed investments in individual stocks, such as Dell Computer or America Online (AOL), pre–Time Warner merger. And they're definitely out there: Quite a few stocks that we've profiled in *SmartMoney* magazine have risen 100 percent or more after we recommended them to our readers. The list includes Microsoft, chip-equipment maker Applied Materials, chip makers Vitesse Semiconductor and Microchip Technology, medical glove supplier Safeskin (now owned by Kimberly-Clark), and PC company Dell Computer.

We won't pretend we know precisely what the next hot sector is going to be. But if all you want is a reasonable chance to succeed, here's what we suggest. It's risky—and by that we don't simply mean it has a lot of stock volatility. We mean it could fail altogether. However, it isn't that different from the approach that many successful fund managers take.

The first step: Concentrate your investments in industries with the best long-term fundamentals—that is, favorable factors that are already in place and would take years to reverse. The aging of the population means health care revenue will continue to grow no matter how badly health care company managements, politicians, and promoters mess up. In addition, the mapping of the human genome has opened new opportunities for drug companies and biotech firms. It's almost certain that scientists over the next 5 to 10 years will find new ways to treat numerous diseases, which will in turn generate considerable revenue and earnings growth for many companies.

Certainly, in any given year, there will always be a hot sector. At *Smart-Money*, every January cover story makes sector predictions based on our investment outlook for the year, complete with a handful of stocks we term the year's "Best Investments." Because these are really year-to-year sectors, however, making them part of your early-retirement strategy will take a strong stomach, a watchful eye, and maybe a bit of luck, too. You have to know when to back out. And you have to accept that sometimes your bets aren't going to go your way.

In any case, when it comes to pinpointing a winning sector, the key is to home in on two factors: valuation and profitability. Are most stocks in the sector under their long-term price/earnings, price/sales, and price/growth-rate ratios? Are corporate profits growing? If profits have had a recent history of falling, have they stabilized?

Good industry fundamentals alone aren't enough. Any hot industry attracts a lot of competitors, all hoping for a piece of the action. Many will burn out eventually. That's why we think your chances get even better if you stick to what some investors term "the arms merchants." These are the firms that supply the know-how, specialized equipment, or new technologies that let all the other participants provide products and compete in the marketplace. Two classic examples from the PC era: Intel and Microsoft. "Figure out which companies are in the most attractive position to cash in on a trend," says Kevin Landis, the top-ranking manager of the technology funds at Firsthand Value. "Consider the PC—it was not immediately obvious that the two companies with the best position were the ones with operating system and microprocessors. I can recall working at [research firm] Dataquest and listening to analysts argue about which was the PC company to buy. The answer was to buy Intel and Microsoft, not to buy any of the PC companies."

In health care today the arms merchants are the drug companies and the medical-device makers. Doctors, HMOs, and hospitals are falling all over themselves trying to grab the money being spent on your aging body. But they can't help you without the drugs and tools of their trade. Five years ago in the telecom industry the arms merchants were the network suppliers that made the switches, routers, wireless base stations, and fiber-optic amplifiers that enabled telecom traffic. You couldn't build a network without them, and that was the direction in which the world was moving.

Start out with the one or two leading arms merchants in each sector. You'll know the leaders because their revenue will be growing faster and their margins will be higher than their competitors'. The key thing is, don't be fooled by companies that are simply growing fast. Lots of companies can acquire other businesses, and thus boost their revenue; that was a recipe that duped many Internet-stock investors. But if the margins don't improve as well, market leadership will remain with the businesses that are both large and efficient.

One caution: No matter how good the arms merchant, don't buy stock when the price is more than 50 times next year's earnings. Since you can't afford to make a mistake, you also can't take the chance that the price/earnings multiple will be sliced down to the market average. Things entirely beyond your control and the control of management may turn investors off from even the best arms merchants. The drug companies, for instance, have had to suffer through several legislative battles that knocked the stuffing out of overly high valuations. Be patient. Price-to-earnings multiples always come down sooner or later, and you don't have to buy all the arms merchants at once.

These rules will not guarantee success, of course. They are really just a guide. And that leads us to the last rule. If you're intent on funding your early retirement by beating the market odds, you'll have to work at it. That doesn't necessarily mean trading the daylights out of your portfolio, but it does mean truly studying the stocks and the business they are in. The typical investor with 20 years until retirement or an already substantial nest egg can afford to ride out periodic disasters. If you want to retire early, you don't have that luxury. When management starts making excuses for performance, assume more bad news will follow. If you have any doubts about the fundamentals of a stock in your portfolio, lose it.

Sure, you'll make mistakes and there will be disasters that you just can't do anything about. The hope is that the market will cooperate and you will learn from your mistakes more quickly than the next guy. If you can do that, early retirement should still be within reach.

Following is our take on two sectors we believe are well-positioned for above-average growth in the years ahead.

## Technology

Every time technology stocks crest a new wave of euphoria, analysts predict that the tremendous cycles of the sector are a thing of the past. And then the stocks come crashing down as orders stop flooding in—and investors lose a ton of money. So a few words to the wise: The cycle lives!

Tech stocks had a miserable 2000 and 2001, yet in early 2002, some strategists were calling the recession in technology capital spending over, and predicting a modest recovery in 2002 and even better growth in 2003. Why? After two years of underspending on technology, much of corporate America would feel the pressure to upgrade existing hardware and software systems just to stay competitive. The onset of the war on terrorism would likely increase government spending on technologies needed to bolster the country's military capabilities. Global demand would also rise—China's preparations for the 2008 Olympics might stimulate tech spending there. And finally, tech spending in early 2002 had fallen to 40 percent below its historical average. "A recovery back to trend, even if it takes five years, implies very good growth rates ahead," according to market strategist Ed Yardeni.

What subsectors then? The tech sector is a beast, easily divided into 100 different areas, from wireless infrastructure, wireless transport equipment, and wireless equipment makers to hardware PCs, enterprise servers, and data storage—and we haven't even mentioned the chip business.

Look at Figure 6.1 and you'll see how two different sections of technology have performed over the past few years, compared to the S&P 500 index. At some time or another, each sector has its heyday. But more important, most have outpaced the broader market over the past seven years.

And that's not likely to change. Over the next three to five years, technology earnings are expected to grow by an average of nearly 20 percent. (See Table 6.1.) The fastest growing areas: Internet services, semiconductors, and wireless communications.

While there's no doubt that the Internet has altered our world forever, many of us still feel pain from the way that bubble burst. So we'd be less inclined to bet on the Internet services group than on such well-known arms merchants as semiconductor makers and communications companies. Yes, they'll slump from time to time. In fact, as of this writing in early 2002, both were in a protracted downturn. But there is simply too much demand for their products over the long term for investors to stay away.

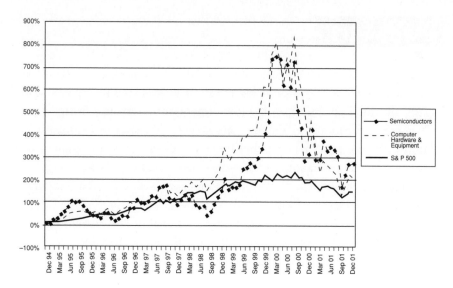

**FIGURE 6.1**    Tech Indexes, 1995–2001

TABLE 6.1    TECHNOLOGY SUBSECTORS–
PROJECTED SHORT- AND LONG-TERM GROWTH

| Subsector | Projected Growth Rate 2002–2003 | Projected 5-Year Growth Rate |
|---|---|---|
| Communications technology | NA | 19.4 |
| Computers | 10 | 14.3 |
| Diversified technology services | 34 | 16.5 |
| Internet services | NA | 27.3 |
| Semiconductors | 59 | 20.7 |
| Software | 14 | 17.9 |
| Technology hardware and equipment | 13 | 13.9 |
| Technology services | 65 | 17.7 |
| Wireless communications | NA | 27.1 |
| Average | | 19.4 |

NA = Not available.
*Source:* First Call.

## Health Care

Of all the future trends we face, the aging of our population and the growing need for medicines is probably the most far-reaching. Everyone is getting older, after all. But probably more important, everyone's living longer. That brings a panoply of different needs when it comes to maintaining a healthy life: not just medicines, but home health care, hospice care, nursing home care, and hospital care. The advancements made in biotechnology will only increase the expenditures (for consumers as well as for the companies that are developing the drugs).

All told, we're talking lots of money. National health expenditures are projected to total $2.9 trillion and reach 15.9 percent of gross domestic product (GDP) in 2010, according to the Office of the Actuary at the Centers for Medicare & Medicaid Services (CMS), formerly called the Health Care Financing Administration. That's more than double what the United States spent in 2000—$1.29 trillion or 13.2 percent of GDP—and it works out to an average annual growth rate of 7.1 percent. The United States spends more than any other country on medical care, with expenditures working out to $4,637 per person in 2000—up 69 percent from $2,738 a decade ago.

The growth in health spending is fueled largely by rapid increases in spending for prescription drugs; drug spending increased 19.2 percent in 1999 and 17.3 percent in 2000, the sixth consecutive year of double-digit growth. By 2010, national spending on drugs is expected to triple. We can thank insurance plans with low-cost co-payments, a higher level of drug advertising, and newer, high-tech therapies that require high-cost branded products for that. All of which, coupled with the fat margins that the top drug companies enjoy, makes the pharmaceutical industry (including biotechnology) a compelling investment.

# Boosting Your Returns with Sector Funds

For some, investing in individual stocks is too risky an endeavor, or they just don't have the time. Enter sector funds. Sector funds concentrate their holdings in a specific industry, typically with about 60 stocks (though some have as few as 10 and others have over 200). Here are our favorites in health care and technology.

### Vanguard Health Care
800-662-7447/VGHCX

There's a reason the minimum investment in this fund is $25,000—it's the best health care offering in the business, in our humble opinion. It's a solid fund, run by Ed Owens, a former Navy submarine officer and nuclear engineer who has been with the fund for over 18 years. Over the past 15 and 10 years, Owens has posted better than 19 percent returns a year. His five-year record is even better: 22 percent, way ahead of the next-best-performing fund in our screen, Merrill Lynch Healthcare (with 20 percent). His secret is a simple buy-and-hold strategy; he turns over a minuscule 21 percent of his portfolio a year, which is good news for investors in taxable accounts. He doesn't chase trends, either. "I'm a value-oriented, bottom-up investor," he says. "I make decisions company by company, not by looking at broader themes within the industry."

### Merrill Lynch Healthcare
800-995-6526/MAHCX (A shares); MCHCX (C shares)

"My interest is in breakthrough growth," says Jordan Schreiber, in charge of this fund since 1983. "I don't care about the drug company that increases its growth rate by one half of 1 percent by cutting costs. I fall asleep with that [kind of story]. But when you have a company that can cure blindness, that's exciting." Hey, it works. In the past five years, this fund has jumped better than 21 percent a year, on average, putting it in the top 13 percent of its peer group. We like that the fund is able to generate market-beating returns while keeping volatility low. In a volatility screen we conducted with the help of Morningstar, the fund scored in the top 13 percent of all equity funds for its ability to keep short-term volatility to a minimum.

### Northern Technology
800-595-9111/NTCHX

Since Northern Technology opened in 1996, it has returned an average of 13 percent a year, compared with the average tech fund's 7.7 percent. Co-managers George Gilbert and John Leo look for companies likely to dominate their respective industries in the next 12 to 24 months. But they're also tough. Executives are hammered with detailed questions about their company's prospects, efficiency, and products in development. If the managers don't like the answers, they walk.

In early 2002, Gilbert and Leo were more cautious, opting for defensive and consumer-oriented stocks like First Data and Electronic Arts. Electronic Data Systems was another favorite. But the managers had sold off what Leo calls high-expectation stocks, including BEA Systems and Veritas Software (in early 2002, both stocks were off their 52-week highs by more than 50 percent). Meanwhile, they were moving more into smaller-cap companies because they think those kinds of companies offer greater earnings visibility—like RF Micro Devices, a $2.9 billion company, which stands to take off when the wireless industry recovers.

### Pimco RCM Global Technology
800-426-0107/DRGTX

This fund has one of the best five-year records (at 22 percent it's better than 98 percent of all tech portfolios) despite a bad turnout in 2001, when it was down 40 percent, the fund's first below-average year since its inception in 1995. Managers Walter Price and Huachen Chen spread their investments around the globe, allowing them to take advantage of technological trends as they migrate from one continent to another. "Plus," says Price, "thinking globally helps us to evaluate U.S. companies, because a lot of their future growth will come from their ability to take their products overseas."

Price and Chen first try to identify the growth themes within technology. They then look for companies in those industries boosting their earnings or sales at least 25 percent a year. Finally, they look for companies that are inexpensive when you compare their P/E ratios with the growth rates.

In 2000, while the average tech fund lost 32 percent, Pimco RCM Global Technology lost only 14 percent. That was due in great part to the managers' fear of heights. As the Nasdaq neared its zenith in March 2000, the managers got spooked by the stratospheric multiples some companies were trading at, and they started selling before the plummet. Eventually they raised their cash position to nearly 25 percent that year. After prices tumbled, Price and Chen snapped up companies that had been unfairly knocked down.

## Gabelli Global Telecommunications
800-422-3554/GABTX

Mario Gabelli heads up this fund, which gets our nod because it has been able to return an annualized 11.3 percent over the past five years—better than 75 percent of its peers—with relatively less volatility than other communications sector funds. (In a Morningstar screen we conducted, it was less volatile on a short-term basis than any other communications fund.)

We also like that it has a value bent, buying stocks on the cheap, so its valuations are lower than the typical communications fund. The average stock in the portfolio has a P/E of 21 and a long-term growth rate of 25 percent. Other communications sector funds carry an average P/E multiple of 28.4 against a growth rate of 29 percent.

In 2001 the fund's performance—down 21 percent—was better than its peers' (down 35 percent) because of a few well-chosen stocks. Two of its top 15 holdings returned better than 20 percent, Commonwealth Telephone Enterprise (a regional telephone service provider in Pennsylvania) and Conectiv (an electric and gas company that until late 2001 had a telecommunications division that has since been sold).

### T. Rowe Price Media & Telecommunications
800-638-5660/PRMTX

Ever since Rob Gensler stepped in as manager in February 2000, this sector fund has ranked in the top decile of all communications funds (some 55 funds). Last year's 7 percent loss, though nothing to write home about, was the second-best showing in the category. His tenure falls short of our three-year requirement, but he has been an analyst for the fund since 1995. And frankly, he's good at what he does. He cut down the fund's holdings in equipment makers and emerging carriers, like Cisco and Nokia, which were some of the worst-performing areas in the sector in 2001. Bets on international wireless holdings—35 percent of the fund is invested in foreign stocks—helped, too. Partner Communications and Vodafone both climbed (47 and 20 percent, respectively) in the last quarter of 2001.

## Exchange-Traded Funds

Looking for a sector fund that invests only in software companies? You probably won't be able to find an ordinary fund that focuses so intently on just one sliver of a sector. In fact, most funds fall in broader groupings—like technology, health care, natural resources, or financial. But you may be able to find an exchange-traded fund (ETF) that fits the bill.

These are essentially index funds, but they trade like regular stocks on a stock exchange so you can buy them (and sell them) at any time during the day through your broker. Ordinary open-end mutual funds, by contrast, can be purchased or sold only at the end of each day.

Exchange-traded funds aren't for everyone, but they can help you diversify your portfolio in ways that couldn't be done otherwise (without large sums of money or stock-picking expertise). For more information on ETFs, visit www.smartmoney.com, www.amex.com, or www.morningstar.com.

# 7

# IS YOUR 401(k) AS GOOD AS IT SHOULD BE?

So you think you have a pretty good 401(k) plan at work? Nice mix of funds—a couple of index funds, a few balanced ones. You can track them from a push-button telephone. Pretty cool. You even have a company match: 25 cents on the dollar. Sure, your plan's not having the best of years, but as your benefits person keeps telling you, "It's one of those so-so years when all investors are taking bite-size gains. Not much you can do but wait it out. Besides, 401(k)s are for the future, not for the present."

We're here to tell you something different: *Wake up people!* Don't listen to the rosy rhetoric. Too many companies are promoting their 401(k) plans—but not improving them. Talk is cheap, and so are some of these plans.

Take PepsiCo. In *SmartMoney's* most recent survey of the biggest companies' 401(k)s, the soft drink giant described its 401(k) as "the most state-of-the-art plan in the market today." It's not state-of-the-art for this generation. The company 401(k) plan doesn't even provide a match, a primary benefit of a 401(k). However, it does give employees stock options, a riskier investment. "We have an entrepreneurial culture," said a spokeswoman, "and people want to be in charge." In charge of what?

Then there's Lowe's Companies. The home improvement chain offered 12 funds in its 401(k) when we last surveyed. Unfortunately, most of them were doing worse than similar funds from other companies. Yet Lowe's director of retirement and incentive plans told us the company is pleased with the results and has no plans to revise its offering. "If it ain't broke," she said, "don't fix it."

Is your 401(k) all that it can be? On the one hand, employers *have* indeed made some significant improvements to their plans in recent years. Increasingly, companies are allowing employees to join plans earlier and are offering them a much wider selection of investment choices. They're also putting more emphasis on service and education. "Employers are paying a lot of attention to their 401(k)s these days," says Martha Priddy Patterson, a director at Deloitte & Touche. "Companies have paid a lot of money to set up these retirement plans. They want to have as many people as possible use them."

Sounds great, but plans still need to improve. In fact, in two critical areas—company contributions and investment performance—progress has been slow or nonexistent. Too many companies just aren't paying enough attention to the bottom line—their employees' bottom line, that is.

Poor-performing mutual funds are a particular problem. "The biggest shortcoming of 401(k)s today is probably that companies don't know how to deal with funds that underperform," says David Wray, president of the Profit Sharing/401(k) Council of America, a group of benefits specialists representing more than 1,200 companies.

Why does performance matter so much? Because the 401(k) is fast becoming workers' principal retirement savings vehicle. For many people today, a 401(k) is their largest asset—bigger even than their home equity.

Following are the attributes we believe should be part of any self-respecting 401(k), from the size of company matches and length of vesting periods to fees and fund performance.

## Company Contributions

This is the single most important factor in your 401(k) plan. After all, company contributions are what make these plans the best retirement investment around. Basically, it's free money. Say your company gives the standard contribution of 50 cents on the dollar up to 6 percent of your pay. You have an automatic 50 percent annual return on your contribution, even if the market takes a dive. That's the power of company contributions. But some kinds of company contributions are better than others. What's good and what's bad? We'll lay it all out for you.

How much does your company match? In an ideal world, your plan would match you $1 for every dollar you put in. But in reality, few companies fork over that kind of money. Only 17 percent of all big employers matched dollar for dollar (but that's up from 12 percent in 1994). More common is a 50 percent match (50 cents on every dollar); some 35 percent of all companies do that.

What's the maximum amount you can expect from your company in its match? A few years ago Costco offered what appeared like a great match: 50 cents on every dollar an employee contributes to the plan. Problem was, the match had a cap on it—only up to $1,000. That meant the most any Costco employee could expect to get from the company was $500 a year.

Is the company match made in cash or stock? A cash match is best, because it offers the most flexibility; you can turn around and invest however you prefer, in a large-cap fund or a bond fund, or even leave it in cash. Unfortunately, as many as 45 percent of companies that offer company stock as an investment option offer a match in company stock, according to a recent Hewitt Associates survey that included midsize to large companies. And of these programs, 85 percent have restrictions on sales of the stock, typically forcing employees to hold on to the stock at least until age 50. That may be all right if you work for a company with a stock like Dell Computer. But unless a stock is continually on the rise, a match in company stock can be worse than no match at all. Just ask the folks at Enron. After the oil company's stock fell to under $1 from a high of $89, Enron's 401(k) plan—which makes its match in company stock—lost more than 90 percent of its value. (See Sidebar 7.1, "What to Do If Your 401(k) Match Comes in Company Stock.")

Some companies give you a certain percentage of your salary in profit sharing. For those that do, the average is about 10 percent of salary. Of course, this figure can change year after year, with the fortunes of the company. And there are companies that don't match at all: In our 2000 survey, there were five.

# What to Do If Your 401(k) Match Comes in Company Stock

Is your company the next Dell Computer ... or the next Enron? That's the only thing you have to wonder about if your company matches your 401(k) contributions in stock, right? Actually, no. Either way, you are being asked to put too many eggs in one basket. Your best bet is to accept the fact that cash would have been a better match and be smart about the rest of your investments—in your 401(k) and outside of it. Here are five tips:

1. **Participate.** First off, while you might not be thrilled with your dollop of company stock, it's still worth receiving. So don't let the Enron fiasco keep you from participating in your 401(k). After all, most companies don't go bankrupt, and even if your employer's stock is a laggard you can eventually invest your money elsewhere—once you reach the approved age or when you leave your company. So a 401(k) with a company match—even if it's in the form of company stock—is still a better deal than an IRA.

2. **But don't go overboard.** That said, no matter how much faith you have in your company, don't hold any more company stock than you have to. So if your match comes in this form, there's no need to invest additional dollars in the stock—inside or outside your 401(k). This means that you might skip participating in an employer stock purchase plan, which allows you to buy company stock, usually at some sort of discount. (Buying company stock at a discount is still a good deal, but only if you can sell immediately.) And certainly it means that you shouldn't allocate your own 401(k) contributions to company stock. Find some other way to express your corporate affection, like joining the holiday party planning committee.

3. **Allocate wisely.** So 40 percent of your 401(k) balance is in company stock; what do you do with the rest of your money? You need to allocate like a champ. First off, review your other investment options, looking for overlap. Clearly you don't want to invest in a fund that has your company as a top holding. And if you work for a large growth company like, say, Cisco Systems, you might want to invest in a solid value fund, rather than a growth fund. Likewise, if you work for a tech company, there's no need to hold a tech fund in your 401(k).

   The same rules should apply to what you hold outside your 401(k). Here, creating some balance should be easier, since you have a universe of investments to choose from. Remember to consider any taxable accounts as well as a spouse's 401(k) and other holdings.

4. **Sell!** If you're allowed to sell on your 50th birthday, that's the day you should start unloading the stock. Don't wait until retirement. Of course, if you have a hefty amount of stock in your portfolio, you might not want to sell it all at once, since you risk selling at a low price. You might want to dollar-cost average out of the holding, selling, say, 25 percent of your stake each quarter over four quarters. Likewise, if you leave your company, don't let your 401(k) sit there indefinitely. You should take control of the account. Assuming that the stock has appreciated, however, you might not want to roll over the entire account into an IRA (as is the conventional wisdom). Instead, for tax purposes, you should consider rolling over your company shares into a taxable account and selling them, since your gains will then qualify for the lower long-term capital gains rate, which could be as low as 18 percent.

5. **Become an Advocate for Change.** Okay, so whining about your company stock might not seem like the wisest move during this era of corporate layoffs. Yet the fact is, employees can—and do—orchestrate change in their 401(k)s. It's simply too important a benefit for you to do anything *but* clamor for change.

## Enrollment and Vesting

When can you start to participate in your 401(k)?

How soon do you vest?

The ideal answer to both questions is immediately. Unfortunately, with most 401(k) plans that's not the case. Indeed, given the amount of job-hopping that went on in the late-1990s tech boom, it seems practically archaic that some companies still have an enrollment term—the waiting period before new employees can start contributing to the 401(k) plan and receive company matches as well. But a vesting period, too? At many companies, employees have to wait up to five years before they can claim money the company has contributed to their 401(k) accounts. That's not a problem if they are going to work there for more than five years. But if they leave before they vest, they forfeit the matching money (their own money, however, they can take with them).

Most large companies don't make new employees wait to sign up anymore; in our 2000 survey of nearly 100 big companies, 92 percent reported that employees can join the 401(k) plan immediately. That percentage drops dramatically, however, to 25 percent, when you look across the board.

Vesting periods, though, are a common thing at many companies: In 2000, 35 percent of the companies we surveyed enforced some kind of vesting period. And nearly half of those made employees wait five years or more (sometimes seven) to get their money. The good news is that the maximum waiting period, by law, is now six years.

Companies enforce their vesting schedules in one of two ways: cliff or graded. In a cliff schedule, the funds typically become 100 percent vested at completion of five full years of service. With a graded schedule, the money vests in 20 percent increments, beginning with the end of the third year of service and ending with the completion of seven years of service. But under the 2001 Tax Act, those time frames were shortened, to a minimum of a three-year cliff or a 20 percent, six-year graded vesting schedule beginning after two years of service (100 percent in the sixth year). It's better, but not perfect. Of course, those are just the minimums—many companies play around within those parameters.

# Investment Options

When it comes to investing options in your retirement plan, less is definitely not more. The more options you have, the more diversified your portfolio can be, the better your chances of finding a great-performing fund, and the greater your chances of building a small fortune in your 401(k).

Luckily, we've found that companies have been beefing up the number of their options: In 1998, when we surveyed 92 large companies, the average number of funds in a company plan was 13. In 2000, it had jumped to 19.

But simply throwing funds into a plan isn't enough. The options must cover a broad array, so employees of any age or risk tolerance can build a retirement portfolio that meets their needs. The best plans will offer at least these seven key investment options: a large-cap fund, a small-cap fund, an international equity fund, an S&P 500 index fund, a balanced fund, a long-term bond fund, and a cash option.

It sounds like a basic grouping, but you'd be surprised at how many companies don't offer all seven options. In fact, only 17 companies in our most recent survey did. Another 41 companies offered six out of the seven core options. Twenty percent of the companies didn't even offer an S&P 500 index fund, the most basic portfolio building block. And 62 percent of the plans failed to offer a long-term bond fund.

# Investment Performance

Great, your plan offers 150 funds. Are any of them good? The best way to measure this is to look at long-term and short-term performance. Do the funds rank in the top 25 percent of their peer group? To figure this out on your own, refer to the benchmarks provided by Morningstar in Table 7.1 and rate the funds on a three-year load-adjusted basis. The best company plans will have top-performing funds in the following five fund categories: large-cap, small-cap, international equity, long-term bond, and balanced funds.

It's not an easy yardstick for companies to measure up to: In fact, in our 2000 survey, only one company, then Time Warner (pre–AOL merger), qualified in each of the five options. Four companies—Albertson's, Bank One, Merrill Lynch, and Tenet Healthcare—had four. And some plans did especially well in certain sectors. For instance, two-thirds of companies had a top-performing large-cap fund.

Still, there were obvious shortcomings. Only 19 percent of companies had a top-quartile small-cap fund. More significantly, 20 companies had no core top-quartile performer at all.

## Fees

Does $165 mean anything to you? It should. That's the amount you're probably paying in mutual fund management and administration charges on your 401(k) account, based on an average balance of $47,000. It's simply subtracted from your fund returns. And they're not the only fees employees often pay for their 401(k). Some companies charge participants per capita fees that cover anything from plan administration to investment education. The rub? Companies often don't provide a detailed breakdown of what employees are paying for. In fact, chances are high that you're not even aware of when the fees are siphoned from your account.

When we surveyed 93 large companies in 2000, the average plan's expense ratio was 0.35 percent. But the results ranged from 0.011 percent at Procter & Gamble to 0.89 percent at DaimlerChrysler. Sound insignificant? Someone with a $47,000 account at P&G would have the balance reduced by $5.30 annually in expense; at DaimlerChrysler the expenses would slice $420.56 off the return.

## Monitoring

How often do companies monitor their plans to ensure funds have been performing up to the stated objective? In our view, quarterly reviews are the most you can expect. In 2000 in our survey, 70 percent of companies said they do so. And just over half the companies (56 percent) said they also have a time frame for removing an investment from the plan if it's underperforming.

## Service

What are we really talking about here? Simple-to-use tools and services: a web site that lets employees easily track and trade their funds; financial modeling tools, either on the web site or through software, so employees can run what-if scenarios on their 401(k)s; the ability to change their investment elections on a daily basis. At a minimum, that's what we think most employers should offer their employees.

Luckily, most big companies do. Of the companies we surveyed, 90 percent allow employees to change their investment elections daily. Also, 90 percent have a web site that employees can use to track their accounts and make trades, too. More than half of the companies we surveyed have financial modeling tools available, either on their web sites or through software.

Of course, that only makes the companies that don't offer this level of tools and services stand out. Back in 2000, for instance, Nabisco offered little in the way of employee education. There were no web sites, no financial modeling tools, no seminars, not even a measly newsletter. Employees could receive daily account updates by phone, but that was about it. Asked whether better tools might help participants make more informed investment choices, a Nabisco retirement plans analyst demurred: "It's hard to say. A lot of that type of information people just throw away."

# Ten Things Your Benefits Department Won't Tell You

SIDEBAR 7.2

### 1. "We just shrunk your pension."

Does your company still have a traditional pension? Enjoy it while it lasts. Already, some 15 percent of Fortune 500 companies have converted to so-called cash-balance plans—to the detriment of employees nearing retirement—and Kwasha HR Solutions, now part of Mellon Financial, expects that figure to climb to as high as 40 percent in the next five years.

Under a traditional pension, you earn the bulk of your benefits toward the end of your career, when your salary is at its peak. With a cash-balance account, your employer annually "deposits" a certain amount (usually 4 to 7 percent of your salary) into a hypothetical account. The problem: By law, it's up to the company to decide the opening balance of these new accounts, and—surprise!—it's often substantially less than the projected value of the pensions they're replacing. If you're close to retirement, you could be in for less money than a pension would have given you. According to a 1997 Society of Actuaries study, the average worker age 61 to 65 with more than 25 years of service would receive $127,908 in a traditional pension plan and just $85,050 in a cash-balance account.

When IBM and AT&T converted to cash-balance accounts in the late 1990s, the official word was that cost was not the primary consideration. Yet in 1999, IBM saved an estimated $184 million after the change. Even worse, in many cases when a company makes the switch, adds David Certner of AARP (formerly the American Association of Retired Persons), "companies have sold cash-balance plans as improvements, without sufficiently explaining to older workers what they've lost."

### 2. "We won't tell you the full story."

Benefits overhauls aside, it can be just as tough to get comprehensive, timely information on your regular accounts. Legally, employers are obligated under the Employee Retirement Income Security Act (ERISA) to supply only annual statements with an account balance, and they must be current only as of the most recent fiscal year.

When Susan McKinney's employer, a Massachusetts consulting firm, announced in early 1998 that it would offer the Vanguard 500 Index fund in its 401(k) plan—it had previously offered only two badly underperforming funds—McKinney told her benefits administrator to move all her money there. When she finally received a statement in December, though, it showed that while her balance had been transferred to the Vanguard fund, her company had been putting her new contributions into the same old underperforming growth fund all year. McKinney was furious. "I got zero information about my investments for the whole of last year," she says. Her employer says that she may not have turned in the right forms. However, shortly afterward, the firm changed its 401(k) provider.

### 3. "If we merge, all bets are off."

If your company is about to be taken over, look out: A corporate marriage usually means one of the two benefits plans is discarded, which can wreak havoc on your retirement security.

There are three things to watch out for during a merger: First, there's the "blackout" period, when your plan switches from the old administrator to the new. You can still contribute during that time, but you won't be able to take loans, check balances, change allocations, and take withdrawals or distributions. According to Key Asset Management in Cleveland, a typical blackout period lasts from one to three months, but others can last longer: The blackout period of one major company (not a Key Asset client) lasted an extraordinary four and a half years.

Second, beware if your former employer's plan is full of complicated assets, like funds with back-end loads, group annuity products, illiquid securities, or real estate investments. According to the Employee Benefits Council in Louisville, Kentucky, new administrators that don't want to deal with complicated assets can either sell them and pass the cost of backing out of them on to you, or freeze them in a separate account until the load or contract expires, in which case you may not be able to get access to that money for loans or even hardship expenses.

Finally, if you have an outstanding loan from your old plan but your new plan doesn't allow you to roll it over, it will be considered a "distribution." If you can't afford to pay back the loan and roll the whole account into an IRA before the 60-day deadline, you'll owe income tax and a 10 percent early-withdrawal penalty.

### 4. "Don't look now, but we switched your funds."

Greg Vossmer didn't learn that KinderCare Learning Centers in Portland, Oregon, his wife Jeanna's employer, had switched 401(k) providers until he saw her annual statement in March 1998. That's when he found out the three mutual funds he had so carefully allocated money to one year earlier had been replaced by what Vossmer calls "no name" large-cap and small-cap growth funds. When contacted, KinderCare's benefits office told him that the company had changed providers and had sent a general notice down through the corporate offices. Unfortunately, it never reached the Vossmers. The worst part? "In [a roaring bull] market, one of the two funds they picked managed to lose money," says Vossmer. A company spokeswoman declined to comment on whether KinderCare employees were kept adequately informed, but says that employees are better served by the new provider.

According to David Wray, president of the Profit Sharing/401(k) Council of America, 4 to 5 percent of U.S. companies change service providers each year for reasons varying from "outgrowing a relationship" to consolidation. Ted Benna of the 401(k) Association, a pension administrator and consulting firm, adds that while mergers and spin-offs often trigger a change, he has also seen situations where a new human resources team comes in and thinks it needs to make its mark by switching providers, whether or not that decision is appropriate.

### 5. "We don't care how much you lose in commissions and fees."

In 1997, when Nancy Lee's firm began a 401(k) program, she chose a variable annuity from the list of offerings. The information systems manager from Silver Spring, Maryland, learned only later that she was charged a commission—and was then assessed another fee when her company decided to switch plan providers a year later and canceled her variable annuity contract early.

Of course, since tax-qualified plan money is already tax-deferred, products like variable annuities have "a layer of fees, administration, and insurance the employees pay for that they don't really need," says Dee Lee (no relation), a certified financial planner and author. Even if you suspect you're getting gouged, proving it can be close to impossible because fees and commissions are usually figured into the formula used to calculate your gains.

So why do such products end up in retirement plans at all? Most likely, it's the result of employers' not doing the research, being suckered into offering high-commission products, or not car-ing since workers wind up paying most fees. Small companies and nonprofits, where decisions are more likely to be made on the basis of personal relationships, are particularly vulnerable, says Ted Benna.

### 6. "Our company stock can be hazardous to your wealth."

Company stock makes up 39.2 percent of all the assets in big company 401(k) plans, according to the Profit Sharing/401(k) Council of America. But owning too much of it can jeopardize your own retirement plans.

First, there are sometimes restrictions on how long an employee must hold company stock before selling or limits on how often allocations can be changed. But even beyond that, there's the simple issue of diversification: If your company falters, not only is your job at risk, but so is your nest egg. The classic example of this: Enron, which matched all contributions in stock and whose collapse wiped out the entire retirement savings of thousands of employees.

### 7. "We'll slash your health coverage after you retire . . ."

When Tom Griffen, a 30-year General Motors (GM) engineering veteran, was weighing the decision to accept an early-retirement package in 1982 at age 55, one of the major factors that swayed him was GM's verbal promise to provide comprehensive health benefits for as long as he and his wife needed them. He was horrified, then, when GM amended its policy in 1987 and informed him that he would have to pay deductibles and co-payments. (In 1993, the company added monthly fees.)

"Without the lifetime health care promise," he says now, "I would never have chosen to retire that early." A GM spokesman replies, "Due to escalating health care costs, GM, like most U.S. companies, added modest cost sharing to its salaried-benefits package."

Disney, Pabst Brewing, and Solutia (Monsanto's chemical spin-off) have all cut retiree health benefits or required cost sharing in recent years. A report released in May 2001 by the federal General Accounting Office notes that only 37 percent of companies nationally offer health coverage to early retirees and 26 percent to those over 65. That's down from about 70 percent in the 1980s, and that number is continuing to decline.

**8. ". . . or we'll make you pay for it."**

Another way employers have gotten around the high cost of health-care coverage: They make the retirees foot the entire bill. According to benefits firm William Mercer, in 1999, 42 percent of large companies required their early retirees to pay 100 percent of their premiums for health coverage. That's up from 31 percent in 1997. Meanwhile, 25 percent of the other companies have increased the share of annual premiums that early retirees must pay; and 10 percent have increased the amount retirees pay to cover annual deductibles and co-payments.

**9. "We can't add."**

Is your company miscalculating your pension? Allen C. Engerman, a "pension detective" at the National Center for Retirement Benefits, estimates the error rate at nearly 30 percent. The firm, which claims to have recovered millions in pension money for its clients, has investigated large corporations, tiny doctor's offices, and everything in between. "There are lots and lots of mistakes," says Engerman, and they often go undiscovered for years.

Some things, though, are even worse than being short-changed. Last year the town of Needham, Massachusetts, discovered that it had made a bookkeeping error in calculating retired library custodian Henry Hinden's first pension check some 17 years earlier. It turns out that over the years he received over $20,000 more than he was owed, and is legally obliged to pay the money back. Legislation is pending, though, that would shift the responsibility back to the town.

"Pension calculations are very complicated, and innocently or not so innocently, mistakes are made all the time," confirms Michele Varnhagen, policy director at the Pension Rights Center.

**10. "We have sticky fingers."**

In 1998, Bella Vista Group, a developer in Bowmansville, New York, got a new pension plan administrator courtesy of the U.S.

Department of Labor (DOL). The DOL charged that former administrator (and company president) Pasquale Cipolla had been lending
pension funds to other companies he owned and had failed to con-
duct credit checks or require security for the loans, which resulted
in substantial losses. "I didn't do a good job of studying the law,"
says Cipolla, who agreed to repay $1.6 million.

You might be surprised at just how many employers are misus-
ing or downright stealing their employees' retirement money.
Since 1995, the DOL has recovered $53.1 million from some 1,200
companies, while another $4.8 million has been collected voluntar-
ily. Though many of those cases involve commingling, lending, or
borrowing employee money, out-and-out theft is not uncommon.

Take the case of former Detroit Tigers pitcher Denny McLain.
After buying the Peet Packing Company in January 1994, McLain
and his partner, Roger Smigiel, raided the Chesaning, Michigan,
company's $12 million pension fund. They were convicted in 1996
of embezzling and laundering more than $2.5 million. In March
1999, the government announced that it had garnished McLain's
baseball pension and plans to distribute it "to the victims of his
greed"—Peet's former employees.

SIDEBAR 7.2

# Grading Your 401(k)

How does your plan compare to the best 401(k)s? Worksheet 7.1 will help
you judge how your company's 401(k) plan compares with the ideal plan.

The worksheet will take only about 10 minutes to complete, but you
may need to refer to your benefits handbook and your 2001 year-end account statement to find some of the information. On your statement, look
for your investments' three-year average annual return ended December 31,
2001. While these numbers may seem outdated, they are probably the easiest
ones to get, as we've found that some employers send account statements only
once a year. (If the figures aren't on the statement, ask your benefits department
for the information.) Then use Table 7.1, "Performance Benchmarks," to determine whether your investment is delivering top-quartile returns. To

remain consistent with *SmartMoney*'s survey, which looked primarily at actively managed funds, do not fill in performance numbers for index funds.

Finally, a note on matching: If your employer offers a graded match, such as dollar for dollar on the first 3 percent of the pay you contribute and 50 cents per dollar on the next 3 percent, skip lines 1 through 3 and complete lines 4 through 7. For each level of matching, use lines 4 and 5 to figure the percentage of your salary given to you. Then use the spaces in line 6 to enter the percentages for grades as necessary.

For the remainder of the questions, simply fill in the information, adding points each time your 401(k) qualifies.

# The 401(k) Worksheet

**Fixed Match**

1.  What is the maximum percentage of salary matched?                                                        _____%

2.  For each dollar contributed to the plan, what is the employer's match?       $_____

3.  Multiply line 1 by line 2 for the percentage of your salary given to you in
    matching funds if you contribute the maximum amount.                                           _____%

**Graded Match**

4.  Percentage of salary matched.                                                                                       _____%

5.  For each dollar contributed at this level, what is the employer's match?        _____%

6.  Multiply line 4 by line 5. This is the percentage of your salary given to
    you for this grade of the match.                                                                               _____%

    Percentage of salary given to you for the next grade of match
    (repeat lines 4 and 5).                                                                                            _____%

    Percentage of salary given to you for the next grade of match
    (if applicable).                                                                                                       _____%

7.  Total graded match. Add all entries in line 6.                                                         _____%

**WORKSHEET 7.1**    The 401(k) Worksheet

8.  If your company has a separate annual profit-sharing plan, what is the annual contribution as a percentage of your salary?                                                       _____%

9.  Total points for company contributions. Add lines 3, 7, and 8.    _____

10.  Multiply line 9 by the number 2.                                              _____

11.  Are after-tax contributions allowed? If yes, add 1 point.       _____

12.  Is the match in cash? If yes, add 3 points.                           _____

13.  Does the plan offer a large-cap fund? If yes, add 2 points.    _____

Is it a top-quartile performer? (See Table 7.1, "Performance Benchmarks.") If yes, add 2 points.                                _____

14.  Does the fund offer a small-cap fund? If yes, add 2 points.    _____

Is it a top-quartile performer? If yes, add 2 points.             _____

15.  Does the plan offer an international fund? If yes, add 2 points.    _____

Is it a top-quartile performer? If yes, add 2 points.             _____

16.  Does the plan offer a balanced fund or a moderate premixed lifestyle portfolio? If yes, add 2 points.                         _____

Is it a top-quartile performer? If yes, add 2 points.             _____

17.  Does the plan offer a long-term bond fund? If yes, add 2 points.    _____

Is it a top-quartile performer? If yes, add 2 points.             _____

18.  Does the plan offer an S&P 500 index fund? If yes, add 2 points.    _____

19.  Does the plan offer a cash option (including money market, stable value, or short-term bond)? If yes, add 2 points.             _____

20.  Can you change investment options daily? If yes, add 1 point.    _____

21.  Do you receive account statements at least quarterly?

If yes, add 1 point.                                                      _____

22.  Does the plan offer a brokerage-window option (which allows 401(k) participants access to a broader array of investment options through a brokerage of the employer's choosing)?

If yes, add 1 point.                                                      _____

**WORKSHEET 7.1**    *(Continued)*

23. Do you pay the load? If yes, subtract 5 points.     _____

24. Are employer contributions immediately vested?

    If yes, add 2 points.     _____

25. If contributions are vested on a graded scale, divide the number of
    years until fully vested by 2, then subtract the result.

    (Example: 7 years divided by 2, subtract 3.5.)     _____

26. If contributions are vested all at once, subtract the number of years
    until fully vested.     _____

27. Total. Add lines 10 through 26.     _____

*What Your Score Means*

   **36+**   Top-of-the-line plan. Your company would rate among our best 401(k)s.

   **26–35**   A good match or good investment choices, but you're probably not getting
   both with this plan.

   **11-25**   You may not like putting all those retirement eggs in this basket. Choose your
   options carefully.

   **Below 10**   It may be time to look into opening a Roth IRA once you've been given
   your match.

---

**WORKSHEET 7.1**   *(Continued)*

---

## TABLE 7.1   PERFORMANCE BENCHMARKS, THREE YEARS ENDED DECEMBER 31, 2001

| Type of Fund | First Quartile Percent | Second Quartile Percent | Third Quartile Percent | Fourth Quartile Percent |
|---|---|---|---|---|
| Large-cap equity | 5.40 | 0.67 | −1.82 | −6.33 |
| Small-cap equity | 21.77 | 12.36 | 8.83 | 2.88 |
| International | 6.38 | −1.03 | −4.10 | −8.39 |
| Balanced | 6.55 | 3.16 | 1.19 | −2.25 |
| Long-term bond | 5.95 | 5.03 | 4.31 | 2.81 |

# The 401(k) Manifesto

Clearly, many 401(k) plans are flawed. Deeply flawed. And apparently it's not a big secret. In a recent poll conducted on the SmartMoney.com web site, 58 percent of respondents said they were dissatisfied with their 401(k) plans; 69 percent also said they had little or no confidence in their companies' benefits departments to manage a plan that had their best interests at heart. Even consultant Ted Benna, the originator of the 401(k) plan, sees "major deficiencies" in today's 401(k) plans. "We need to dramatically overhaul the investment structure of these plans," says Benna.

Such complaints—combined with the recent drubbing many accounts have taken—may have left you wondering: Can I really depend on my 401(k)? Well, we believe you can, provided it's designed properly. We've come up with five demands you need to make—to your company, your legislators, your 401(k) provider—so that your account is and will continue to be running in peak condition. Some of these demands, if acted upon, will overcome the devastating effects such things as company stock matches can potentially have on your portfolio. Others will make your 401(k) a much more finely tuned employee benefit. But all are worth making a case for.

In other words, rock the boat. It may be your only safe passage to the peaceful waters of retirement.

## Demand No. 1: Reduce the Fees That Are Nibbling Away Our Retirement Money

Rob Lever, an editor for the French news service Agence-France Presse (AFP), discovered a 1.5 percent wrap fee in his 401(k) about five years ago that he'd never been told about. Annoyed, he and members of his newspaper guild complained to management to get the fee dropped. But AFP's provider, Great-West Life & Annuity Insurance, didn't drop the fee completely until about a year ago. "It really felt that we were getting ripped off," Lever says of the fee.

Folks, fees can fleece your 401(k). The wrap fee in Lever's case was on *top* of any individual mutual fund expenses incurred. To see how small fees add up, consider this example: Suppose over a 30-year period you invest $10,500 a year and estimate an 8 percent annual return. If your average expense ratio—the annual amount you pay for fund operating and management expenses—is 0.28 percent, you'd end up with about $1.2 million. But if your expense ratio is 1.25 percent, you'd have only about $970,000—or $230,000 less. Not a small chunk of change.

You probably wouldn't have noticed a 1 percent fee when the market was cranking out double-digit returns. But these days participants are being rudely awakened. Attorney Eli Gottesdiener says he has received dozens of calls in recent months from angry 401(k) participants about fees they had little knowledge of. One reason: Half of all employers don't actively communicate fees to their participants, according to a study by research firm BARRA RogersCasey. (Though most will disclose fees if you ask.) To find out what you're paying, check fund prospectuses, summary plan descriptions, or quarterly statements; you may also have to call your benefits departments.

Many companies absorb record-keeping and administrative fees, but the trend is to pass them on to employees. According to Hewitt Associates, 22 percent of companies required employees to pay record-keeping fees in 1991. In 2001, 33 percent did. Plus, some companies aren't getting providers to reduce fees or offer lower-cost share classes. "If a company has a billion dollars they're bringing to the table, they have the ability to negotiate," says Michael Scarborough of the Scarborough Group, which specializes in 401(k) planning. "They're not always doing that."

What to do? Push your employer to change providers if your plan is an annuity, which often includes expensive wrap fees. Next, think twice about selecting funds with high expense ratios. And be aware of other administrative costs. While some employers charge either nothing or a flat fee, others charge a percentage of assets, which hits big account holders the hardest.

In the end, your best bet at getting the fees in your plan lowered may be sharing the bad news with your boss. If the fees are dragging down your investments, just think what they're doing to your boss's.

## Demand No. 2: Give Us Better Funds Not Just More Funds

Your company is touting that it increased your fund options from 5 to 40—but that doesn't necessarily mean you'll be truly diversified. All too often, plans still lack key investment options. Fact is, almost 60 percent of plans still don't offer a mid-cap equity fund, and only 45 percent of plans offer an intermediate- or long-term bond fund (a necessity in a tumbling market).

And value funds—about the only consistent winners these days—routinely crop up far less often than growth funds in most 401(k) plans. In fact, a recent survey by the Spectrem Group that looked at what kind of options are available in 401(k)s plans didn't break out value funds as a separate category.

But there's more to diversification than just having different fund types. Many 401(k) plans offer a variety of funds that have heavy holdings in the same stocks. Say your plan is run by Fidelity, the largest 401(k) provider, and includes several of its popular 401(k) funds. Looking to diversify, you allocate your large-cap assets among Fidelity Blue Chip Growth, Fidelity Growth & Income, and Fidelity Equity-Income, which have growth, blend, and value investing styles, respectively. But if General Electric, Citigroup, and Philip Morris all take a hit, you'll feel the sting in each fund—all three stocks are in each fund's top 15 holdings. "I often see four or more [large-cap] funds with different names in a plan, but they're all S&P surrogates," says Paul Brahim, a Pittsburgh certified financial planner.

Plus, there's probably a fund or two in your plan that your company seemingly must have used a dartboard to choose—and worse, that it won't replace. One reason: More than 40 percent of employers don't have a written investment policy. Such a policy serves as a formal road map for the way the company will monitor performance and replace funds if needed. And according to a study by BARRA RogersCasey, more than half of these employers, astonishingly, aren't considering adding one in the future.

Getting new funds added or those dartboard dogs replaced isn't impossible. It may actually be too simple. Some experts say one reason there are too many tech-heavy large-cap funds in plans now is because employees asked for them.

The trick is demanding the right funds.

George Pehanich knows the drill. A steelworker at Wheeling-Nisshin Steel in West Virginia who's on the company's retirement plan committee, Pehanich has been pushing to expand fund offerings for the past 10 years. The results: Between 1991 and 1999, Wheeling-Nisshin's 401(k) plan grew from three funds to 11, and now includes everything from three large-cap growth funds and a large-cap value fund to a mid-cap fund, an international fund, and a fixed-income fund. Most recently, Pehanich, 40, helped convince the company to add an index fund because he wanted a lower-fee option to round out the plan.

Is Pehanich satisfied? Hardly. "After these last negotiations," he says, "I looked at [our benefits administrator] across the table and said, 'I don't care what position I'm in. As long as I'm working in this company, I'll be over here asking for improvements in the 401(k).'"

## Demand No. 3: Let Us Max Out Our Contributions

So you just got a fat raise. It's going to be easier now, you figure, to max out your 401(k) and sock away that $12,000 next year. Well, think again. If you make $85,000 or more this year, you may have a hard time getting to that magic number.

Take Richard Geist, for example. With his 2001 promotion, the Studio City, California-based finance manager for CNA Insurance had his salary bumped to just above $85,000. What else did he get? A notice telling him that his pretax 401(k) contribution would be reduced to just 6 percent of his salary—or $5,500. "It sort of blindsided me," says Geist. "That's $5,000 less that's hidden from taxes."

Here's why: Uncle Sam wants to ensure that rank-and-file workers are encouraged to join 401(k) plans. For that to happen, the Internal Revenue Service (IRS) requires tests that determine how much highly compensated employees (anyone who made more than $85,000 the prior year) can contribute based on the amount lower-paid employees put in. So if lower-paid employees don't contribute enough, companies must either lower the amount higher earners put in or return part of their contributions. In 1999, about half of all plans either limited or refunded highly paid employees' contributions in order to pass the tests.

Some experts worry about the fairness of these tests. "The question is, given where the overall level of [401(k)] participation is now, whether it's fair to penalize the highly compensated employees," says Karen Field, senior tax manager at KPMG. Field notes that 403(b)s, cousins to the 401(k) for teachers and nonprofit employees, don't run these tests.

To prevent being penalized, gather the troops and push lower-paid employees to contribute more. Then encourage your employer to reach "safe harbor" status. Essentially, any company that matches 4 percent of an employee's salary or gives a 3 percent nonmatching contribution is exempt from the IRS rules. But good luck. Currently, less than 20 percent of plans have that status.

At the very least, whether you're highly paid or not, make sure you don't miss out on maximizing your employer's contribution. Say you make $100,000 a year, and your company matches up to 3 percent. If you contribute 20 percent of your salary each month, or $1,667, you'd reach this year's $11,000 limit by mid-July. That's also when your employer would have to stop matching—after giving you just $1,650 of a possible $3,000. The smarter strategy: Evenly distribute your contributions over 12 months. How do you calculate the amount? It's simple: Divide $11,000 by 12 (it comes out to $917). Then divide $917 by your monthly salary to arrive at the percent you should contribute.

## Demand No. 4: Don't Delay Rolling Over Our Money

These days we have real-time online trading and electronic transfers. Pretty sophisticated stuff. So you'd think that rolling over your money from a 401(k) to an IRA when you leave a job would happen as fast as your boss can say "layoff."

Too bad companies don't execute rollovers as swiftly as they do firings. Typically, such transfers take at least 30 days to complete. However, in many cases (especially with small businesses), rollovers can take several months to a year. And, says John Hotz, deputy director of the Pension Rights Center in Washington, D.C., there are no regulations mandating speedy transfers. "There need to be strict deadlines and consequences for not making a distribution [in a timely manner]," says Hotz, who ranks delayed distributions as one of the top 401(k)-related complaints he receives.

Technically, your company could hang on to your money until you reach 65 (or the plan's "retirement" age) even if you request a transfer. In practice, that rarely occurs. Companies don't want to continue administering an account any longer than they need to. Still, delays occur because some companies value the funds in their plans only monthly or quarterly rather than daily. Also, many small businesses don't have the resources to ensure that the transaction occurs quickly.

While a delay shouldn't endanger your retirement savings, it can be frustrating, especially if you want the flexibility and choice that come with moving your money into an IRA. Unfortunately, there's little you can do to make the process go faster. Your best hope is to make it happen more smoothly. Here's how: First, if you have any control over when you're leaving a company, consider making your last day around the end of the month or quarter if your company values its plan that way. Then go ahead and set up the IRA where you want the money transferred; don't wait for the distribution check to be cut.

# Demand No. 5: Keep the Company Stock—Give Us Cash

Talk about the Curse of the Pink Panther. Like many companies, Owens Corning, maker of that pink insulation you use in your home, made the matching contributions to its 401(k) plan in company stock. Nice perk. The problem: It didn't let employees reallocate the match into more diversified investments, leaving them unguarded when the stock started reeling more than two years ago.

Due in part to billions of dollars of asbestos-related lawsuits, Owens Corning's stock fell 45 percent in 1999. In January 2000, the company let employees move just a portion of the match into other investments. Then, six days before it filed for bankruptcy last October, employees were finally allowed to move the rest. By that time, though, the stock was trading for around $2 a share. Parker Lichtenstein, 56, a former Owens Corning research technician from Newark, Ohio, lost $250,000 in his 401(k) because he had so much tied up in company stock. "It was completely disastrous," says Lichtenstein.

Disastrous, indeed. Roy Diliberto, a Philadelphia financial planner, has another word for when employees are forced to keep their matches in company stock: outrageous. "Not only your career but your retirement is wrapped up in one single company," says Diliberto.

About 30 percent of companies still match exclusively in company stock. What's worse: Two-thirds of those companies don't let you move that match into other investments until at least age 55.

Bulking up on company stock goes against everything you've heard about diversification. So why do companies do it? David Wray, president of the Profit Sharing/401(k) Council of America, says company stock "builds a bond with the workforce." Um, okay. But that bond won't mean much when the stock starts sinking and you can't do anything about it.

Here's another reason: Companies save money when they match in stock. Unlike a cash match, a stock match is not charged against the company's bottom line. For example, say a company gives a typical 3 percent match to its 5,000 employees, who make an average of $40,000. A cash match would produce a $3.6 million cash hit on its income statement (assuming every employee participates). A stock match would usually cost the company only a dilution in stock value.

Thankfully, some companies that match in stock do let you move the stock into other fund options earlier. If that's the case, reallocate as soon as possible. Also, check to see if your plan is one of the few that offer "in-service withdrawals," which let you take the money out of the plan for any reason. If so, make sure you can roll it into an IRA, which will give you more options (and let you avoid any penalties).

For those without these options, be careful about how you invest the rest of your portfolio. Don't buy any additional company stock with your own money, and stay away from all mutual funds that have heavy weightings in your company or its particular sector. And when you reach age 55 and leave your company, you may be able to get a big tax break from your company stock. Here's how: Before you roll your 401(k) into an IRA or take a distribution, you are allowed to withdraw some or all of the company stock penalty-free. You'll pay income tax only on the stock's original cost, not on its current value. Then when you actually sell the stock, you'll pay only capital gains taxes (generally 20 percent) on your earnings.

## The 401(k) Crusaders

So, as luck has it, your plan is lacking. It doesn't offer an index fund; you have to wait a year before you can join it; or you hate that your company match comes in company stock. Feeling powerless? Think you can't get your employer to make a bad 401(k) plan better? Well, you're wrong.

Throughout the country, at companies big and small, scores of employees no longer believe that any retirement plan is better than nothing at all. Instead, they're risking the ire of their bosses, the sidelong glances of their colleagues, and the wrath of their human resources departments to do the one thing that is almost unheard-of in the workplace: agitate for change. That's because this new breed of activist understands the single most important truth about the 401(k) revolution sweeping corporate America: If employees don't take charge of their 401(k)s, no one else will.

And by taking charge, these employees don't mean spending hours trying to decide which of the four or five underperforming mutual funds in their 401(k)s they should invest in. Or figuring out which is better, a high-fee annuity or a mutual fund with a hefty back-end load. These crusaders know the true meaning of a self-directed retirement plan: It's one in which employees decide which investment options are offered, what kind of customer service is provided, and how much investing education is necessary.

And at some smaller firms, it is employees who persuade their bosses to offer a 401(k) in the first place.

Not all of these retirement activists have been successful—yet. But they are fostering a grassroots movement that may, in the end, prove to be more powerful than the 401(k) revolution itself. Want proof? Just look at what people are doing out there.

- Until a few years ago, employees at Chicago-based Boeing, the world's largest aerospace manufacturer, received a 401(k) account statement only once a year. And that meager offering reported beginning and ending balances only—no transaction details. Frustrated, one of the company's webmasters went underground (so underground he asked us not to use his name) and created an unofficial site providing weekly share prices for each of the 11 fund options in Boeing's plan. Within weeks the site was the talk of the watercooler and the subject of plenty of interoffice e-mails. Hundreds of employees began logging on regularly. Boeing and State Street Bank, the plan provider, got the hint. Employees can now get daily automated account information through an 800 number as well as detailed transaction histories.

- One curriculum specialist was convinced that Vanguard was the perfect provider for her employer's 403(b) plan, the 401(k) equivalent for nonprofits. But the bank in charge of running the plan was pushing Putnam funds instead. So the employee did a little detective work and found out whose funds the bank offered in its own 401(k) plan. The answer: Vanguard. Later that month, when a bank representative gave a presentation to employees at the nonprofit, the woman confronted him with that little irony in front of the crowd. It wasn't long before her company began offering Vanguard funds.

- In the late 1990s Duane Whitney, the director of retirement plans at American Stores, a Salt Lake City food and drugstore chain, didn't usually have much contact with the company's 70,000 401(k) participants. But he'll never forget a particular pharmacist from California who called and e-mailed Whitney regularly, pounding away with the idea that employees wanted more investment choices in their plan. While American Stores had recently conducted an employee survey that came to the same conclusion, the pharmacist still made a real impression. "He was relentless," says Whitney. "But as long as employees are pleasant, I don't mind their persistence. Sometimes they make us think about things that we otherwise might not have." American Stores (now owned by Albertson's) has gradually added more than 150 funds to its 401(k).

"In recent years I've seen a groundswell of interest by employees in changing their 401(k)s," says Ted Benna, the benefits consultant who, in the early 1980s, identified the arcane tax loophole that led to the 401(k) revolution. "Employers are getting feedback, sometimes solicited, sometimes not."

No matter. All the stonewalling, red tape, and curt responses in the world won't stop the true believers in what may ultimately be the *real* 401(k) revolution: Employees demanding—and sometimes getting—a retirement plan that they can truly retire on. Here, then, are four particularly instructive tales from the front.

## Do Your Homework

One of the best ways to get a company to change a 401(k) plan is to do the research for them. That's what Luita Persyko, a former store manager for Papyrus, a national chain of paper stores, did. After scrutinizing her plan's choices, she was dismayed to discover that not one of the nine funds in her plan offered a socially responsible portfolio. Politically aware but inexperienced as an investor, Persyko started making phone calls. An outfit called Franklin Research (now part of Trillium Asset Management), an investment management firm that specialized in socially responsible investing, sent her a newsletter called "Investing for a Better World." Franklin Research suggested she also call the *GreenMoney Journal*, a publication concerned with ethical business and investing issues. With information from these two groups, Persyko was able to gather a list of more than 30 socially responsible funds. She then called her plan's administrator, Western Pension Service, and got the go-ahead to send them her information. She didn't hesitate to point out that many of the funds on her list had managed to beat their peer-group averages despite the fact that they avoided investing in tobacco, alcohol, and other so-called sin stocks.

Weeks passed, and Persyko heard nothing from Western. So she continued her lobbying campaign with coworkers and anyone in management who would listen. More than a few people thought she was nuts. "They said, 'Why are you doing this? Why are you rocking the boat?' " Persyko remembers. But she persisted, always stressing the performance angle in each of her conversations. When she mentioned, say, that the Domini Social 400 index had a consistent record of outperforming the Standard & Poor's 500-stock index, she could usually keep people's attention. Four months later, at a managers meeting, the president of the company tapped her on the shoulder and said, "Your efforts have paid off. We're adding a socially responsible fund."

## Size Doesn't Matter

There's good news and bad news for 401(k) crusaders who work at small companies. While the typical Fortune 500 employee may have to make a dozen phone calls simply to find out which human resources executive handles retirement benefits, an employee at a small firm probably has much better access to the decision makers. The bad news: A small company has nowhere near the resources needed to find the best 401(k) providers, nor the leverage to negotiate with them. "Lots of big providers won't look at a company unless its portfolio is over $10 million," says Greg Viviani, a benefits attorney with Squire, Sanders & Dempsey in Cleveland. With the average 401(k) balance at about $49,000, a company needs more than 200 employees to come close to that number.

Joe Walsh, then a partner at Howell & HaferKamp, a St. Louis intellectual property law firm that employs 45 people (the firm has since merged with another firm), has firsthand experience with this small-company dilemma. Seven years ago, when the firm converted from a Keogh plan to a 401(k), big providers turned it down. So the firm hired a self-described specialist in small-company retirement plans.

The headaches began almost immediately. Employees received quarterly account statements, but they showed only how much an employee had in total; no share prices or transaction histories were recorded. The provider kept promising to improve his software. But two years later the firm was still waiting.

For Walsh, the last straw was when his mortgage lender asked for a written statement of his 401(k) account balance. A simple request, but Walsh had to delay the closing on his house until the provider sent it.

At the partners meeting in January 1998, Walsh and a colleague proposed looking for another 401(k) provider. Convincing other partners wasn't hard, as many of them had their own horror stories to share. Finding another provider, however, was tough. Walsh contacted law firms around town and got the names of providers those companies used. He called consultants who specialized in 401(k)s and asked for their advice. Then he scheduled presentations for the half dozen candidates who were willing to consider a small plan. None seemed quite right: Fees were too high, the provider offered only proprietary funds, there was no index fund. "Finally we ran out of candidates," Walsh remembers.

One night that summer Walsh and his wife were having dinner with three other couples. On the patio, over cocktails, Walsh was grumbling about his plan to other guests. "Man, am I disappointed in our 401(k)," he said. "In fact, I'm embarrassed to share the details of this plan."

"Really?" said one of the guys, a banker at State Street. "It seems to me our 401(k) people have some sort of relationship with the American Bar Association. Let me have someone call you."

The next week State Street met with the partners. For just a bit more than it was currently paying, the law firm could get an 800 number for daily account valuations, transfers, and other service requests, and a brokerage window for buying and selling individual stocks. The plan was precisely what the lawyers wanted. "Once we found the ABA program, it was easy to decide," says Walsh. "But when you're a small firm, people aren't going to go overboard to attract your business. You have to do the legwork on your own."

## You *Can* Start Something from Scratch

At Leonard Kunkin Associates, a Hilltown, Pennsylvania–based steel fabricator, employees had to start a 401(k) from scratch.

Shaun L. O'Connor was ready for the job. Known as the "lead man" at Kunkin, he makes sure that the girders, plates, and other chunks of metal that arrive daily at the plant get from the yard to the right spot on the shop floor. When O'Connor decided the company needed to add a 401(k) plan to the pension plan that was already in place, he didn't hesitate to take charge. "My father-in-law retired from this place, and I knew the pension wasn't going to be enough," says O'Connor. "I wanted to do something for myself and the guys at the plant."

It's a casual work environment, so one afternoon about two years ago, O'Connor stopped by company president Matthew Kunkin's office and asked whether the company would consider adding a 401(k). "A 401(k)? I don't know much about them," said Kunkin. O'Connor quickly sketched out how the plans worked. "Interesting," said Kunkin. "If it doesn't conflict with the pension plan, we might be able to do it. Let me think about it." Wanting to be prepared in case he got the thumbs-up, O'Connor started calling fund companies to get information. He chose only brand-name companies—Merrill Lynch, T. Rowe Price, Vanguard, and Strong—because he wanted people to feel as comfortable as possible with the idea.

Right away O'Connor dropped some brochures from the potential providers on his boss's desk. Every couple of days O'Connor would stop by Kunkin's office and ask if he'd had a chance to look over the materials. "I was kind of relentless; I wasn't going to let it drop," O'Connor remembers. Finally, Kunkin said they could go ahead.

The selection process went smoothly. A committee made up of O'Connor, Kunkin, the chief financial officer, and the controller reviewed the companies. All were close on costs, but Strong made the best presentation. For an annual $2,000 in administrative fees, plus about $25 per participant, the committee could select six Strong funds.

## It Never Hurts to Ask

American Airlines started its 401(k) back in 1986 with four investment options that mirrored those of its pension plan—a cash account, a bond fund, a balanced fund, and an equity fund. In 1991 the airline added an international fund at the suggestion of AMR Investment Services, the finance subsidiary of American Airlines' parent company. But employee dissatisfaction with the plan was growing, and William Quinn, president of AMR Investment, knew it. "Frankly, for years there has been ongoing demand for more fund options," he says.

It wasn't until October 1998, when union negotiations were under way (retirement benefits were one of the top items on the agenda) and the flight attendants' grassroots campaign was in full swing, that the company finally held focus groups with employees to find out what they wanted in their 401(k) plan. At the top of the list: an S&P 500 index fund. Just two months later, the company announced it was adding one to the 401(k), along with five other choices. "If employees hadn't asked for that index fund, we wouldn't have added it," says Quinn.

# 8

# THE BEST AND WORST
# FUNDS FOR YOUR 401(k)

ake a look around your office. You probably think you have the same
retirement benefits as your coworkers. After all, your company matches
all employees' 401(k) contributions uniformly, and you all choose from
a single list of mutual funds.

Maybe you should take a closer look. Five years ago, the guy sitting to
your right put the lion's share of his money into Fidelity Dividend Growth.
You opted for the more hotly promoted Fidelity Magellan. Now, after socking away an identical $5,000 annually, you've got only $33,314 in your account while he's got $38,152—a difference of 14 percent.

So much for financial equality.

The bottom line is that while the terms of your company's 401(k) plan
can have a major impact on your retirement savings, so can the choices you
make within that plan. With the leverage of tax-deferred compounding, the
difference between picking good funds and picking mediocre ones can
mean the difference between affording a lavish retirement or settling for a
chintzy one.

So which are the funds worth investing in, and which should be
avoided? We couldn't possibly answer that question for every 401(k) on
earth; there are simply too many funds to choose from. However, we *have*
gone through and rated the most commonly held 401(k) funds. Because

these funds are so popular in retirement accounts, we figure there's a good chance that you will encounter at least some of them in your plan.

We focused our research on the 10 mutual fund companies with the most 401(k) assets, as tracked by the publication *Pensions & Investments*. Then we probed the most popular 401(k) funds at each of those fund companies, using an exclusive rating system created with the help of Morningstar. How does the system work? We compared each fund against its peers in the entire universe of all funds with five-year records, dividing them into four broad groups—domestic equity, international equity, taxable bond, and municipal bond.

The first test was designed to measure consistency. The funds were ranked by the number of rolling 12-month periods (48 in all) that they returned more than 10 percent—and by how wide a margin. The second screen gauged short-term volatility. It looked at each fund's rolling *three-month* returns. How often did the funds turn in a negative return in each three-month period (58 in all) over the past five years, and how big was the shortfall? Our system penalized funds with frequent and large short-term losses.

The percentile ranks in Table 8.1—1 is best, 100 is worst—are designed to help you decide what's most important to you: return or volatility. It depends on both your level of comfort as well as how much time you have before you retire. And remember: You needn't feel compelled to buy, say, your 401(k)'s international fund just for the sake of getting some foreign-stock exposure. Allocate your 401(k) money into the best funds available, and then invest in an international equity fund outside of your plan to get the diversification you want.

All returns are through November 30, 2001.

## Fidelity

Drum roll, please: The best overall fund for your money—in terms of high returns and relatively lower volatility—is **Dividend Growth**. It's the quintessential sleeper. Because the word "dividend" figures so prominently in its name, you might brush it off as a cautious fund more concerned with stability than with high-octane returns. But through late 2001, this portfolio had

TABLE 8.1   RATING THE MOST POPULAR 401(K) FUNDS

| Fund Family | Fund Name | Category | 5-Year Return* | Percentile Rank in Broad Group | Percentile Rank in Volatility | Percentile Rank in Growth |
|---|---|---|---|---|---|---|
| Fidelity | Asset Manager | Domestic hybrid | 9.22 | 38 | 7 | 68 |
| Fidelity | Blue Chip Growth | Large growth | 9.06 | 40 | 46 | 26 |
| Fidelity | Contrafund | Large blend | 9.85 | 31 | 34 | 32 |
| Fidelity | Dividend Growth | Large blend | 15.16 | 6 | 10 | 32 |
| Fidelity | Equity-Income | Large value | 9.38 | 36 | 29 | 72 |
| Fidelity | Growth Company | Large growth | 12.80 | 12 | 73 | 6 |
| Fidelity | Growth & Income | Large blend | 10.00 | 29 | 12 | 55 |
| Fidelity | Magellan | Large blend | 10.28 | 27 | 47 | 30 |
| Fidelity | Puritan | Domestic hybrid | 8.83 | 42 | 5 | 88 |
| Fidelity | Spartan 500 Index | Large blend | 9.86 | 31 | 32 | 40 |
| Vanguard | 500 Index | Large blend | 10.03 | 29 | 31 | 38 |
| Vanguard | Institutional Index | Large blend | 10.16 | 28 | 31 | 38 |
| Vanguard | LifeStrategy Moderate Growth | Domestic hybrid | 8.19 | 50 | 5 | 74 |
| Vanguard | Primecap | Large blend | 16.22 | 5 | 52 | 13 |
| Vanguard | Total Bond Market Index | Intermediate-term bond | 7.27 | 6 | 37 | 11 |
| Vanguard | U.S. Growth | Large growth | 2.78 | 90 | 70 | 23 |

(Continued)

## TABLE 8.1 (Continued)

| Fund Family | Fund Name | Category | 5-Year Return* | Percentile Rank in Broad Group | Percentile Rank in Volatility | Percentile Rank in Growth |
|---|---|---|---|---|---|---|
| Vanguard | Wellington | Domestic hybrid | 9.98 | 30 | 4 | 79 |
| Vanguard | Windsor | Large value | 9.93 | 30 | 52 | 70 |
| Vanguard | Windsor II | Large value | 9.57 | 34 | 34 | 57 |
| American Funds | Amcap A | Large growth | 15.32 | 6 | 8 | 21 |
| American Funds | American Balanced A | Domestic hybrid | 11.34 | 19 | 2 | 70 |
| American Funds | Bond Fund of Amer. A | Intermediate-term bond | 6.15 | 42 | 36 | 75 |
| American Funds | EuroPacific Growth A | Foreign stock | 7.30 | 14 | 26 | 23 |
| American Funds | Fundamental Investor A | Large value | 11.22 | 20 | 18 | 41 |
| American Funds | Growth Fund of Amer. A | Large growth | 17.43 | 3 | 29 | 8 |
| American Funds | Income Fund of Amer. A | Domestic hybrid | 9.18 | 39 | 4 | 88 |
| American Funds | New Perspective A | World stock | 11.56 | 5 | 7 | 12 |
| American Funds | Investment Company of Amer. A | Large value | 12.55 | 13 | 7 | 48 |
| American Funds | Washington Mutual A | Large value | 11.61 | 18 | 14 | 58 |
| Putnam | Asset Allocation: Balanced Y | Domestic hybrid | 6.83 | 64 | 17 | 80 |
| Putnam | Fund for Growth & Income Y | Large value | 7.63 | 56 | 35 | 79 |

| | | | | | | |
|---|---|---|---|---|---|---|
| Putnam | George Putnam Fund of Boston | Domestic hybrid | 7.93 | 53 | 8 | 91 |
| Putnam | Global Growth Y | World stock | 3.42 | 35 | 53 | 9 |
| Putnam | International Growth Y | Foreign stock | 10.42 | 7 | 19 | 10 |
| Putnam | Investors A | Large growth | 7.18 | 61 | 64 | 20 |
| Putnam | New Opportunities Y | Large growth | 5.26 | 79 | 88 | 8 |
| Putnam | OTC Emerging Growth Y | Mid-cap growth | −7.03 | 99 | 100 | 9 |
| Putnam | Vista Y | Mid-cap growth | 6.78 | 65 | 86 | 12 |
| Putnam | Voyager Y | Large growth | 8.87 | 42 | 79 | 13 |
| Janus | Balanced | Domestic hybrid | 12.71 | 12 | 8 | 32 |
| Janus | Enterprise | Mid-cap growth | 5.83 | 74 | 91 | 2 |
| Janus | Flexible Income | Multisector bond | 6.68 | 20 | 44 | 29 |
| Janus | Growth & Income | Large growth | 14.89 | 6 | 48 | 9 |
| Janus | Janus | Large growth | 9.17 | 39 | 74 | 11 |
| Janus | Mercury | Large growth | 13.02 | 11 | 81 | 2 |
| Janus | Olympus | Large growth | 14.66 | 7 | 85 | 2 |
| Janus | Overseas | Foreign stock | 9.09 | 10 | 46 | 7 |
| Janus | Twenty | Large growth | 11.23 | 20 | 79 | 4 |
| Janus | Worldwide | World stock | 9.24 | 9 | 35 | 6 |
| T. Rowe Price | Balanced | Domestic hybrid | 8.08 | 51 | 4 | 86 |
| T. Rowe Price | Blue Chip Growth | Large blend | 9.89 | 31 | 26 | 31 |
| T. Rowe Price | Equity Index 500 | Large blend | 9.75 | 32 | 32 | 42 |
| T. Rowe Price | Equity-Income | Large value | 10.40 | 26 | 17 | 68 |
| T. Rowe Price | Growth Stock | Large blend | 11.67 | 17 | 30 | 29 |

*(Continued)*

TABLE 8.1 *(Continued)*

| Fund Family | Fund Name | Category | 5-Year Return* | Percentile Rank in Broad Group | Percentile Rank in Volatility | Percentile Rank in Growth |
|---|---|---|---|---|---|---|
| T. Rowe Price | International Stock | Foreign stock | 0.50 | 56 | 35 | 66 |
| T. Rowe Price | Mid-Cap Growth | Mid-cap growth | 12.88 | 12 | 45 | 31 |
| T. Rowe Price | New Horizons | Small growth | 6.47 | 68 | 84 | 43 |
| T. Rowe Price | Science & Technology | Specialty-technology | 1.55 | 93 | 99 | 5 |
| T. Rowe Price | Small-Cap Stock | Small blend | 11.23 | 20 | 39 | 47 |
| American Century | Equity Growth Inv. | Large blend | 9.30 | 37 | 42 | 42 |
| American Century | Growth Inv. | Large growth | 9.90 | 30 | 65 | 17 |
| American Century | Income & Growth Inv. | Large value | 9.86 | 31 | 29 | 49 |
| American Century | International Growth Inv. | Foreign stock | 7.87 | 13 | 33 | 11 |
| American Century | Select Inv. | Large growth | 9.56 | 35 | 43 | 26 |
| American Century | Strat. Alloc.: Mod. Inv. | Domestic hybrid | 8.43 | 47 | 10 | 67 |
| American Century | Ultra Inv. | Large growth | 8.17 | 50 | 73 | 21 |
| American Century | Value Inv. | Mid-cap value | 11.24 | 20 | 37 | 60 |
| Merrill Lynch | Balanced Capital A | Domestic hybrid | 6.46 | 68 | 16 | 96 |
| Merrill Lynch | Basic Value A | Large value | 9.81 | 32 | 27 | 73 |

| | | | | | | |
|---|---|---|---|---|---|---|
| Merrill Lynch | Davis NY Venture A | Large value | 11.19 | 20 | 19 | 47 |
| Merrill Lynch | Fundamental Growth A | Large growth | 11.90 | 16 | 65 | 15 |
| Merrill Lynch | Global Allocation A | International hybrid | 9.50 | 8 | 1 | 62 |
| Merrill Lynch | MFS Emerging Growth A | Large growth | 3.17 | 89 | 93 | 22 |
| Merrill Lynch | MFS Massachusetts Investors A | Large blend | 7.22 | 60 | 40 | 70 |
| Merrill Lynch | Pimco Total Return Administrative | Intermediate-term bond | 7.72 | 3 | 42 | 8 |
| Merrill Lynch | Small Cap Value A | Small blend | 17.76 | 3 | 54 | 19 |
| Merrill Lynch | Van Kampen Emerging Growth A | Large growth | 14.01 | 8 | 88 | 2 |
| Franklin Templeton | Franklin Balance Sheet Investment A | Small value | 11.07 | 21 | 17 | 63 |
| Franklin Templeton | Franklin Small-Mid Cap Growth A | Mid-cap growth | 9.56 | 34 | 86 | 10 |
| Franklin Templeton | Franklin U.S. Gov. Securities A | Intermediate government | 6.92 | 13 | 23 | 42 |
| Franklin Templeton | Mutual Beacon A | Mid-cap value | 12.00 | 15 | 8 | 60 |
| Franklin Templeton | Mutual Discovery A | World stock | 11.15 | 5 | 2 | 35 |
| Franklin Templeton | Mutual Shares A | Mid-cap value | 11.80 | 16 | 9 | 61 |
| Franklin Templeton | Templeton Foreign A | Foreign stock | 4.85 | 26 | 23 | 86 |
| Franklin Templeton | Templeton Growth A | World stock | 8.72 | 11 | 6 | 81 |
| Franklin Templeton | Templeton World A | World stock | 7.80 | 13 | 13 | 79 |

*(Continued)*

163

## TABLE 8.1 *(Continued)*

| Fund Family | Fund Name | Category | 5-Year Return* | Percentile Rank in Broad Group | Percentile Rank in Volatility | Percentile Rank in Growth |
|---|---|---|---|---|---|---|
| Scudder Kemper | Balanced S | Domestic hybrid | 8.49 | 46 | 9 | 68 |
| Scudder Kemper | Growth & Income S | Large blend | 4.49 | 82 | 59 | 94 |
| Scudder Kemper | Income S | Intermediate-term bond | 5.77 | 57 | 39 | 61 |
| Scudder Kemper | International S | Foreign stock | 3.76 | 33 | 44 | 25 |
| Scudder Kemper | Large Company Growth S | Large growth | 7.71 | 55 | 72 | 18 |
| Scudder Kemper | Large Company Value S | Large value | 8.30 | 48 | 41 | 70 |
| Scudder Kemper | Pathway Conservative S | Domestic hybrid | 4.50 | 82 | 3 | 100 |
| Scudder Kemper | Pathway Moderate S | Domestic hybrid | 4.70 | 81 | 16 | 91 |

*Data as of November 30, 2001.
*Source:* Morningstar, Inc.

# How to Evaluate the Funds in Your 401(k) Plan on Your Own

Here's a clue: Funds that have underperformed their peers in every time period that is typically tracked—one-year, three-year, and five-year—are *bad*. So, too, are funds that take larger than average risks, charge high expenses, and cost you a fortune in taxes.

Of course, if you don't want to do the work that's required to investigate your 401(k) funds, you can simply choose an index fund and hold on to it for the long haul. They're cheap. They're tax efficient. And they routinely beat the vast majority of actively managed funds. Over the past 10 years, through early 2002, only 25 percent of diversified domestic equity funds beat the S&P 500. Go out 15 years, and only 21 percent have, according to fund-tracking firm Morningstar.

So what are the chances of one of those funds being in your 401(k)? Not as remote as you think. Consider this: Even if only 25 percent of all domestic equity funds have outpaced the S&P 500 over the past 10 years, that amounts to over 160 solid fund portfolios. Unless you really don't know what you're doing—you're chasing last year's hot fund, for instance—we think it is possible to pick one, even a few, winners. It helps, of course, to have a game plan.

First, hit the fund company's web site for reports, prospectuses, and (sometimes) updated commentary from fund managers. At www.smartmoney.com, you can pull up basic information you'll want to know on U.S. and foreign funds—annualized returns for the past 10, 5, and 3 years as well as returns in the past 12 months, year-to-date, and 3 months. There's also information on portfolio composition: What are the fund's top holdings? How much of the portfolio is invested in tech stocks or utilities or consumer durables? At Morningstar's web site, www.morningstar.com, you can also find analyst reports for nearly every fund (look under "Morningstar Analysis" in the left menu). After a 30-day free trial, access to these reports through Morningstar's Premium service runs $11.95 each month. These include short reports on management, strategy, risk, as well as a three- or four-paragraph summary of whether Morningstar thinks the fund is worth investing in.

Three things you ought to focus on when weighing a fund: its performance, its riskiness, and its manager's track record.

**Performance**

Of course, "past performance is no guarantee of future results." But those who ignore a mutual fund's historical record do so at their own peril. It's the best measure we have of a fund manager's competence.

And in fact, studies show that past performance is probably a better predictor for really bad funds than it is for highfliers. A 2000 study of ongoing fund performance by Fordham University professors found that while Morningstar's four- and five-star funds (the best performers) didn't necessarily remain at the top of the charts, one- and two-star funds continued to flounder.

What does that tell you? Don't buy into a loser fund thinking it's going to turn around anytime soon. By the same token, don't hang on to a longtime loser, either. Although the decision to sell is never easy ("What if it finally turns around this year?"), your plan should have other funds from which to choose.

The best way to evaluate a fund's performance is to examine multiple periods and compare the returns against other similar funds (small-cap to small-cap, large value against large value, etc.) and a broader index, like the S&P 500 or the Russell 2000 (for small caps).

Whatever you do, don't get seduced by a fund if all it has going for it is a single hot year, unless you want to get burned. Take the American Heritage Fund. It finished 1997 with a blazing 75 percent gain, then plunged 61 percent the following year, ending up at the bottom of the barrel. Had you been wowed by the 1997 gain but checked the fund's five-year record (a negative 30 percent annualized return in early 2002), you would have seen its erratic history. That's a pretty clear red flag.

What if you have a more ordinary fund with, say, 7 percent, 15 percent, or 20 percent annual returns? How do you tell how good—consistent—that fund really is? As we have mentioned earlier,

everything is relative. Compare its numbers to a relative benchmark index (compare a large-cap fund to the large-cap S&P 500 for
instance; a small-cap growth fund with the Russell 2000) as well as
other funds with similar objectives.

### Risk

If your fund choice is going to make you sick with worry, what's
the point? That's why it pays to make sure you're comfortable with
a fund's risk profile and its propensity for short-term volatility.

Risk is generally a function of investing style. Growth funds
—run by managers who chase popular but risky companies with
huge earnings growth—tend to suffer wider short-term price
swings and more turnover. Value funds—in which the managers
look for undiscovered bargain stocks, hoping that their prices
will pick up over time—are less volatile on the downside, but
you sometimes pay for that with less dramatic upside. The les-
son (true for stock investing as well): The lower the risk, the
lower the potential return; the higher the risk, the higher the potential return.

How do you go about assessing the risk of a fund? Morningstar has a simple, generally well-regarded way to do it. The
firm quantifies the risk-return trade-off of each fund. Its ratings,
which range from one to five stars (five being the best), take into
account both a fund's performance and its risk for the life of the
fund. Basically, Morningstar subtracts the fund's risk score from
its performance score. A five-star rating means a fund has scored
in the top 10 percent of its broad investment class. Funds with
four stars fall into the next 22.5 percent of their broad class, and
so on down the line.

You can find the rating for any fund on Morningstar's web site
(www.morningstar.com) or in www.smartmoney.com's "Fund
Snapshots."

"Beta" is another measure of a fund's volatility relative to its
benchmark—typically the S&P 500 for stock funds. The beta of the
benchmark is always 1.00; so it follows that if a fund has a beta of
1.00, it has experienced roughly the same up and down movements as the S&P 500. A fund with a beta of 1.25, on the other

hand, is expected to do 25 percent better than the S&P 500 in an up market and 25 percent worse in a down market.

Sometimes you'll hear fund industry people talk about a fund's "r-squared" number. This measures a fund's correlation to the market on a scale from 0 to 100 (100 means the fund is 100 percent correlated to the market).

## The Manager

We can look at all kinds of performance numbers and risk factors, but at the end of the day, those statistics won't tell us what kind of manager is behind it all. And given that fund managers tend to come and go like flies through an open window, that is often the hardest part.

You can find the manager's name and tenure on the fund company's web site (and it will typically include a short biography). Or click onto www.morningstar.com or www.smartmoney.com. Obviously, the longer a manager has been around generating good returns, the better. Keep in mind, though, that only a handful of managers—Bill Miller of the Legg Mason Value fund is one of them—have been around for longer than 10 years. The average for fund manager tenure is just 4.5 years.

If it turns out a fund manager is new—he has been running the fund for less than two years—track down his or her previous record. If the manager's history is cloudy, consider holding off before you buy shares in it. You should also keep in mind that a change in fund management can often lead to high portfolio turnover (and high taxes) as the new manager shapes the fund to his or her own liking.

Probably the best sources of information about mutual fund managers, however, are web sites like SmartMoney.com or the general business press. The mutual fund industry's spectacular rise has spurred a concurrent boom in mutual fund coverage. A quick trip to the library or even a Web search engine like Yahoo! will likely turn up a lot of good information—especially on old-guard managers like Miller, who is one of the industry's brightest stars.

delivered a 15.1 percent five-year annualized return, lifted in part by its heavy weighting in technology, health, and financial services stocks. It stands up to its peers outside of Fidelity, too: It ranks in the top 7 percent of all growth funds, according to Morningstar. And its volatility? After the two hybrid funds, **Asset Manager** and **Puritan** (more than 30 percent of both portfolios are invested in bonds), Dividend Growth has the best volatility ranking of the top 401(k) funds at Fidelity.

If volatility is something you're trying to avoid, then stay away from **Growth Company**. Although this growth fund is one of the best performers in Fidelity's stable—its five-year 12.8 percent return ranks in the top 15 percent of all growth funds—with it comes more volatility than most funds (in or outside of Fidelity). Our short-term volatility screen shows that not only does Growth Company often post a negative three-month return, but the size of the shortfall is larger than most. For instance, Growth Company posted a negative return in 36 percent of all the three-month periods we tested—as did other Fidelity funds, like **Magellan** (39 percent), **Contrafund** (36 percent), and **Equity-Income** (38 percent). But in those periods, the degree of the shortfall was far greater than other Fidelity funds; Growth Company's worst three-month return was a negative 26.5 percent, while the rest hovered more in the 15 percent range.

Better bets for a stable fund would be the domestic hybrid funds, Asset Manager and Puritan. Of the two, our research shows that Asset Manager, which is just as good as Puritan at keeping a lid on volatility, is also more consistent. In the 48 one-year periods we tested, Asset Manager delivered a return of 10 percent or more 63 percent of the time. That's in keeping with aggressive growth funds like Growth Company and Magellan. (Puritan, however, exceeded 10 percent returns only 40 percent of the time.) So why does Asset Manager fetch a low ranking in the consistency screen? Because we also took into account the amount by which its returns topped 10 percent. While Asset Manager is generally consistent, its returns are not high-octane.

And what of Magellan? It's been years since the fund headlined for Fidelity, but it's not a dog of a fund, either. Morningstar gives Peter Lynch's former fund a rating of three stars (out of five), and its 10.3 percent five-year record outpaces the S&P 500, ranking it among the top 33 percent of its peers. That's not outstanding, but it's not shabby, either.

## Vanguard

Vanguard doesn't sell itself as an actively managed fund firm—its best fund managers aren't stock pickers; they're index fund managers. So it should come as no surprise that the only actively managed large-cap growth fund on Vanguard's top-10 401(k) list, **U.S. Growth**, is a dud. The fund has a 3 percent five-year record, which may not be completely awful considering the market in recent years. But that return ranks in the bottom 80 percent of its peer group (other large growth funds). And as our screens show, the sheer drop of its returns on the downside dwarfs its returns on the upside; when it's bad, it's so bad that when it's good it doesn't matter. Luckily there are other equity funds in its stable that are worth investing in.

**Primecap** is one: The blend fund—so-called because it can buy shares in companies that are growing fast, like Microsoft, as well as companies trading on the cheap, like Bank One—has a 16.22 percent five-year record, which ranks at the top of the charts against all other large-cap blend funds. Although it does experience some bumps along the way—it ranks in the middle of the pack in our volatility screen—the upside returns over the longer term tend to smooth them out. Primecap wins the best score in our growth screen of all Vanguard equity funds, because of the size of its upside returns as well as its consistency in delivering them. The minimum investment for regular investors is $25,000, so you're lucky it's in your 401(k) plan.

Three of the funds aren't actually managed by Vanguard, technically speaking. The fund company outsources to Wellington Asset Management several funds including **Wellington**, **Windsor**, and **Windsor II**. All three have strong five-year records that are very similar (in the upper 9 percent range). Of the three, Windsor II tends to be more consistent in delivering returns over 10 percent during 12-month periods. It also is relatively less volatile than its twin, Windsor. But if volatility is a concern, the Wellington fund shines in this category. That's because the fund is a domestic hybrid (33 percent of the portfolio is invested in bonds), which makes it an excellent choice for investors looking for decent returns with less risk.

A word about Vanguard's LifeStrategy funds: Only **LifeStrategy Moderate Growth** made the top-10 401(k) list, but there are others (Growth, Income, and Conservative Growth). They are basically funds of funds, made up of a combination of different Vanguard offerings. Moderate Growth consists of four funds: Total Stock Market Index (35.2 percent); Total Bond Market Index (30.2 percent); Asset Allocation (25.0 percent); and Total International Stock Index (9.7 percent). Should you invest in it? If you like index funds, it's one way to go. This is one-stop shopping asset allocation at its simplest. Just be aware that you're limited to this strict weighting—the fund's makeup doesn't change much—and that you're investing in indexes, which can, as we've seen lately, underperform a good actively managed fund.

A final word on Vanguard's index funds: Vanguard is, without argument, the biggest retail index fund family in the country. If you want to invest in the S&P 500 index, there's no question that Vanguard **500 Index** is a great choice. Manager George Sauter has even managed to narrowly beat the index he mimics in some good years. In addition, bond lovers need not worry about **Total Bond Market Index.** It is what its name implies, and according to our research, it's a standout on all measures.

## American Funds

As far as overall performance goes, this may be the best group of funds in this chapter. Over the past 10 years, all but one fund—Investment Company of America—rank in the top 15 percent of their peer groups. Over the past five years, all but one—this time the Bond Fund of America—rank in the top 20 percent of their peer groups.

The two best funds for your money are **Amcap**, a large-cap growth fund, and **New Perspective**, a world stock fund.

Amcap is that rare breed—a fund that can post strong returns consistently and keep a lid on volatility as well. It has posted better than 10 percent returns over 75 percent of the past 48 rolling 12-month periods. What's more, of all the large-cap growth funds in this chapter (20 in all), Amcap boasts the lowest volatility. You can't ask for more in a mutual fund.

New Perspective does more than hold its own with other world stock funds. Morningstar gives the fund a five-star rating for the past five and 10 years, based on its ability to generate above-average returns (the fund's five-year return of 11.6 percent ranks in the top 11 percent of all world stock funds, and the top 5 percent compared to all international equity funds) with below-average risk. The fund earns an enviable 7th percentile ranking in our volatility screen.

If those two funds aren't on your list of options, go for the **Growth Fund of America**. The fund has the strongest five-year return of any fund in American Funds' top-10 list (and of any fund we surveyed), ranking it in the top 3 percent of all domestic stock funds in the country. But with that comes some volatility—not a lot, as it ranks in the 29th percentile range in our short-term volatility screen, but enough to make note of it.

**EuroPacific Growth**, the fund company's No. 1 401(k) portfolio, is also a strong choice, with top-quartile (or nearly) rankings in all of our screens. And as for the remaining equity funds, **Fundamental Investors**, **Investment Company of America**, and **Washington Mutual**, it's a toss-up. All three have nearly identical five-year returns, and they score similarly well in both our volatility and our growth screens. (That should come as no surprise, given that all of these funds have multiple managers, most of whom manage at least one or two other funds in the American Funds family.)

You'll notice that the bond funds or funds heavily weighted in bonds, like **American Balanced** and **Income Fund of America** (both domestic hybrids) and **Bond Fund of America**, earn shoddy records in the growth screen. That's to be expected. After all, if most bond funds were able to exceed 10 percent returns in most one-year periods, we'd all be in bonds, wouldn't we? But that's not what these funds are designed to do.

How well do they do what they're designed to do—offering investors relatively safe, stable investments? So-so. The American Balanced fund and the Income Fund of America both earn near-perfect scores in our screen for short-term volatility. But the Bond Fund of America ranks in the middle to top third of all bond funds, with a 36th percentile ranking in that particular screen.

Of the two hybrids, we like the American Balanced fund over the Income Fund of America. If you look at the way the two funds stand up to our growth screen, you'll notice that American Balanced turns in a stronger result: It posted a 10 percent or higher return in 70 percent of the 48 one-year periods we tested. It's a steadier fund, and thus its five-year record, 11.3 percent, beats the Income Fund of America's 9.2 percent return. As for the Bond Fund of America, it's mediocre compared with other bond funds. Even though it earns four stars from Morningstar, we think there are better funds on offer here. If you really need the stability of bonds, it's not a poor choice, but you could buy a stronger bond fund outside of your 401(k)—in your IRA or Roth IRA, for instance—and keep your 401(k) money invested in the American Funds' equity portfolios instead.

## Putnam

The best thing about Putnam is its international funds, **Global Growth** and **International Growth**. Otherwise, there's not much to choose from. If you can get your hands on some shares of International Growth—and your asset allocation calls for some foreign stock exposure—we'd start there. This fund has a 10.4 percent five-year record, which ranks in the top 7 percent of all foreign funds (Global Growth ranks in the top 35 percent). But more important, compared to its foreign fund peers, International Growth is relatively stable—it ranks in the top 19 percent in our volatility screen—and it scores well in our consistency screen, too.

A lot of Putnam's funds score well for consistency. Overall, Putnam **Investors** fund, for instance, delivered 10 percent or greater returns in 70 percent of the periods we tested. Other domestic equity funds, like **New Opportunities** and **Voyager**, rank higher than the Investors fund in this category because of the margin by which they beat 10 percent in each of those periods. Still, as a whole, Investors offers a better return for the risk, for it scores a better volatility ranking than either of those funds. If Investors isn't one of your options, consider Voyager. It's the next best (albeit by default), given its overall score for volatility and consistent returns.

If avoiding volatility is your biggest concern, we'd choose the domestic hybrid funds, **George Putnam Fund of Boston** or **Asset Allocation: Balanced**. Like most funds of this ilk, a large percentage of the portfolio—36 percent and 25 percent, respectively—is invested in bonds.

One last thing: The **OTC Emerging Growth** fund. When it's good, it's very good. When it's bad, it's simply horrible. The fund has a negative 7.0 percent five-year record, a bottom-of-the-barrel return for the group. Overall, the fund makes a poor choice for your 401(k) money.

## Janus

Given how far these funds have fallen from the perch they held in the 1990s, it's kind of surprising how strong they look based on their five-year returns. There isn't really a loser in the bunch, except for the **Enterprise** fund, whose 5.8 percent annual return over 5 years ranks it in the 63rd percentile of all mid-cap growth funds. Manager James Goff has been running the fund for nine years, but looking at his year-by-year returns, he's given his shareholders a bit of a roller-coaster ride. He posted a 121 percent return in 1999, but in 2000 and 2001 returns were negative 30 percent or worse. In addition, as our two screens show, the fund, when it is good, tends to outperform by a wide margin—and vice versa on the downside, too.

Of course, Janus is a growth house, and that kind of ride is par for the course because it's an investment style that tends to be more volatile and a little more risky. In good years, the returns can be phenomenal. But in bad years, the downside can be horrific. Recent returns for many of these funds (three-year and one-year, for instance) are abysmal.

Nevertheless, when the market settles down, and growth stocks begin to win Wall Street's favor again, there are plenty of funds from which to choose at Janus.

There's one hybrid fund in the bunch: **Balanced**. And as far as stability goes, it does a good job. (Its total returns, at 12.7 percent for the last five years, aren't bad, either.) The fund ranks in the top 8 percent of all equity funds in our short-term volatility screen. Surprisingly, the one bond fund—**Flexible Income**—doesn't rank so well in that screen, with a 44th percentile ranking (keep in mind it is ranked against other bond funds). What gives? With a 6.7 percent five-year return that ranks in the top 20 percent of all bond funds, it's a strong performer. But it is a multisector bond fund, and as such, according to its prospectus, it may own an unlimited amount of high-risk, high-yield bonds. In addition, some of its portfolio invests in preferred stock.

The remaining equity funds are all strong performers, as you can see from their five-year returns. The two foreign funds, **Overseas** and **Worldwide**, are two of the best in the business, co-managed by superstar manager Helen Young Hayes. (Worldwide has 45 percent of its portfolio invested in U.S. stocks; Overseas has 10 percent.) Consider yourself lucky if either of these funds is in your plan. They're both closed to new investors in the outside world.

It should come as no surprise that Balanced and **Growth & Income** secured top rankings. Balanced is a hybrid, as we mentioned, and Growth & Income invests part of the portfolio in dividend-paying stocks. It's worth reiterating that the other equity funds, **Janus**, **Mercury**, **Olympus**, and **Twenty**, are all top-notch *growth* funds. Just be prepared to hang on tight when the market gets rough—as it has been in recent years.

## T. Rowe Price

T. Rowe Price's portfolios may not make headlines or top the charts all that often, but this is not a bad group of funds. Here's what are worth investing in: Best overall funds are **Growth Stock** and **Mid-Cap Growth**. And it's not just because the funds have the two highest five-year returns of the group. They scored relatively well in our volatility and consistency screens, too. There are T. Rowe Price funds that do better in both screens, but taken as a whole Growth Stock and Mid-Cap Growth are winners.

**Small-Cap Stock**, for those seeking exposure to small companies, is a good choice as well. It doesn't rank as high as the two funds we just mentioned, but keep in mind that it's ranked against all domestic equity funds. Given the spectacular performance of larger companies in the late 1990s (and the corresponding underperformance of small-cap stocks), we're not surprised it doesn't compare well. Take Small-Cap Stock and compare it to other small-company funds and you get a different picture. It ranks among the top third of all small blend funds (funds that invest in both value and growth stocks), according to Morningstar and earns five stars for its three-year record (13 percent) and an "average" rating for risk.

T. Rowe Price **Science & Technology** scores in the 99th percentile for volatility and the top 5 percent for consistent returns that outpace 10 percent. That shouldn't seem unusual. That's what tech funds are like—high risk, high returns. But what's up with its five-year record? At an annualized 1.6 percent, Sci-Tech lags behind 77 percent of other tech funds, which have an average five-year return of 8.3 percent. If you want a dose of high exposure to tech stocks, there are better funds from which to choose; you'll just have to look outside your plan.

Less adventurous investors should head straight to the **Balanced** fund or **Equity-Income**. Both funds win the best rankings of all T. Rowe Price funds for stable returns, which naturally means they make less impressive showings in our screen for outsized returns. Balanced has 40 percent of its holdings invested in bonds, so it doesn't have as strong a five-year record as Equity-Income, which relies more on dividend-paying stocks for stability.

## American Century

The best fund for your money at American Century is **International Growth**. This foreign stock fund, which had about 4 percent of the fund invested in U.S. stocks and the rest worldwide, has a mouth-watering—for foreign funds, at least—five-year return of 7.9 percent. That's better than 89 percent of its peers. What's more, it's consistent. It ranks in the top 7 percent of all foreign funds for its 10-year record, which is 10.7 percent, and in the top 25 percent for three-year returns (1.9 percent). Our screens show it is consistent at delivering strong returns (better than 10 percent), too, on a 12-month rolling basis: International Growth finishes in the 11th percentile in our consistent growth screen. And it's fairly stable, too. To wit: It is less volatile than two-thirds of the other international funds we ranked.

Whatever happened to American Century **Ultra**? In the mid-1990s, Ultra was the brand name of the group, with a better than 20 percent average annual return over the previous five years. Now it's a decidedly mediocre fund with an 8.2 percent five-year return, placing it in the 47th percentile of all large-cap growth funds. As our screens show, its shareholders are paying for that mediocre return with a lot of volatility: Ultra ranks in the 73rd percentile of all domestic equity funds in our short-term volatility screen. The depth of its downward volatility and the repeated offenses earns it that poor score.

A better choice, if you're looking for growth, is the aptly named **Growth** fund. You're going to get a good dose of volatility with this fund, but it has an above-average three- and five-year record compared with other large-cap growth funds. However, it's worth noting that this fund has a bedraggled 10-year record (10.3 percent, which lags the S&P 500 by nearly 4 percentage points and ranks in the bottom quartile of its peer group). The fund has a relatively new manager: C. Kim Goodwin, who also assists on **Select**, has been with the fund since October 1997, and since then the fund has been performing better. Maybe it's a sign of things to come. If Growth isn't an option in your plan, **Equity Growth** stands up to our tests, too—but it doesn't score as well in our growth screen as Growth.

Aside from that, American Century's funds are generally solid. That is, they're not dogs, but they're not going to make us jump up and down with excitement, either. The Select fund has a decent five-year average annual return, and it scores well in our two screens. But the fund has a new manager who has only been at the helm for just over two years. We'd wait and see how the fund fares, given that our scoring is based on five-year returns.

And then there's the **Value** fund. According to our screens, the fund looks passable—not a poor choice, but not an exceptional one, either. Compared with other mid-cap funds, Value is simply average. Its five-year record ranks in the 53rd percentile of all mid-cap value funds. The fund ranks in the top 20 percent in our table because it is compared to a broader group—all domestic equity funds. Part of the reason for that good showing, however, is that the fund didn't load up on tech funds in the late 1990s, so that in 2000 and 2001 the fund's 7 percent tech weighting helped the fund beat the S&P by more than 20 percentage points each year.

That leaves **Income & Growth**. If a lower-risk fund is what you're looking for, then Income & Growth fits the bill. This fund, which gets four stars from Morningstar, has a five-year return of 9.9 percent, which is essentially as good as the straight equity growth funds in American Century's stable. Yet its volatility ranking—29th percentile—is relatively low.

## Merrill Lynch

Trying to find an overall winner here—one that can provide strong returns consistently with limited short-term volatility—isn't easy. Of Merrill's top-10 401(k) funds (not all of which carry the Merrill Lynch brand name), the ones that score well for short-term volatility earn below-average rankings for steady growth—and vice versa.

If we had to make a choice, however, we'd go with a fund that doesn't happen to be a Merrill fund: **Pimco Total Return Administrative**. Pimco's bond funds are among the best in the country, so we shouldn't be surprised.

This one invests in intermediate-term bonds and has a top-of-the-charts five-year return. At first glance, it doesn't score well in our short-term volatility screen—42nd percentile—but its worst three-month return was just negative 2 percent. We'll take that for a five-year record that stands at 8 percent.

Of course, finding a good bond fund isn't always everyone's top priority. Don't worry—there are plenty of good growth funds in this bunch, too; you just have to be willing to take on some volatility. There's a fund for every purpose. Looking for a small-cap fund? There's Merrill Lynch **Small Cap Value**. Large-cap growth? Two good options are Merrill Lynch **Fundamental Growth** and **Van Kampen Emerging Growth**. Of the two large-cap value funds in Merrill's top 10, we'd opt for **Davis NY Venture** over the Merrill Lynch **Basic Value** fund—it scores better than the Merrill fund in both of our screens.

Then there's Merrill Lynch **Global Allocation**. This is an aggressive fund, because it invests in foreign stocks (a quarter of the portfolio is invested outside the United States), but that risk is tempered by its North American equity holdings (30 percent, including Canada) and bonds (24 percent of the fund). Whatever the recipe, the ingredients are working: This fund ranks in the top 1 percent for its 10-year 12 percent return. What's more, this fund is consistent—its five- and three-year returns rank among the top 5 and 6 percent of all international hybrid funds.

With some of the remaining funds, however, you'd better tread carefully. **MFS Emerging Growth** was once a superstar fund, but now the fund has a pathetic five-year record, 3.2 percent, that ranks it in the 79th percentile of all large-growth funds. **Massachusetts Investors**, another MFS offering that happens to be the oldest mutual fund in the country, ranks below average, too.

We dug a little deeper into Merrill Lynch **Balanced Capital**, because it's a domestic hybrid fund (31 percent of the portfolio is invested in bonds) and might not stack up well against all-equity funds. That could explain its embarrassing performance in the growth screen—96th percentile—and its uplifting score in our short-term volatility screen—16th percentile. But on closer examination, even compared to other domestic hybrid funds, the Balanced Capital fund doesn't stand out. Its five-year average return, 6.5 percent, falls just shy of the *average* domestic hybrid fund (which comes in at 6.7 percent). And the Balanced Capital fund is relatively more volatile than the average domestic hybrid fund, too, according to Morningstar. Bottom line: With a good bond fund to choose at Merrill (Pimco Total Return Administrative) and plenty of decent growth funds, why would anyone go for the Balanced Capital fund?

# Franklin Templeton

This is one impressive group of funds. All of them are above average in their respective categories, with many ranking in the top quartile. This is the kind of performance every 401(k) investor craves. But there are a couple of things to keep in mind about these funds: Three of them—**Templeton World**, **Mutual Discovery**, and **Mutual Shares**—have relatively new managers. Still, on closer examination, we noticed that each of the new managers (all on the job for more than a year) posted strong performances in 2001—a difficult market to say the least. All funds ranked in the top 10 percent or better within their respective peer groups.

So which ones should you invest in?

Mutual Discovery is the No. 1 fund of the bunch, according to our screens. This world stock fund is one of four of Franklin Templeton's top-10 401(k) funds to win five stars from Morningstar. Don't be fooled by its 5 percent ranking for its five-year record, though. That's up against all international funds, and this fund, as a world fund, has 30 percent of its portfolio invested in U.S. stocks. Still, compared to other world funds, Discovery still ranks high—top 12 percent—over the past five years. All that aside, what impresses us most was how well this fund scores in our two screens—2nd percentile for stability, 35th percentile for growth.

Among Wall Streeters, Templeton is well known for its international funds. Three made Franklin's top-10 list: Templeton **Foreign**, **Growth**, and **World**. The funds hold their own against their peers for overall returns. Two of them, Growth and World, won five stars from Morningstar. And they rank high for low short-term volatility. But the flip side is they don't score well in our growth screen, which looks at 12-month rolling returns of greater than 10 percent. International stock markets haven't been exactly booming lately, so that could explain the lack of oomph in this screen. It's worth noting, though, that these funds were stacked up against other international funds when they were ranked. So keep in mind that there are other foreign funds that are better at posting outsize returns on a 12-month basis—but those funds may be more volatile, too.

There's one other five-star fund on Franklin's list: **Balance Sheet**. This small-cap value fund ranks high in our table—based on its five-year return—because it is compared to all domestic equity funds. But when you look at its five-year return compared to those of other small-cap value funds, it doesn't. According to Morningstar, it ranks in the top 42 percent. So why does it fetch five stars? Because of its 15.2 percent 10-year record, which ranks in the top 22 percent. Still, according to our screens, this fund is reasonably stable, ranking in the 17th percentile against all domestic equity funds in our volatility screens. Its score isn't as good in our growth screen (63rd percentile ranking), but small caps have only recently experienced a renaissance. Until 2000, small caps had been in a bear market. And compared to the other small- or mid-cap selection on Franklin's list, **Small-Mid Cap Growth**, which is also a strong performer (its five-year record, 9.6 percent, ranks in the top 34 percent of all mid-cap growth funds), Balance Sheet is a more stable option.

The Mutual Series funds **Beacon** and **Shares** are two top-notch mid-cap value funds. Both funds have respectable five-year records and, being value funds, they score well in our volatility screen. But their growth screen rankings fall slightly below average for all domestic equity funds.

Finally, there's a great bond fund in here, too. Franklin **U.S. Government Securities** wowed us with the way it scored in our two screens relative to other bond funds. The fund earns a four-star rating from Morningstar because its long-term record (any which way you look at it, 15-year, 10-year, 5-year, or 3-year) ranks it in the top 20 percent of all intermediate government bond funds. The U.S. Government Securities fund invests in exclusively AAA-quality government bonds, and the fund has an average maturity of 3.3 years.

## Scudder Kemper

"Mediocre" is the word that comes to mind for these funds. No single fund here is an overall stunner, though there are a few decent performers when it comes to stability and low volatility. These include a pair of **Pathway** offerings and **Balanced** (but that comes in part from a 40 percent weighting in bonds). For consistent, steady growth, there's **Large Company Growth** and **International**. But despite those good showings, overall the funds here are just average. Bottom line: Most Scudder funds do what they need to do to get by and not much more.

**Growth & Income**, though, does not. You'd expect a little stability, a little oomph in returns from a large-cap blend fund like this. Growth & Income does neither. It ranks below average—59 percent—in our volatility screen and far below average—94 percent—in our screen for consistent returns over 10 percent. The clincher: Over every single time period possible—fifteen-, ten-, five-, three-, and one-year—this fund has a bottom-of-the-barrel record.

Some of Scudder's 401(k) clients offer funds outside the Scudder family—like Vanguard Institutional Index (the institutional version of the 500 Index fund), Janus Mercury, or Worldwide. If those are offered in your plan, consider investing in them instead. Scudder's Balanced fund might have won our nod as a decent—but not good—overall fund, because it has a fairly strong five-year record (8.5 percent ranks in the top 26th percentile of its peers). But it has a new manager who has been running the fund for just two years, and the three-year record is nothing to write home about (3.2 percent; ranks in the top 47 percent). That leaves International, which has a five-year record of 3.8 percent. Sounds poor, but it beats the Morgan Stanley Capital International EAFE index by more than 3 percentage points.

# What If the Funds in My Retirement Plan Are Dogs?

SIDEBAR 8.2

First ask yourself what you mean by "dogs." Just because a fund you own hasn't had the gains of popular market indexes such as the Nasdaq Composite or the Standard & Poor's 500, that doesn't mean the fund is a bust. In recent years, the movements of just one asset class have dominated those indexes: large U.S. technology stocks.

So if some of your dogs are international funds, small-cap funds, or bond funds and they trail the S&P 500, they could still be beating indexes such as Morgan Stanley Capital International's EAFE (a leading international index), the Russell 2000 (the leading small-cap index), or the Lehman Brothers Long-Term Bond index (printed every day on the first page of the *Wall Street Journal*'s "Money & Investing" section). A fund is a dog only if it's not doing what it was designed to do.

**SIDEBAR 8.2**

That said, we recognize that many funds *by any measure* fail to live up to their mandate. What then? An employer's matching contribution can make an underperforming fund acceptable. But where there is no match to be had, don't hesitate to put your money in the best fund available and ignore the rest as long as you get the diversification you need (foreign, small stock, etc.) from your other investment accounts. You might have a rollover IRA from the plan of a previous employer, for instance. Or your spouse's plan may have winning funds for investing in the asset classes that your plan lacks.

# PART THREE

# THAT OTHER LONG-TERM GOAL, PAYING FOR COLLEGE

# 9

# SAVING FOR COLLEGE: HOW MUCH CAN YOU PUT ASIDE?

**N**othing kills the buzz you feel after the birth of a child faster than the frightening notion that in 18 years time, you'll have to pay the first chunk of a $150,000 four-year college tuition bill. Oh, and you have your heart set on Harvard? Make that $400,000.

Wait a minute. Can that be right? Five years ago, the College Board said it would cost $280,416 to send a child to a private college in the year 2014. Now they're telling us it will cost $326,736 (and the price tag is expected to top $400,000 in 2018). That's an increase of 17 percent in five years. Of course, that includes everything: tuition, room and board, books, and other expenses. Nevertheless, the scary truth is that college is expensive, and it's getting more expensive every year.

How are you ever going to pay for one college education, let alone two or three? Unless you're rolling in dough and your retirement is already fully funded, if you want to pack off your child to college you may have to cut back on your spending, and you'll definitely have to save and invest wisely. It sounds dreadful, doesn't it?

Still, this is not the impossible dream that many experts would have you believe. Plenty of parents send their kids to school with no thought put into a "college savings strategy." Most families, in fact, *don't* cover every penny their children need to get through college. They cobble together their savings, some financial aid, and loans to cover the cost. Close to 50 percent of all full-time students receive some sort of grant or government-sponsored loan. What's more, many universities now take into account other demands on your family budget when they calculate how much aid they'll give you: elementary and secondary tuition costs, unusually high child-care expenses, and unemployment or other changes in family finances.

Meanwhile, tuition hikes have settled somewhat; they still figure in the 5 to 7 percent range, but that's not the 16 percent jumps of years past. A handful of colleges have even announced tuition freezes. The trend may continue as enrollment rises with the echo boomers—the children of baby boomers. But the single best thing to happen to saving for college is the 529 plan. These plans allow you to save and invest money for your child's college education tax-free. Some states even allow you to deduct from your state taxes a chunk of (or all of) your annual contributions. The states run the program for you (and you don't have to be a resident of one to participate), and you choose an investment track that allows you to invest in stocks or bonds or a combination. When you withdraw the money for required college supplies or tuition, it's tax-free. What's more, changes in the tax law (pre- and post-George W.) have made saving and investing for college easier than ever before.

What can you scrape together? And, equally important, how should you invest it? In this chapter, we'll help you find the answers to both of these questions.

We start with "The SmartMoney College Savings Worksheet" (Worksheet 9.1), which will help you figure out how much you *should* save every month, plus how much it will grow over time until your child starts college. When you finish that worksheet, the dollar figure you end up with—"How much do you need to save each month?"—may seem like a stretch given the reality of your household finances. If you're just getting going on your savings program (meaning you haven't saved a penny yet) and your child will start college in 2019, you'll have to save more than $262 a month to send him or her to a state university; $763 a month for a college in the Ivy League. For many parents, $763 a month is just ridiculous—and $262 isn't that easy to set aside, either.

# The SmartMoney College Savings Worksheet

Think about how much tuition and other costs have risen since you went to school. Then multiply a college education price tag by the number of booster seats you've seen at your breakfast table over the years. It's easy to jump to the conclusion that your projected college savings budget could rival that of the Department of Defense. Now relax. In this worksheet we'll help you quickly figure out how big that number really has to be and take stock of what you already have. When you're done, you'll know how much you should be socking away each month into a 529 plan. Do it now: It could ultimately mean the difference between the Ivy League and the Envy League.

### How Much Should You Expect to Pay?

**1.  What are the expected costs for four years?**

Check Table 9.1 for an estimate of four-year college costs, including tuition, room and board, books, and other expenses. Separate projections are provided for public and private colleges. Of course, if you're expecting your child to get a financial aid package from the chosen school, the final amount will be lower. List each child separately. For more than one child, add the amount for each child.                                                   $_____

### Where Are You Now?

**2.  How much have you saved on your own so far?**

Enter the amount you've saved at this point for each child. If you have funds for all of your kids in one account, divide it accordingly.          $_____

**3.  How much will your current savings be worth when your kids enter college?**

Choose a figure from Table 9.2 and multiply by amount on line 2 for each child.                                                                $_____

**WORKSHEET 9.1**   The SmartMoney College Savings Worksheet

## TABLE 9.1    FOUR-YEAR COST OF ATTENDING COLLEGE

| Year Beginning | Public College* | Private College† |
|---|---|---|
| 2002 | $ 55,730 | $162,378 |
| 2003 | 59,074 | 172,120 |
| 2004 | 62,618 | 182,447 |
| 2005 | 66,375 | 193,394 |
| 2006 | 70,358 | 204,998 |
| 2007 | 74,579 | 217,298 |
| 2008 | 79,054 | 230,336 |
| 2009 | 83,797 | 244,156 |
| 2010 | 88,825 | 258,805 |
| 2011 | 94,154 | 274,333 |
| 2012 | 99,804 | 290,793 |
| 2013 | 105,792 | 308,241 |
| 2014 | 112,139 | 326,736 |
| 2015 | 118,868 | 346,340 |
| 2016 | 126,000 | 367,120 |
| 2017 | 133,560 | 389,147 |
| 2018 | 141,573 | 412,496 |
| 2019 | 150,068 | 437,246 |

Based on data from *College Board, †The Independent College 500 Index and College Board, and SmartMoney.

4. **Do you expect any gifts or awards?**

Enter the amount you expect to receive from family members and
other sources before your kids start college.                                   $_____

5. **How close does this get you to your goal?**

Add lines 3 and 4 for each child.                                               $_____

6. **How much do you still need to save?**

Subtract line 5 from line 1 for each child.                                     $_____

**WORKSHEET 9.1**    *(Continued)*

## TABLE 9.2     LUMP-SUM MULTIPLIER

| Years Until Child Begins College | Multiplier |
|---|---|
| 18 | 4.0 |
| 17 | 3.7 |
| 16 | 3.4 |
| 15 | 3.2 |
| 14 | 2.9 |
| 13 | 2.7 |
| 12 | 2.5 |
| 11 | 2.3 |
| 10 | 2.2 |
| 9 | 2.0 |
| 8 | 1.9 |
| 7 | 1.7 |
| 6 | 1.6 |
| 5 | 1.5 |
| 4 | 1.4 |
| 3 | 1.3 |
| 2 | 1.2 |
| 1 | 1.1 |

7. **How much do you need to save each month?**

For this section, we're assuming that you're putting your money in a tax-advantaged 529 plan with an annual return of 8 percent. We're also assuming that you'll keep contributing—and earning those returns—through your child's sophomore year.

To calculate the figure for each child, divide line 6 by the appropriate figure in Table 9.3.                                     $_____

**WORKSHEET 9.1**   *(Continued)*

TABLE 9.3 MONTHLY SAVINGS DIVISOR

| Years Until Child Begins College | Divisor |
|---|---|
| 18 | 572.7 |
| 17 | 518.7 |
| 16 | 468.7 |
| 15 | 422.4 |
| 14 | 379.5 |
| 13 | 339.8 |
| 12 | 303.0 |
| 11 | 269.0 |
| 10 | 237.5 |
| 9 | 208.3 |
| 8 | 181.3 |
| 7 | 156.3 |
| 6 | 133.1 |
| 5 | 111.6 |
| 4 | 91.8 |
| 3 | 73.4 |
| 2 | 56.4 |
| 1 | 40.6 |

**WORKSHEET 9.1**   *(Continued)*

The sad truth is, life is never as simple as financial planners and tuition guides make it out to be. It would be nice to set aside even $200 or so a month starting at birth and then gradually build a nest egg over the years—increasing the monthly savings every year—but in the real world this isn't how things usually work. Far more likely is that tuition savings will go in waves. Years where summer camp and piano lessons take priority may render saving for college nonexistent. Other years that bring a financial windfall will translate into a bonus for the college account. While it's impossible to calculate the specifics of each situation, for most parents this kind of fits-and-starts saving can be just as productive as dogged month-by-month planning. Say you save $100 a month from the time your child is born, for a total of $21,600 by the time he or she goes off to college. Assuming you earn an 8 percent return, you'll have nearly $50,000 by the time the tuition bills come due.

But let's say your savings habits are slightly less routine. If you manage to stash away $5,000 by the time your child is three (think gifts from grandparents), add $3,000 when your child turns five, invest $5,000 about the time your child turns eight, add $6,000 more when your child hits 13, then add $2,600 two years before your child starts freshman year of college, you'll end up with just under $47,000—not radically different from the once-a-month saver.

Still, you can't get anywhere if you don't know where you're going. And that's where our worksheet comes in; it gives you a target of what, in an ideal world, you need to save. Use the "private college" estimate for four-year college costs and you have an upper-end idea of what you need to save every month; use the "public college" estimate and you'll have the low-end approximation.

Whether you can save that much money is another question. So, how much can you *actually* afford to save? Check out Worksheet 9.2, "Where to Go from Here."

This worksheet will tell you what you can set aside every month after all of your monthly bills, credit card payments, and other expenses have been accounted for—not what you *should* be saving. And it starts with one basic premise: that all parents should save as much as possible for their retirement first and kids' college second. There are several reasons for this, the first one being that nobody else is going to fund your retirement (unlike college, where there are plenty of resources to tap). Second, when it comes time to apply for financial aid, colleges don't look at the assets you have saved in retirement accounts. Finally, in the game of college financing, it's the one trump card parents have—if you're using the money for education-related costs, you can tap into IRA or Roth IRA funds early with no early withdrawal (10 percent) penalty.

To fill out the worksheet, you'll need to have an idea of what your monthly expenses run—including your fixed costs like mortgage or rent, utilities, insurance, car payments, loan and credit card payments, as well as discretionary items like food, entertainment, travel, and clothing. Be conservative. It will help if you have a rough idea of what your cash outflow is like month to month (Quicken users won't have a problem here). If you're at a loss for what your monthly expenses run, it's worth it to sit down and look at some old bills (or just look at the last three to six bank account statements for a quick and rough estimate of your monthly outlay) before you fill out the worksheet.

# Where to Go from Here

**How Much Can You Afford to Save?**

1. **Monthly inflow.** Enter your current monthly income after taxes.    $_____

2. **Retirement account savings per month.** Ideally, after maxing out in your 401(k) plan first, you should be putting away the maximum allowed by the IRS for IRA or Roth IRA accounts ($3,000 in 2002).    $_____

3. **Income after retirement savings.** Subtract line 3 from line 2.    $_____

4. **Monthly outflow.** Enter your household and other expenses.

   | | |
   |---|---|
   | Mortgage/rent | $_____ |
   | Utilities (electricity, cable, water, gas) | $_____ |
   | Insurance (health, auto, home) | $_____ |
   | Car payments | $_____ |
   | Loans (school, home-equity, etc.) | $_____ |
   | Credit card payments | $_____ |
   | Medical costs | $_____ |
   | Travel | $_____ |
   | Entertainment | $_____ |
   | Other | $_____ |
   | **Total** | $_____ |

5. **The maximum you can save for tuition per month.** Subtract line 4 from line 3.    $_____

6. **How much your savings will grow.** Multiply line 5 by the appropriate line in Table 9.3 (page 190). This is the amount your money will be worth when your child reaches college age, assuming your money goes into a tax-advantaged 529 plan with an annual return of 8 percent. We're also assuming that you'll keep contributing—and earning those returns—through your child's sophomore year.    $_____

**How Much Will Financial Aid Cover?**

If nearly 50 percent of all kids in school get financial aid, will your child get any?

**WORKSHEET 9.2**   Where to Go from Here

7. **Your net worth.** Enter the value of your current assets—cash, stocks, bonds, mutual funds, and real estate—excluding your home equity and retirement account savings. (If you plan to send your child to a private or elite college, add your home equity back in.)     $_____

8. **The amount you can afford to save per month for college.** Enter line 5.     $_____

9. **How much your savings will grow.** Enter line 6.     $_____

10. **What your future savings mean in today's dollars.** Divide line 9 by the amount in the divisor column of Table 9.4 that corresponds to your child. For more than one child, use the appropriate divisor for each child. Then add the results for all children.     $_____

## TABLE 9.4     PRESENT-VALUE DIVISOR

| Years Until Child Begins College | Divisor |
|---|---|
| 18 | 2.03 |
| 17 | 1.95 |
| 16 | 1.87 |
| 15 | 1.80 |
| 14 | 1.73 |
| 13 | 1.67 |
| 12 | 1.60 |
| 11 | 1.54 |
| 10 | 1.48 |
| 9 | 1.42 |
| 8 | 1.37 |
| 7 | 1.32 |
| 6 | 1.27 |
| 5 | 1.22 |
| 4 | 1.17 |
| 3 | 1.12 |
| 2 | 1.04 |
| 1 | 1.04 |

**WORKSHEET 9.2**   *(Continued)*

11. **How much you've saved on your own.** Enter the amount you've saved at this point for each child. If you have funds for all of your kids in one account, divide it accordingly.    $_____

12. **How much your current savings will be worth when your kids enter college.** Choose a figure from Table 9.2 (page 189) and multiply it by the amount on line 11 for each child.    $_____

13. **Total assets available for tuition.** Add lines 7, 10, and 12.    $_____

14. **Percent paid by financial aid.** Refer to Table 9.5 using the information on line 7 and your family's current pretax income.    _____%

15. Multiply line 14 by 0.01.    _____

16. **Estimated amount of financial aid you can expect based on today's aid standards.** (This figure may include government-guaranteed student and parent loans, depending on the type of aid awarded by individual schools.) Multiply line 1 of Worksheet 9.1, the expected cost of four years of college, by line 15.    $_____

## TABLE 9.5   HOW MUCH WILL FINANCIAL AID COVER?

**Annual Pretax Income**

| Total Family Assets* | $30,000 Public | $30,000 Private | $50,000 Public | $50,000 Private | $70,000 Public | $70,000 Private | $90,000 Public | $90,000 Private |
|---|---|---|---|---|---|---|---|---|
| $  20,000 | 87% | 94% | 45% | 74% | 0% | 45% | 0% | 16% |
| 40,000 | 87 | 94 | 44 | 73 | 0 | 44 | 0 | 15 |
| 60,000 | 87 | 94 | 33 | 68 | 0 | 39 | 0 | 9 |
| 80,000 | 87 | 94 | 21 | 63 | 0 | 33 | 0 | 4 |
| 100,0000 | 87 | 94 | 9 | 57 | 0 | 28 | 0 | 0 |

*Excluding retirement account savings and home equity. Assumes a family of four, with one child in college.

**WORKSHEET 9.2**   *(Continued)*

*If you will have two children in college at once:*

a. Subtract the amount on line 15 from 1.0.    _____

b. Multiply line a by 0.5.    _____

c. Add line b and line 15.    _____

d. If the children will be in college together all four years, repeat the entry from line c. If they will be together for one year, multiply line c by 0.25; for two years, by 0.5; for three years, by 0.75.    _____

e. If the children will be in college together all four years, enter zero. If they will be together one year, multiply line 15 by 0.75; for two years, by 0.5; for three years, by 0.25.    _____

f. Add line d and line e.    _____

g. Multiply line 1 of Worksheet 9.1 by line f. Replace line 16 with this amount.    _____

## How Much Might You Need to Borrow?

17. Add the amounts on line 16 and line 9.    $_____

18. Subtract line 17 from line 1 in Worksheet 9.1. This is the estimated amount you may have to borrow (in addition to any loans in your aid package) to pay for four years of college for your children. If the number is negative, it means you're in the clear.    $_____

---

**WORKSHEET 9.2**    *(Continued)*

# 10

# LETTING SOMEONE ELSE DO IT FOR YOU: 529 COLLEGE SAVINGS PLANS

O kay. So you have a game plan for how much you're going to set aside for college. Now what? How do you invest it? Do you open a separate account or open an account in your child's name? Savings account? Brokerage account? Mutual fund or stocks?

The answer is very simple: a 529 state savings plan.

Up until a few years ago, your best choices for college savings were either Education IRAs, tax-friendly accounts which are now called Coverdell Education Savings Accounts (ESAs), or custodial accounts, which parents maintain in their child's name and which, depending on their earnings, are taxed at various rates (these are commonly called UGMAs or UTMAs, for the Uniform Gifts to Minors Act and Uniform Transfers to Minors Act). But now the revamped Section 529 savings plan—each sponsored by a different state—gives you new degrees of investing freedom and tax advantages that will help your regular contributions, no matter how small, grow at a mercifully brisk rate. You'd be crazy not to consider stashing your college savings money in a 529 plan.

If you haven't heard of these savings plans before, don't worry, you're not totally clueless. These plans are relatively new, based on a tax break the IRS created in 1996, and are named 529 plans because of their governing set of rules in Section 529 of the Internal Revenue Code. Just two years ago, in 2000, only 17 states had 529 plans. Nearly all states offer one.

In this chapter, we'll tell you all the ins and outs of these state-sponsored plans and which ones are best for you. Settling on the best college savings plan—or reconciling a new plan with your old one—can be more confusing than that calculus course you took at your own alma mater. For one thing, this year a host of new laws went into effect, changing many of the rules regarding 529 plans and ESAs. (Thank President Bush's tax-cut package.) And over the past several months, states debuted 529 plans—or altered existing ones—at a dizzying pace.

To help you make sense of the changes, we analyzed all of your viable options—nearly 50 in all, including all the participating states' plans. We'll tell you the best all-around 529 savings plans in terms of options and fees, as well as how they work best with funds that you may have already set up. In short, we'll help you chart a financial course to cover your child through his or her summa cum laude.

## Why 529s Are Such a Great Deal

A very high (or nonexistent) cap on annual contributions. Tax-free withdrawals. A portfolio that is managed and allocated appropriately by pros. What more can a parent ask for? That's what makes a 529 plan a logical centerpiece for a college savings strategy.

One big misperception lingers: that they're limited to residents of the state running them, or that the beneficiary has to go to a college in that state. In fact, there are two distinct types of 529 plans: prepaid tuition plans and college savings plans. Prepaid plans often carry residency requirements and are directed at paying for a particular state university system—essentially paying tomorrow's tuition at today's prices; you can often transfer the funds out of state, but you'll have to pay any difference in tuition. We don't like prepaid plans: They cover only tuition bills and, because of the way colleges view them when determining financial aid, they can cut your aid packages dollar for dollar.

Savings plans, however, are more akin to 401(k)s for college, albeit with a few more restrictions: Your contributions are invested in a portfolio of mutual funds managed by the state or an outside financial institution (like Fidelity, T. Rowe Price, Vanguard, or TIAA-CREF, to name a few). They generally don't have residency rules and can usually be used at almost any college in the United States, and even some foreign schools.

Plus, earnings in these plans are tax-free at the federal level as long as they're used to pay "qualified college expenses" (tuition, books, supplies, and room and board). Most states are expected to exempt earnings from state taxes for residents, too (in many states, such legislation is still pending). Until 2002, the earnings were taxed at either your rate or your child's, depending on your youngster's age.

If you take money out of a savings plan for anything but those expenses, you'll still get taxed, and hit with an extra 10 percent penalty; but the new laws make that situation less likely. Say your youngster decides to join a thrash band rather than go to college. You've always been allowed to roll over a 529 to your son's more studious sister, but now you can even punt it to a niece (the new law broadens "immediately family" to include cousins).

You also get more power in the way your money is invested. The IRS traditionally forbade 529 participants from "directing" investments as they would in a 401(k). In most states that meant you had to invest in preset portfolios of mutual funds and keep your money there. No longer. Now states *may* let you change your investment track with a particular plan once a year. (That's not saying every state actually *will*, but still. . . .)

Finally, you can usually give as much as you want. As with any gift, you can kick in up to $11,000 a year without having to file a gift tax return. And while all plans have cumulative maximums, most are generously high (usually at least $200,000). The only hitch: The tax bill calls for these rules to sunset in 2010, unless Congress passes new legislation. But most experts agree that it's unlikely these new laws will die. "Once a provision gets in the code, it's extremely difficult to get it out," says Buffalo, New York–based financial planner Anthony Ogorek. "If [529s] take off like 401(k)s, it would be ill-advised for politicians to change them."

In early 2002, 42 states offered a 529 plan, and only three had residency restrictions (Kentucky, Louisiana, and New Jersey). We wouldn't be surprised if the remaining eight states follow suit shortly. Which state's plan is best for you? It's natural to feel a tug toward your home plan—and it's not a bad idea to consider the benefits before you look at other state offerings. Some offer residents lower fees or grants that match a small percentage of contributions (Minnesota, for instance, offers a $300-a-year match for families who live in the state with incomes that fall below $80,000).

And several plans make 529 contributions state-tax deductible up to certain limits (like Wisconsin, Virginia, and New York). A few states (including Colorado, New Mexico, and Illinois) offer unlimited tax deductions for state residents' contributions.

# Should You Roll Over Your Child's UGMA or UTMA Funds into a 529 Plan?

With all the benefits that 529 plans offer, plenty of parents are wondering whether they should convert their old UGMA or UTMA accounts to a state-sponsored plan (even with the possible financial aid repercussions).

For instance, John Daniel III, an internist from Richmond, Virginia, has kept a custodial account since 1988, when his son John IV was three years old. But in 1999 Daniel sold some funds in that account and was looking for a way to save on taxes when he learned about Virginia's new 529 savings plan: "It was a good option because I wouldn't have to pay [taxes] the next time I sold"— and neither would his son later.

Since then Daniel has transferred about 10 percent of his son's college fund into the 529, and only when selling funds that he has wanted to liquidate anyway. Another good time to move your UGMA to a 529 is when you have a loss on your investments, as many parents do in today's market conditions, since you won't be hit with any capital gains when you cash out.

But if you still have healthy gains on your custodial account, "It doesn't make sense to pay a boatload of taxes up front to convert to something that's going to give you a tax benefit," says Steven Weydert, a financial planner in the Chicago area. A good guideline: If your account gains are enough to put you into a higher tax bracket when you sell, leave it alone.

Keep in mind, too, that when you convert a custodial account to a 529, you miss out on some of the 529 advantages. The money remains legally the child's, so you don't regain control, and for that reason the account will likewise be hit harder at financial aid time. In this case, Weydert suggests opening two 529 accounts: one with the UGMA cash and a second for new contributions. (While your child will retain the rights to the former, you get control of the latter—and likely, larger—kitty.) Since UGMA funds have broader uses than 529 withdrawals—say, a car for your student—it can be used to supplement 529 funds.

Granted, financial aid won't matter much to John Daniel if his son gets into his first-choice school, the Naval Academy in Annapolis, Maryland. In that case, the Navy will pay all the young midshipman's expenses. "All you have to pay for is some initial supplies—uniforms and such," says Daniel, "and I'm sure the 529 would cover those. And you never know, he may want to get some other education later on, and this can cover it."

No amount of perks, however, can make up for a dog of a plan. Here's how to assess the one in your state (or any other, for that matter).

## What to Check For

### The Investment Tracks You Want

Montana's state plan offers a single investment option, and it's a certificate of deposit (CD) (it pays 4 percent annually or the college inflation rate, whichever is greater; last year it was 5.2 percent). That's fine if you're extremely risk-averse or your nest egg is already well into six figures and all you care about is preserving what you've accumulated. But if you're going for growth, chances are it won't get you to your goal. Better plans offer at least one age-based track (in other words, you're mostly in stocks while your child is young and gradually move toward fixed-income investments as he or she ages), as well as one or more static portfolios (including all equity, all bonds, or some mix of the two) and one money-market option. The best plans offer multiple age-based options, some more aggressive than others, so you can find one that suits your risk level and your time frame.

## Strong Fund Performance

We won't lie to you: Assessing the fund performance for these plans is difficult. It has to do with the way the portfolios in these programs are set up. Most are a blend of different funds, like an equity fund (several funds in some cases), a bond fund, and a money-market fund, allocated aggressively or conservatively depending on the age of your child. And more important, you might have to dig a little into the glossy literature that the state puts out or read the program prospectus to learn which funds make up each portfolio (Maryland and Virginia, for instance, fall guilty there). The program prospectus details which fund company or companies are managing the plan, and the style of fund in each portfolio.

It might be buried deep, though. On page 53 of the file we downloaded off Maryland's web site, for instance, we found exactly what we were looking for: a percentage breakdown of each fund in each age-based portfolio. The most aggressive portfolio, called Portfolio 2021, is made up of six stock funds. Most of it (42 percent) goes into T. Rowe Price's Equity Index 500 fund, with smaller amounts going into the Blue Chip Growth fund, the Value fund, as well as Mid-Cap Growth, Small-Cap, and International stock funds. Armed with that information, you can go from there to www.smart-money.com to dig up the goods on each fund.

Yes, this will require you to do a little bit of work on your own, but it's the most important step in your assessment of your state plan. If the funds stink, after all, your money won't grow like it should.

## Low Fees

Analyzing fees is more complicated, since states vary widely on how they assess them. You'll find everything from a flat annual account fee to a sliding scale, depending on your investments and what class of shares you choose. One new trend: Some states are offering a broker-sold plan, frequently with a more diverse menu of funds than the basic plan. Just be aware that often increased options mean slightly higher fees, too. For instance, Alaska has an alternative plan sold by Manulife Financial that, like the state's regular plan, is managed by T. Rowe Price. It features investment options from a wider variety of fund families, including a "future trends" portfolio invested in tech, health care, and financial-services sector funds. Some of those funds regularly outpace T. Rowe's large-cap funds, but the annual fees are also higher—0.15 and 0.4 percentage points higher than Alaska's regular plan—and the portfolio's expense ratios are generally higher, too.

With all this in mind, we took a look at all the savings plans currently open to out-of-state investors, putting them through a series of tests to determine which ones combine the best investment options with the lowest fees. We rated plans based on the typical fees and expenses faced by investors in three types of tracks—age-based equity, non-age-based equity, and money market—and we deducted points for states that charged additional enrollment or termination fees. We awarded points to plans with a wide range of investment options, and with at least one track adequately exposed to equity (at least 85 percent) until the child reaches age five. We also eliminated plans with very low contribution ceilings (such as Minnesota's, with its comparatively lean $122,484). Finally, we scored investment performance, looking at the overall track record of the fund family or families constituting the bulk of a plan's funds.

Our top four states: Nebraska, Utah, Virginia, and New York. The first three invest primarily in Vanguard funds, known for their all-around low fees. Nebraska narrowly led the pack with a total of 10 investment tracks, including four age-based options, each moving to fixed income at a different rate, plus six static portfolios. (Aside from Vanguard, the plan's investments include funds from Janus, Fidelity, and American Century.)

Utah has fewer options, but they're strong ones: two age-based tracks that gradually shift from a Vanguard index fund to a bond fund, a 100 percent equity portfolio invested solely in the index fund, and a money-market portfolio. Expenses are typically just under 0.6 percent for age-based investors. In many lesser plans, fees pass the 2 percent mark.

Another winner, New York, is managed by TIAA-CREF, which handles 12 states' plans. While most of the TIAA-CREF plans are solid (albeit conservative) bets, New York recently added three new options—including a more aggressive age-based option—to its previous moderate age-based track (expenses run 0.65 percent a year). Likewise, Virginia gets a lift from several new options. In addition to its age-based track, it now offers four static portfolios—three with mixes of equity and fixed income, plus one money-market fund (families include Vanguard, Franklin Templeton, and Pimco). And though we're not fond of Virginia's $85 enrollment fee—or its $25 fee if you roll over to another state—the plan still has reasonable annual expenses, at about 1.0 percent for the typical age-based investor.

Besides our top four, seven others also performed well in our analysis: Alaska, Wisconsin, Nevada, Rhode Island, Ohio, New Hampshire, and Massachusetts. See Table 10.1 "College 529 Plans," for a breakdown of the top 12 state plans and why we like them. Still others just debuted this year: South Carolina, Georgia, South Dakota, and Alabama. For links to these state plan web sites and more information on these plans and others, visit the College Savings Plan Network at www.collegesavings.org.

## Looking at 529s versus Custodial Accounts

Starting from scratch with one of these plans will set you on a good course, but what if you've already socked away money in one of the traditional savings vehicles? Depending on how much you plan to put aside, a Coverdell ESA or UGMA/UTMA may still be worthwhile.

The ESA, which has been tax-free since 1998, is in some ways the opposite of the 529 in terms of benefits and restrictions. Unlike 529s, you get a lot of control: You can invest in whatever stocks or funds you choose, limited only by your brokerage firm's offerings. However, there's an annual contribution cap of $2,000 (up from a paltry $500 in recent years).

You can contribute to both an ESA and a 529 for the same beneficiary in the same year, which makes an ESA a nice complement to a 529 plan. That's especially good if you want to fund education expenses not covered by a 529, such as private elementary and secondary schools, as well as tutoring or a computer. (A 529 plan covers "qualified" expenses, which means anything the institution requires your student to have to attend the college—and technically speaking, computers are not usually required.)

Custodial accounts also offer total investor discretion and can be used even more broadly than ESAs (for any expenses before or during college). The downside: UGMAs and UTMAs are subject to taxes and become the child's asset once he or she hits adulthood—which may make parents of free spirits think twice.

But the biggest problem you may face with an UGMA, an UTMA, or an ESA—and a good reason to limit them to supporting roles—is the effect they have on financial aid. Generally, the federal aid formula expects families to contribute 35 percent of the student's assets toward college expenses, but only 5.6 percent, tops, of the parents' assets. Since ESAs, UGMAs, and

TABLE 10.1   COLLEGE 529 PLANS: STATE FINALISTS—OUR TOP 12

| State | Savings Plan | Toll-Free Number | Web Site | Fund Manager | Fees | Age-Based Portfolios? | Static Portfolios? | State-Tax-Deductible? | Maximum Account Level |
|---|---|---|---|---|---|---|---|---|---|
| Nebraska | College Savings Plan of Nebraska | 888-993-3746 | www.planforcollegenow.com | Union Bank (and various funds) | Sales load on class A shares; $24 annual maintenance fee, waived for $50,000 balances or $25,000 with automatic deposit; 0.6% management fee; .02% to 1.12% expense ratio. | Yes | Yes | $1,000 | $250,000 |
| Utah | Utah Education Savings Plan Trust | 800-418-2551 | www.uesp.org | Vanguard and State Treasurer | None for fixed-income portfolios; $5 per $1,000 up to $25 in annual maintenance fees; 0.25% management fee; 0.06% to 0.10 % expense ratio | Yes | Yes | $1,410 ($2,820 for married filing jointly) | $175,000 |
| Virginia | VEST | 888-567-0540 | www.virginia529.com | Various (Vanguard, Pimco, Franklin Templeton, American Funds) | $85 enrollment fee; 0.85% to 1% expense ratio | Yes | Yes | $2,000 | $250,000 |
| New York | New York College Savings Program | 877-697-2837 | www.nysaves.com | TIAA-CREF | 0.65% management fee | Yes | Yes | $5,000 ($10,000 for married couples filing jointly) | $235,000 |

(Continued)

TABLE 10.1 (Continued)

| State | Savings Plan | Toll-Free Number | Web Site | Fund Manager | Fees | Age-Based Portfolios | Static Portfolios | State-Tax Deductible | Maximum Account Level |
|---|---|---|---|---|---|---|---|---|---|
| Alaska | The University of Alaska College Savings Plan | 800-478-0003 | www.uacollegesavings.com. | T. Rowe Price | $30 annual maintenance fee, waived for $25,000 balances or automatic deposit; 0.30% management fee; 0.3% to 0.97% expense ratio | Yes | Yes | NA | $250,000 |
| Alaska | Manulife College Savings Plan | 866-222-7498 | www.manulifecollegesavings.com | Distributed by Manulife Financial and managed by various fund companies (T. Rowe Price, AIM, Davis, Franklin Templeton, MFS, Oppenheimer) | $30 annual maintenance fee, waived for $25,000 balances or automatic deposit; class A shares carry a 3.5% load and 0.75% annual fee; 0.45% to 1.38% expense ratio | Yes | Yes | NA | $250,000 |
| Wisconsin | EdVest | 888-338-3789 | www.edvest.com | Strong Capital Management | $20 enrollment fee; $10 annual management fee waived for $25,000 balances or automatic deposit; 1.25% management fee | Yes | Yes | $3,000 | $246,000 |
| Nevada | America's College Savings Program | 877-529-5295 | www.americas529plan.com | Strong Capital Management | $20 enrollment fee, waived for $25,000 balances or automatic deposit; 1.3% management fee | Yes | Yes | NA | $246,000 |

| State | Plan | Phone | Website | Manager | Fees | | | | Amount |
|---|---|---|---|---|---|---|---|---|---|
| Rhode Island | CollegeBound | 888-324-5057 | www.collegeboundfund.com | Alliance Capital | $25 annual maintenance fee, waived for $25,000 balances or automatic deposit; 0.9% to 1.1% management fee | Yes | Yes | No | $265,620 |
| Ohio | CollegeAdvantage | 800-233-6734 | www.collegeadvantage.com | Putnam Investments | $25 annual maintenance fee, waived for $25,000 balances or automatic deposit; fund share classes include sales charges and annual management fees; 0.55% to 1.15% expense ratios | Yes | Yes | $2,000 | $232,000 |
| New Hampshire | Unique College Investing Plan | 800-544-1722 | www.fidelity.com/unique | Fidelity Investments | $30 annual maintenance fee, waived for $25,000 balances or automatic deposit; 0.3% management fee; 0.48% to 1.19% expense ratio | Yes | Yes | NA | $233,240 |
| Massachusetts | U. Fund College Investing Plan | 800-544-2776 | www.fidelity.com/ufund | Fidelity Investments | $30 annual maintenance fee, waived for $25,000 balances or automatic deposit; 0.3% management fee; 0.38% to 1.19% expense ratio | Yes | Yes | No | $230,000 |

UTMAs are considered to be your child's, any aid you qualify for will be reduced by 35 percent of their value. Since 529 savings plans are considered the asset of the account owner, not the beneficiary, they're subject only to the 5.6 percent financial aid hit, assuming the parent owns the account. (And if the owner is a grandparent or another relative, it won't affect initial aid at all.)

One catch you ought to know about: Up until now, any earnings on qualified withdrawals your child made from a 529 were considered income, which could take a bite out of financial aid eligibility after the first year. But it's still too early to tell how the new tax laws will change that. "I don't expect that it will be treated as a student's earnings, but as parents' earnings," which are assessed at a slightly lower rate, says Joseph Hurley, a 529 expert who runs the web site Savingforcollege.com. However, the *Chronicle of Higher Education* recently reported that some colleges want to treat savings plans as they do prepaid plans—that is, as a resource reducing aid dollar for dollar.

Still, a few dings to the financial aid package shouldn't scare parents off. Most aid is given in the form of loans anyway, and while a low-interest loan (or for parents with more resources, a home-equity loan) may be a tempting last-ditch approach as a high school graduation nears, it's no substitute for saving even a modest amount now. "The key thing to remember," says Judy Miller, principal of College Solutions, a college financial planning firm in Alameda, California, "is that savings represent dollars that don't have to be borrowed and repaid in the future."

# 11

# Asset Allocation: A Year-by-Year Guide to Investing Wisely for Your Child's Tuition

Few financial products come without one or two drawbacks. The 529 college savings accounts offered by most states are no different. The tax-free character of these savings plans is a big benefit, without a doubt. But in most of the plans we've looked at you sacrifice investing flexibility once you commit your money. You can't choose who is going to manage the investment accounts or precisely how they will be managed. On top of that, your ability to diversify among different managers and investing styles is usually limited because there just aren't that many options offered.

The limitations on your choice of investing style, asset types, and managers means you probably won't get market-beating performance from these funds. But that shouldn't be a deal killer for you. The tax breaks will give you enough of a head start to ensure that your 529's after-tax total return nudges out the after-tax total return from all but the best-performing taxable mutual funds and investment managers.

Once you've made the choice of a 529 program to save for your children's education, you have effectively segregated your college savings plan from the rest of your wealth-building investments. Since you have less money in the college savings accounts, that probably means you should be more conservative with the way you invest it. You shouldn't be trying to hit a home run. The investment choices you'll be offered aren't likely to be home run hitters in any event. Instead you should be concentrating on making sure all the money you save will be there and working for your kids when they are ready for college. This is called "managing downside risk."

Diversification among assets—large-cap stocks, small-cap stocks, bonds, and short-term fixed-income investments like T-bills and money-market funds—is the best way to reduce your risk. Your risk will be greater the closer your children are to college age. If the stock or the bond market crashes within a year or two of starting college, there will be little you can do to make up for the loss. That's why you need to limit your exposure to any single market.

If your 529 program offers only one type of investment, you may have to start a parallel, taxable investment in another type as your student nears college and cut back on your contributions to the 529 program. It will be hard to give up the tax advantages, but once your child hits 15, minimizing risk should be a much greater priority, anyway.

What's risky and what's safe? Good questions. Table 11.1 is *SmartMoney*'s guideline. The table assumes your child enters college at age 18 and finishes in four years. The investments start out being slightly conservative when your child is young and get increasingly more conservative as the child becomes older. Yet the choices in the table still allow for growth of your savings.

Each suggested allocation of stocks, bonds, and cashlike assets has been tested against 77 years of data provided by the Center for Research in Security Prices at the University of Chicago and Ibbotson Associates. The results are in the table. Pay particular attention to the minimum gain column, which is the second from the far right. It shows the *worst-case* scenario of that particular combination of stocks, bonds, and cash over the past 77 years. All the allocations were chosen so that even in the worst-case scenario the mixture would still give you a positive increase in your college savings account.

In half of the historical scenarios we tested, the overall investment gains were between the minimum gain and the number in the median return column (the scenario exactly halfway between the best scenario and the worst in the series of scenarios tested). In the other half of the historical sample, the returns are better than the median.

Note that for younger children we included a small-cap stock allocation. Most states don't have a small-cap fund available as an option, but where it exists—or where the stock fund offered includes small-cap

## TABLE 11.1   INVESTING FOR COLLEGE—ASSET ALLOCATION GUIDELINE

| Child's Age | Percentage of Large-Cap Stocks (Such as Found in the S&P 500) | Percentage of Small-Cap Stocks If Option Available (Such as Found in the Russell 2000) | Percentage of Bonds (Such as 10- to 30-Year Treasuries) | Percentage of Cashlike Investment (Such as Treasury Bills of Funds Consisting of T-bills) | Minimum Historical Gain in Time until College Payments | Median Historical Gain in Time until College Payments |
|---|---|---|---|---|---|---|
| Newborn | 35 | 35 | 30 | 0 | 129% | 745% |
| Newborn | 40 | — | 60 | 0 | 98 | 432 |
| 3 | 30 | 30 | 40 | 0 | 91 | 503 |
| 3 | 35 | — | 60 | 5 | 78 | 280 |
| 6 | 15 | 15 | 60 | 10 | 44 | 199 |
| 6 | 30 | — | 60 | 10 | 44 | 174 |
| 9 | 30 | 0 | 55 | 15 | 29 | 110 |
| 12 | 15 | 0 | 55 | 30 | 18 | 46 |
| 15 | 10 | 0 | 45 | 45 | 6 | 23 |

stocks—it's possible to be much more generous with the overall percentage of savings placed in a stock market fund. That's because good years in small-cap investments often balance out bad years in large-cap investments. The last time that happened was quite recently. In 2001, while the large-cap stocks lost a total of 14.1 percent, the small caps were up 13.3 percent.

If there is no small-cap option available, you have to be even more conservative, because large-cap stocks on their own have had negative returns for several years at a time in the past. Sometimes those periods—as in the Great Depression, in the 1970s, and at the beginning of the current decade—are so severe that the steadier gains of bonds and cashlike investments cannot make up the difference.

# PART FOUR

# LIFE IN RETIREMENT

# 12

# BEING THERE: INVESTMENT MOVES FOR RETIREES (AND THE NEARLY RETIRED)

The day, at last, is within your reach. Sometime in the very near future you're going to stop dreaming about retirement and start *living* it.

Believe it or not, it's time to get busy—really busy. Because you've got important decisions to make. You've got to figure out what to do with your 401(k) plan when you quit working; how to start withdrawing your money from tax-deferred investments while owing the least amount possible to the IRS; how to reallocate your investments so your portfolio is more about *preserving* your capital than increasing it; and more.

This chapter will walk you through all these issues, starting with a guide to what to do with your retirement accounts at retirement—from your 401(k) to your IRA. From there we'll help you create a new asset allocation to render a portfolio geared more to preservation and safety than to growth.

## Exit Strategies

The final few years before retirement can be a tax nightmare, what with your earnings at their peak and your big deductions (kids and mortgage) often gone or nearly nonexistent. So as you struggle to keep your tax bill under control, you long for the end of your working days, when your tax worries—along with your income—will fall.

Sorry to break the news to you, but the sad truth is that retirement brings on a whole new set of tax worries. In fact, some people might actually see their tax rates go up (see Sidebar 12.1, "Limiting the Tax Bite"). What's worse, mistakes you make when you retire can haunt you and your heirs for years to come.

## Limiting the Tax Bite

**SIDEBAR 12.1**

After you retire, and your portfolio gets more conservative, you might find your tax bill on your investments actually rising. It bites, but it's true: That's because you'll be earning more interest from bonds, which is taxed as income (rather than capital gains from stocks). And you will be withdrawing money from your tax-deferred accounts—also taxed as income (unless it comes from a Roth IRA account).

Here's one way to keep it under control: As you begin shifting your assets from stocks to bonds, move the money in your tax-deferred accounts first, and keep your stocks in taxable accounts as long as possible. This is especially wise if you expect to leave something behind for your heirs. The income-tax liability for your capital gains on assets held in taxable accounts vanishes when you die, while assets in tax-deferred accounts are taxed as ordinary income for your heirs.

## Your 401(k)

Your first big decision will involve the money you've saved in your company's retirement plan. You generally have three choices: withdraw the money in a lump sum and pay the (often substantial) tax bill; keep the money in the plan and take annuity payments; or roll the account into an IRA and defer taxes until you start making withdrawals.

In most cases, cashing out of the plan is the worst move because you will pay taxes now that could be deferred. So it should be considered only if you will need the money immediately—to fund the purchase of that condo in

Naples or the yacht you've been eyeing. Some company plans don't let you take the money in one lump sum, so annuity payments are your only choice. The third move, rolling over the money tax-free into an IRA, is both the most common and the most complicated.

If you've decided to roll over your retirement money, be careful. You must set up your IRA account and find out how the check from the plan should be made out (for example, to "Mammoth Bank as IRA trustee for Joe Smith") before you talk to your company's 401(k) administrator. In other words, the check cannot be payable to you, unless you want to fork over the tax bill for it. Then tell your plan administrator you want a direct rollover without any withholding, and when you get the check, deposit it into your new IRA account within 60 days. Your company might even send it directly to the brokerage.

There is more than enough incentive to make sure you do this right. Here's why: If the check is made out to you, the government assumes you are cashing out of your retirement plan, and your employer will withhold 20 percent of the money for taxes. Then you have to come up with the missing 20 percent to accomplish the tax-free rollover. (This is true in any rollover situation, not just when you retire.) You can't touch the remaining 80 percent of the rollover money without being liable for even more taxes, so that 20 percent must come out of your own pocket. If you can't come up with the money, you will have to pay income tax on the 20 percent, and if you're under age $59\frac{1}{2}$, you might also be hit with a 10 percent early-withdrawal penalty.

For example, if your distribution is $500,000, the plan will withhold $100,000. If you can't come up with that amount, meaning your rollover falls short, then you'll owe income tax on the $100,000. If you're in the 27 percent bracket, your bill will be $27,000. The excess of the withholding—$73,000—will be returned to you in the form of a tax refund, but you can't collect the money until you file that year's tax return.

There's one situation when it pays to cash out rather than roll over your retirement money into an IRA: When a retirement account contains employer stock that has appreciated quite a bit and is part of a lump-sum distribution.

In this case, you may be better off withdrawing the shares, paying the tax, and holding them outside your IRA. Why? (Bear with us, because it gets kind of tricky, but it's worth it.) The deal is, when you withdraw the shares from your retirement account, you will pay tax only on the value of the shares at the time they were acquired for your account. If your account has held the shares for a long time, that value could be a fraction of what they are actually worth when you withdraw them. You won't owe any tax on your gains until you sell the shares, and even then you will pay only at the new, low 18 percent rate for long-term gains (effective beginning 2006).

If you roll the stock over into your IRA, by contrast, you won't have to pay any taxes up front—but you will be hit with the higher ordinary income-tax rates when you withdraw the money. And if you die before withdrawing the shares, your heirs will pay taxes at the same rate on the full value of the account. By contrast, if you hold the stock in a taxable account your heirs will have no tax liability.

Here's an example: Say you have $50,000 in company stock that cost your employer $20,000. If you withdraw the shares from your plan and hold them outside your IRA, you will pay income tax (say at the 27 percent rate) on the $20,000. So your initial bill is $5,400. If the shares keep rising in value and you eventually sell them for $100,000, you will have two capital gains bills. The first will be for the $30,000 in profit you made while the stock was in the plan. That type of gain will always be considered long-term so it will be taxed at the 18 percent rate, giving you a $5,400 tax bill (assuming you acquired the shares after the beginning of 2001—otherwise it's 20 percent; for people in the 15 percent income-tax bracket, the rate is 8 percent). You'll also owe tax on the $50,000 gain that you realized after you got your hands on the shares. The tax rate on that gain will be determined by how long you held the shares outside the plan. If it's more than five years, the rate is 18 percent again, or another $9,000. Tallying up the initial $5,400 tax bill with the $5,400 and $9,000 capital gains tax bills gives you a total tax liability of $19,800.

If you never sell the stock, however, your heirs will get the shares, and all of your capital gains will vanish—it will be as if they bought the stock for $100,000. So in this case, the only income taxes paid on the $100,000 of stock would be the initial $5,400 payment you made when you took the stock out of your company's plan.

Still with us? Good. Now let's say that, instead, you roll the stock over into an IRA. You will pay income tax on the money when you withdraw it. If you pay at the 27 percent rate, that bill will be $27,000, roughly 36 percent more than what you would have paid if you had withdrawn the shares immediately from the plan (the scenario that ended up with a $19,800 total tax bill). That's pretty rough, considering your heirs could have inherited the entire $100,000 tax-free if you had shelled out a mere $5,400 when you retired.

One far-reaching caveat: You probably shouldn't follow this strategy if your company's stock hasn't performed well and your shares are worth about the same as they were when they were given to you. In that case, hold the shares outside your IRA only if you expect the stock to rise dramatically, or if you plan on leaving it to your heirs.

# Your IRA

What about all the money in your IRA? Ah yes. Well, here's the one thing about IRAs to remember: You must start withdrawing money from your IRAs the year after you turn 70½. (It's one of those great ironies of life: The government created IRAs to encourage you to save for retirement, but it will penalize you if you keep saving.) The rules used to be extremely complex, but thanks to the new tax law, they're not only simpler, they could also be worth thousands of dollars in tax savings.

The tax law hasn't changed a few things. You still have to take mandatory payouts starting no later than April 1 of the year after you turn 70½. (So if you reach 70½ this year, you have to take your first minimum withdrawal no later than April 1 of next year.)

Tapping your IRA, of course, means you'll also get stuck with the resulting income-tax bills. In fact, the whole reason your friends in Congress enacted the minimum withdrawal rules was to force you to hand over the government's share of your IRA sooner rather than later. If you fail to take at least the minimum withdrawal amount each year, you'll owe a 50 percent penalty on the shortfall. Of course, you can always take out more than the minimum and pay the extra income taxes. In fact, the IRS will be delighted if you do.

Before you get too depressed, let's get back to the good news: The new withdrawal rules are beneficial to nearly everybody. They essentially change the ways you must calculate your minimum withdrawals, and the net result is that you'll most likely be required to take out less than you would have under the old rules. You'll see what we mean when we give specific scenarios shortly.

Keep in mind, the IRA minimum withdrawal rules also apply to simplified employee pension (SEP) accounts as well as SIMPLE IRAs, since they're both considered IRAs for this purpose. But Roth IRA owners are exempt from the minimum withdrawal rules as long as the original account owner is alive.

# Tax Penalties for the Retired Set

Between the ages of 59$\frac{1}{2}$ and 70$\frac{1}{2}$, you can do pretty much what you want with your retirement savings. But outside of those age brackets, you'll have to watch out for a slew of taxes and penalties. Here are some mines to watch out for.

### Overfunding an IRA

If you put more than you're allowed into an IRA, the government will charge you. You'll have to pay 6 percent in excise taxes for each year the excess is in your account. You should withdraw the excess as soon as you realize your mistake.

### Withdrawing Early

There are ways to get at your money before you turn 59$\frac{1}{2}$ without incurring penalties. Generally IRA withdrawals are allowed for qualified education expenses, certain medical expenses, a first home purchase (limited to $10,000), or permanent disability. Be sure to review the IRS strict guidelines, to ensure you won't be nicked with a 10 percent penalty on top of all the taxes you'll owe.

### Not Withdrawing Enough after Age 70$\frac{1}{2}$

After you turn 70$\frac{1}{2}$, you are required to start making withdrawals from your IRA by the following April 1. People who don't need the income and want their IRAs to grow tax deferred for as long as possible must use special IRS tables (tied to your life expectancy) to calculate the minimum they must withdraw each year. Withdraw too little from your account and you'll be gouged with a 50 percent penalty on the shortfall. The only exception is if you continue to work into your 70s, you don't have to touch the money in your employer's plan until you retire (as long as you don't own more than 5 percent of the company). But keeping a job does not excuse you from making the minimum withdrawals from your regular IRA.

# When to Start Withdrawals

Since nothing the IRS does is ever simple, knowing when you need to start taking mandatory withdrawals, is—but of course—tricky. As you approach $70\frac{1}{2}$, you're faced with a choice. You can take your first minimum withdrawal during the year you turn $70\frac{1}{2}$, or you can take it by April 1 of the year after you turn $70\frac{1}{2}$. Then for that year and each subsequent year, you must take at least the required minimum withdrawal by December 31 of that year.

Why does it matter when you start tapping your IRA? Well, it can have significant tax implications. After all, if you don't take your first minimum withdrawal during the year you turn $70\frac{1}{2}$, you must take two—and pay the resulting double dip of taxes—in the following year.

# Calculating Minimum Withdrawals

The amount of each minimum withdrawal depends on your IRA account balance at the end of the previous year divided by a joint life-expectancy figure for you and your account beneficiary found in tables published by the IRS. The younger you are, the longer your life expectancy and the bigger the divisor. And the bigger the divisor, the lower the minimum withdrawal amount. Lower minimum withdrawals mean lower taxes—which, obviously, is good.

The new minimum withdrawal rules automatically assume you've designated a person at least 10 years your junior as your IRA beneficiary. Don't worry—it doesn't matter to the IRS whether your actual designated beneficiary is older than the assumed age. In fact, it generally doesn't matter whether you've actually designated a beneficiary. This might strike you as odd, but there is some history behind it. (We'll spare you the titillating details.) All you really need to know is that it's probably the best set of taxpayer-friendly assumptions you could hope for.

The only exception to the new automatically-10-years-younger-beneficiary rule is when your spouse is designated as the sole IRA beneficiary and he or she is *more* than 10 years younger. In this somewhat unusual circumstance, you're allowed to calculate your IRA minimum withdrawals using more favorable joint life-expectancy figures based on the actual ages of you and your spouse. This is also a good deal.

# The Right Mix for Retirees

Yes. It's one more worksheet. But we promise it's the last one. And though Worksheet 12.1 looks like our SmartMoney One asset allocation worksheet (the one you filled out in Chapter 4), this one has been designed primarily for readers nearing or already in retirement. The results, as you'll see, are geared to more conservative investments. The more time you expect to spend retired, the more asset growth you'll need to keep up with inflation. A richer equity mix will increase the growth potential of your investments, although stock investments will also make the value of your retirement assets jump around from year to year. The more time you have to keep money in stocks, the better the chances that such volatility will resolve itself in your favor.

Part One will give you a starting point for setting your equity allocation. Begin with Table 12.1, "How Long Should You Plan on Your Money Lasting?" Transfer the appropriate numbers from there to the first part of the

## TABLE 12.1   HOW LONG SHOULD YOU PLAN ON YOUR MONEY LASTING?

| At Age . . . | You Have at Least a 20 Percent Chance of Living . . . | |
| | (Female) | (Male) |
| --- | --- | --- |
| 54 | 37 more years | 33 more years |
| 55 | 35 | 31 |
| 56 | 33 | 29 |
| 58 | 31 | 28 |
| 60 | 29 | 26 |
| 62 | 28 | 24 |
| 64 | 26 | 22 |
| 66 | 24 | 20 |
| 68 | 22 | 19 |
| 70 | 20 | 17 |
| 72 | 19 | 16 |
| 76 | 17 | 14 |

*Source:* National Center for Health Statistics.

worksheet. Part Two provides adjustment factors that will help you customize your allocations to reflect your individual circumstances. Part Three puts it all together for you, setting allocation guidelines and computing a long-term average growth rate for your retirement assets. Use this in Table 12.2, "How Much Can You Spend Each Year?" to find how much you can draw down from your investment each year. (To make the worksheet easier to fill out, we've included sample numbers in italics.)

## TABLE 12.2    HOW MUCH CAN YOU SPEND EACH YEAR?

To see how much income you can safely extract from you retirement portfolio each year, divide the current value of your investments by $1,000 and multiply the result by the appropriate dollar amount below. Thus, someone expecting to live 20 more years in a world of 2 percent inflation could withdraw $33,485 each year from a portfolio worth $500,000 if it earned 7 percent a year after taxes (500 × $66.97 = $33,485). If inflation rose to 4 percent, the retiree could safely spend only $27,550.

| Years Remaining after Retirement | Your Expected Inflation Rate | Average Annual After-Tax Investment Growth | | | | |
|---|---|---|---|---|---|---|
| | | 5% | 6% | 7% | 8% | 9% |
| 10 | 2% | $81.03 | $86.07 | $91.23 | $96.50 | $101.85 |
| | 3 | 76.01 | 80.88 | 85.87 | 90.98 | 96.19 |
| | 4 | 71.22 | 75.92 | 80.74 | 85.68 | 90.73 |
| 15 | 2 | 64.94 | 70.31 | 75.86 | 81.56 | 87.39 |
| | 3 | 59.66 | 64.79 | 70.10 | 75.59 | 81.22 |
| | 4 | 54.68 | 59.56 | 64.64 | 69.89 | 75.32 |
| 20 | 2 | 55.42 | 61.09 | 66.97 | 73.06 | 79.31 |
| | 3 | 49.90 | 55.26 | 60.86 | 66.68 | 72.70 |
| | 4 | 44.76 | 49.80 | 55.10 | 60.64 | 66.40 |
| 25 | 2 | 49.19 | 55.12 | 61.32 | 67.75 | 74.37 |
| | 3 | 43.45 | 49.02 | 54.88 | 61.01 | 67.37 |
| | 4 | 38.16 | 43.35 | 48.85 | 54.65 | 60.71 |
| 30 | 2 | 44.82 | 51.01 | 57.50 | 64.25 | 71.19 |
| | 3 | 38.88 | 44.65 | 50.76 | 57.18 | 63.85 |
| | 4 | 33.46 | 38.78 | 44.48 | 50.52 | 56.86 |
| 35 | 2 | 41.63 | 48.05 | 54.81 | 61.84 | 69.08 |
| | 3 | 35.49 | 41.45 | 47.79 | 54.58 | 61.43 |
| | 4 | 29.95 | 35.38 | 41.27 | 47.54 | 54.15 |
| 40 | 2 | 39.21 | 45.86 | 52.87 | 60.15 | 67.63 |
| | 3 | 32.89 | 39.02 | 45.59 | 52.52 | 59.72 |
| | 4 | 27.22 | 32.78 | 38.84 | 45.33 | 52.18 |
| 45 | 2 | 37.33 | 44.19 | 51.43 | 58.94 | 66.63 |
| | 3 | 30.84 | 37.14 | 43.92 | 51.07 | 58.49 |
| | 4 | 25.04 | 30.72 | 36.95 | 43.65 | 50.72 |

*Note:* These figures include a five-year safety cushion in case you live longer than you expect or the initial years of your retirement coincide with a major bear market. They also assume that you increase your withdrawals in step with the inflation rate.

# The SmartMoney Retirement Worksheet

**Part One: Your Life Expectancy**

| Question | *Example* | Your Answer |
|---|---|---|
| 1. How many more years should your retirement money last? (If you are investing for yourself only, enter appropriate number of years from the table and skip to line 5.) | *27* | _____ |
| 2. How much longer do you expect your spouse to live? (If the expectation is greater than 50 years, enter 50.) | *31* | _____ |
| 3. Add lines 1 and 2. | *58* | _____ |
| 4. Divide line 3 by two. | *29* | _____ |
| 5. Enter result from either line 1 or line 4. (If you are single, enter line 1; if you are married, enter line 4.) | *29* | _____ |

**Part Two: Customizing Your Allocation**

For each answer, circle the entire row under columns A through D.

**Income**

| | A | B | C | D |
|---|---|---|---|---|
| A. Percentage of your retirement savings currently invested in tax-deferred retirement accounts such as IRAs, SEPs, 401(k)s, and 403(b)s. (NA = Not applicable.) | | | | |
| 0 to 20 percent | 4 | NA | 5 | 6 |
| 21 to 50 percent | 3 | NA | 4 | 8 |
| 51 to 75 percent | 2 | NA | 3 | 9 |
| More than 75 percent | 1 | NA | 2 | 10 |
| B. Your federal tax bracket in retirement. | | | | |
| 15 percent | 0 | NA | 0 | 4 |
| 27 percent | 1 | NA | 2 | 8 |
| 30 percent | 2 | NA | 4 | 8 |
| 35 percent or more | 5 | NA | 5 | 10 |

**WORKSHEET 12.1**   The SmartMoney Retirement Worksheet

|  | | A | B | C | D |
|---|---|---|---|---|---|
| C. | Number of years you or your spouse plan to work part time after retirement. | | | | |
|  | None or less than 3 years | 1 | 2 | 0 | 6 |
|  | 3 to 7 years | 2 | 5 | 4 | 8 |
|  | 8 to 12 years | 4 | 6 | 4 | 8 |
|  | More than 12 years | 5 | 8 | 5 | 12 |
| D. | Subtract your expected part-time income from you retirement income. What portion of the emainder will come from noninvestment sources, such as pensions, Social Security, rental real estate, and fixed annuities? | | | | |
|  | 0 to 10 percent | 2 | 3 | 2 | 6 |
|  | 11 to 30 percent | 4 | 5 | 3 | 8 |
|  | 31 to 50 percent | 5 | 6 | 4 | 10 |
|  | More than 50 percent | 6 | 8 | 5 | 12 |

**Wealth**

|  | | A | B | C | D |
|---|---|---|---|---|---|
| E. | Minimum portion of your current wealth you want to leave to your heirs or to charity. | | | | |
|  | None | 1 | 4 | 1 | 7 |
|  | 0 to 10 percent | 2 | 7 | 4 | 8 |
|  | 11 to 25 percent | 3 | 8 | 6 | 10 |
|  | More than 25 percent | 6 | 10 | 6 | 12 |
| F. | The amount you still owe on your home. | | | | |
|  | None (you rent) | 1 | NA | NA | 6 |
|  | More than half its value | 0 | NA | NA | 8 |
|  | Less than half its value | 2 | NA | NA | 10 |
|  | None (your home is paid off) | 3 | NA | NA | 12 |
| G. | Your other debt balances. | | | | |
|  | Less than 5 percent of your net worth | 3 | NA | NA | 6 |
|  | Between 5 and 10 percent | 2 | NA | NA | 4 |
|  | Between 10 and 20 percent | 1 | NA | NA | 2 |
|  | More than 20 percent | 0 | NA | NA | 0 |

**WORKSHEET 12.1**   *(Continued)*

**Economic Conditions (Optional)**

|   | | A | B | C | D |
|---|---|---|---|---|---|
| H. | Your view of the U.S. economy in the next five years. | | | | |
|   | Prolonged downturn | −3 | 3 | −4 | 10 |
|   | Recession, then weak recovery | 0 | 4 | 0 | 6 |
|   | Recession, then strong recovery | 3 | 2 | 10 | 2 |
|   | Steady growth | 5 | −2 | 5 | −6 |
| I. | Your outlook for annual inflation increases over the next five years. | | | | |
|   | Less than 1 percent | −2 | NA | NA | 12 |
|   | Between 1 and 2.5 percent | −1 | NA | NA | 6 |
|   | Between 2.5 and 4 percent | 1 | NA | NA | 0 |
|   | More than 4 percent | 5 | NA | NA | −6 |
| 6. | Add up the circled values in each column for Items A to I, and enter the results on this line. | ___ | ___ | ___ | ___ |
|   | *Example* | 26 | 17 | 17 | 52 |

**Part Three: Your Overall Allocation**

| Question | *Example* | Your Answer |
|---|---|---|
| 7. Add the sum from the first column of line 6 to line 5 from Part One. If greater than 80, enter 80. *This is your equity portion.* | 55% | _____% |
| 8. Subtract line 7 from 100. *This is your fixed-income portion.* | 45% | _____% |
| 9. Divide the second column of line 6 by 100. | .17 | _____ |
| 10. Multiply line 9 times line 7 (if number is less than 3 percent, enter 0). *This is your foreign equity allocation.* | 9.4% | _____% |
| 11. Subtract line 10 from line 7. *This is your U.S. equity portion.* | 45.6% | _____% |
| 12. Divide the third column of line 6 by 100. | 17 | _____ |
| 13. Multiply line 12 times line 7 (if number is less than 4 percent, enter 0). *This is your small-cap allocation.* | 9.4% | _____% |

**WORKSHEET 12.1**    *(Continued)*

| Question | Example | Your Answer |
|---|---|---|
| 14.  Add lines 10 and 13. Subtract the result from line 7. *This is your large-cap allocation.* | 36.2% | _____% |
| 15.  Divide the fourth column of line 6 by 100. | .52 | _____ |
| 16.  Multiply line 15 times line 8. *This is your intermediate- and long-term bond allocation.* | 23.4% | _____% |
| 17.  Subtract line 16 from line 8. *This is your cash and short-term bond allocation.* | 21.6% | _____% |

**Expected Return**

18. Multiply the long-term after-tax growth rates for each asset by the percentage allocations obtained, then add the results to get an estimate of the average annual returns on your portfolio. Use the withdrawal table to determine your safest initial withdrawal rate.

| | Example | Your Answer | | Example | Your Answer |
|---|---|---|---|---|---|
| Line 10 | 9.4% | _____ | times 0.10 = | 0.94% | _____ |
| Line 13 | 9.4% | _____ | times 0.11 = | 1.03% | _____ |
| Line 14 | 36.2% | _____ | times 0.10 = | 3.62% | _____ |
| Line 16 | 23.4% | _____ | times 0.04 = | 0.94% | _____ |

19. If you manage your own stock portfolio, enter 0; otherwise enter –1.0 percent as a rough estimate of fees.    –1.0%    _____

20. Expected after-tax portfolio growth rate (add the four items in line 18 as well as line 19).    6.2%    _____%

**WORKSHEET 12.1**   *(Continued)*

# Reallocating Your Portfolio

Now here's the last step: How do you decide what to sell from your current holdings to create your newly balanced portfolio?

First, look around for your losers. If nothing else, you can use your losses to offset your capital gains at tax time. Here are a few things to look for in a losing stock:

Are earnings falling either for the company or for the industry?

Is the industry at the wrong end of the economic cycle?

Has the company cut its dividend?

Has management changed for the worse?

Has the stock fallen below $10 a share? (Many institutions are reluctant to buy below that price, so the stock may languish there.)

If you answered "yes" to two or more of these questions—and you have capital gains to offset—you should consider selling.

Of course, you could be a total whiz and have more winners to choose from than losers. The simplest strategy for investments that are in the money would be to sell your stocks with the highest price-to-earnings (P/E) ratios. Another common selling discipline: Trimming back all stocks that have given you total gains of more than 50 percent. But formulas can be too simplistic sometimes. It may be simply the wrong time to bail out of a winner. Instead, we suggest you ask yourself the same questions you did with your losers, with these additions:

Is the stock trailing its sector in sales, net profit margins, or return on equity?

Is the rate of its projected earnings growth less than the stock's P/E ratio?

Any "yes" answers indicate it's time to get out.

Selling funds is easier. Has your fund consistently lagged its peer group in recent years? If so, sell it—or at least trim it back.

Here's what *not* to sell at a profit: stocks or funds you've held for one year or less. Why? Because you'll be stuck paying short-term capital gains, which are taxed at the same rate as your regular income. In other words, you could have to pay as much as 38.6 percent on the sale in 2002. (The rates are scheduled to ratchet down in two stages so that in 2006 the highest tax bracket will be 35 percent.) Meanwhile, most long-term capital gains (on investments held for more than one year) are taxed at 20 percent. In 2006, if you have held on for longer than five years, the rate slips to 18 percent. The difference between 20 percent and 38.6 percent works out to roughly $190 on a capital gain of $1,000. For most of us, that's reason enough to hang on for at least a year.

# 13

# FEELING FINE: AFFORDABLE HEALTH CARE FOR RETIREES

Ah, the good life: Waking up when you want to, doing what you will with your days. This is what you've worked for all your life, right?

Of course it is. And apparently it's going to be pretty nice. Says Tom Otwell, spokesman for the AARP (formerly the American Association of Retired Persons) in Washington, D.C.: "This generation of seniors is probably better off than any previous generation."

He's basing that assessment on statistics like these: The average household income for those 65 and older is up 33 percent since 1981 and up 8 percent since 1996. Nearly 50 percent (47 percent) have an annual income of more than $35,000. And beyond the monthly checks from Social Security, pensions, and investment dividends, many seniors are finding that they've got a cushion of assets, too. According to U.S. Census Bureau statistics, median net worth for those 65 and older is $92,399—more than double the U.S. average of $40,200. In fact, one in six is worth at least $250,000.

Today's retirees can thank an exceptional confluence of benefits for this wealth: pensions from long-term jobs, 401(k) self-directed retirement plans, employee stock option plans, individual retirement accounts, strong real estate prices, and a tax law that lets home sellers keep a bigger chunk of their profits. Oh yeah, and that long bull market in the 1980s and 1990s didn't hurt, either.

Despite all that good news, there is one looming concern that touches every retiree, no matter how wealthy: health care. In this chapter, we'll cover the types of government-sponsored health coverage that will be available to you as a retiree, and whether you should consider long-term care insurance, which would pay for an extended stay in a nursing home.

## Health Insurance

There are three key things to know about when it comes to health care as a retired person: Medicare, Medigap, and Medicare+Choice.

If you're like most seniors, Medicare will be your basic health insurance policy. If you are 65 or older, or have been on Social Security disability for at least 25 months, you're eligible for Part A—hospital insurance—and Part B—medical insurance.

## SIDEBAR 13.1

# What's Not Covered by Medicare Part A and Part B in the Original Medicare Plan

- Acupuncture.
- Cosmetic surgery.
- Custodial care (help with bathing, dressing, using the bathroom, eating) at home or in a nursing home.
- Deductibles, co-insurance, or co-payments when you get health care services.
- Dental care and dentures.
- Health care while traveling outside the United States (except in limited cases).
- Hearing aids and hearing exams.
- Orthopedic shoes.
- Outpatient prescription drugs (with only a few exceptions).
- Routine foot care (with only a few exceptions).
- Routine eye care and most eye exams.
- Some screening tests and some shots.

# What Medicare Helps Pay For

- Ambulance services (when other transportation would endanger your health).
- Artificial eyes.
- Artificial limbs that are prosthetic devices, and their replacement parts.
- Braces: arm, leg, back, and neck.
- Chiropractic services (limited), for manipulation of the spine to correct a subluxation.
- Emergency care.
- Eyeglasses: one pair of standard frames after cataract surgery with an intraocular lens.
- Immunosuppressive drug therapy for transplant patients as long as you are covered by Medicare (transplant must have been paid for by Medicare).
- Kidney dialysis.
- Macular degeneration (an age-related eye disease) treatment, using ocular photodynamic therapy with verteporfin.
- Medical supplies—items such as ostomy bags, surgical dressings, splints, casts, and some diabetic supplies.
- Outpatient prescription drugs (very limited), like some oral cancer drugs.
- Preventive services (like flu shots, mammograms, cancer screenings).
- Prosthetic devices, including breast prosthesis after a mastectomy.
- Services of practitioners such as clinical psychologists, social workers, physician assistants, and nurse practitioners.
- Telemedicine services in some rural areas (medical information exchanged using electronic communications).
- Therapeutic shoes for people with diabetes (in some cases).
- Transplants—heart, lung, kidney, pancreas, intestine, bone marrow, cornea, and liver (under certain conditions and when performed at approved facilities).
- X-rays, MRIs, CAT scans, EKGs, and some other diagnostic tests.

Part A is free, with hospitalization covered at 100 percent for the first 60 days (after a deductible) and the next 30 days covered with a $203 co-payment per day. Part B requires a small monthly premium ($54 in 2002) and a $100 annual deductible. The amount of each doctor's bill that is covered depends on whether your doctor "accepts assignment" of the Medicare-approved amount as full payment of the bill. Assuming he or she does, it works like a traditional indemnity plan, with Medicare paying 80 percent of the bill and you being liable for the other 20 percent. If your doctor doesn't accept assignment, you may have to pay more—up to another 15 percent of the bill. (Doctors who charge more than 15 percent above Medicare-approved rates don't receive Medicare reimbursement at all, so most charge less.) See Table 13.1 for Medicare plan descriptions.

Those rate gaps are the reason many people have taken out Medicare supplement—or Medigap—insurance policies. These fill in where Medicare leaves off, paying annual deductibles and at least some portion of noncovered doctor and hospital bills. Basic policies run an average of $877 a year, according to a recent survey by the U.S. General Accounting Office (GAO), while the most comprehensive policies average $1,672. (The national average for Medigap plan premiums is $1,311.) If you live in Massachusetts, Minnesota, or Wisconsin, the standard Medigap policies are not an option. You'll have to call your state insurance department for your options, or visit the www.medicare.gov site and click on "Medigap Compare." (There are similar options, and the average annual premium for these kinds of policies is $1,311, according to the GAO.)

How do you shop for them? First, get in early. Unless you buy your policy during the first six months after you turn 65—called the open enrollment period—insurers can turn you down for preexisting medical conditions. Sign up during the first six months and insurers cannot deny you coverage. They can't place conditions on your policy, such as making you wait to start. Nor can they change the price of the policy because of past or previous health problems.

Next, pick the policy that fits your needs. Throughout most of the country, insurers offer 10 different plans, designated "A" through "J." "A" is the most basic—its features include co-payments for doctors' visits as well as hospital co-payments (for up to 150 days) and reimbursement for an additional year of hospital expenses (with some restrictions) after Medicare taps out. "J" has the most to offer; its benefits include

## TABLE 13.1  MEDICARE PLAN DESCRIPTIONS

| Plan | What It Is | Where It Is Available | How It Works | Where to Go for More Information |
|---|---|---|---|---|
| Original Medicare plan | The traditional pay-per-visit (also called fee-for-service) arrangement offered by the federal government. | Nationwide. | You go to any doctor, specialist, or hospital that accepts Medicare. After you pay a $812 (in 2002) deductible, Medicare covers 100 percent of your costs for the first 60 days. After that, for the next 30 days, you pay $203 (in 2002) per day and Medicare pays the rest.<br><br>You pay the monthly Part B premium of $54 (in 2002). There's a $100 deductible and you pay 20 percent of the doctor's bill without an out-of-pocket limit.<br><br>You get an "Explanation of Medicare Benefits" or a "Medicare Summary Notice" in the mail. These are sent by a company that handles bills for Medicare. The notice lists the amount you may be billed. | Call 1-800-MEDICARE (800-633-4227) and ask for a free copy of *Medicare & You* or go to www.medicare.gov and select "Publications" to read or print it out. |
| Original Medicare plan with Medigap policy | The traditional pay-per-visit plan plus one of up to 10 standardized Medigap policies sold by private insurance companies. A Medigap policy fills gaps in original Medicare plan coverage. | Every state: however, Massachusetts, Minnesota, and Wisconsin offer a slightly different option of plans. If you live in one of these states, call you state insurance department or look on the Internet at www.medicare.gov and select "Medigap Compare." | Generally you may go to any doctor, specialist, or hospital that accepts Medicare, unless you have SELECT policy. With Medicare SELECT you need to use specific hospitals and doctors to get full insurance benefits (except in an emergency).<br><br>Medigap policies work only with the original Medicare plan. Depending | Call your state insurance department to find out what Medigap policies are available and which companies sell them.<br><br>Call your State Health Insurance Assistance Program to get free counseling to help you decide which policy is best for you. |

*(Continued)*

TABLE 13.1 *(Continued)*

| Plan | What It Is | Where It Is Available | How It Works | Where to Go for More Information |
|---|---|---|---|---|
| | | | on which Medigap policy you buy, you will have coverage for some of the costs the original Medicare plan doesn't cover. You pay the monthly Medicare Part B premium of $54 (in 2002). The Medicare carrier will process the claim and send it to the Medigap insurance company. The carrier will send you an "Explanation of Medicare Benefits" or "Medicare Summary Notice." Your Medigap insurance company will pay your doctor or provider directly. | Look on the Internet at www.medicare.gov and select "Medigap Compare." Look on the Internet at www.medicare.gov and select "Publications" to read or print out the *Guide to Health Insurance for People with Medicare.* |
| Medicare managed care plan | A Medicare managed care plan, sometimes called an HMO, is offered by private insurance companies. | Available in many areas of the U.S., but not all states. | In most cases, you can only go to certain doctors and hospitals that agree to treat members of the plan. Generally, you can only see a specialist (like a cardiologist) when you get a referral, which means your primary care doctor says it is okay to go. Some managed care plans offer a point-of-service option. This allows you to go to other doctors and hospitals outside the plan. Most of the time this option costs | Call 1-800-MEDICARE (800-633-4227) and ask for a free copy of *Medicare & You.* Or go to the web site, www.medicare.gov, and select "Publications" to read or print out *Medicare & You* or select "Medicare Health Plan Compare." |

| Private fee-for-service plan (do not confuse with the original Medicare plan, which is also sometimes called a fee-for-service plan and is offered by the federal government.) | Health care plan offered by private insurance companies. | Available in some areas of the country. | you more, and gives you more choices.<br><br>You must pay the monthly Part B premium of $54 (in 2002).<br><br>Medicare pays a set amount of money every month to a private insurance company.<br><br>You may have to pay an additional monthly premium.<br><br>Most plans charge you a set amount (called the co-payment), like $5 or $10 every time you see your doctor.<br><br>You must live in the plan's service area (the area in which the plan accepts members) and get your services there.<br><br>You can often get extra benefits, like prescription drugs.<br><br>You can go to any doctor or hospital that accepts the terms of the plan's payment.<br><br>You may have prenotification requirements (for example, a requirement that you notify the plan of any planned inpatient admissions).<br><br>You must pay the monthly Part B premium of $54 (in 2002).<br><br>Medicare pays a set amount of money every month to a private insurance company. | Call 1-800-MEDICARE (800-633-4227) and ask for a copy of Your Guide to Private Fee-for-Service Plans, or go to www.medicare.gov and select "Publications" to read or print a copy of it. |

(Continued)

TABLE 13.1 (Continued)

| Plan | What It Covers | What You Pay |
|---|---|---|
| | | You may have to pay an additional monthly premium. |
| | | The insurance company provides health care coverage to people with Medicare who join this plan. |
| | | You pay and the insurance company pays a fee for each doctor visit or service you get. |
| | | The insurance company, rather than the Medicare program, decides how much it pays, and how much you pay, for services you get. |
| | | You must live in the service area, but you don't have to get services there. |
| | | You may be able to get extra benefits, like coverage for additional days in the hospital. |
| Medicare Part A or hospital insurance | Hospital stays | A deductible of $812 for the first 60 days; $203 per day for days 61–90 of a hospital stay; $406 per day for days 91–150 of a hospital stay; all costs for stays beyond 150 days. |
| | Skilled nursing facility care | Nothing for the first 20 days; up to $101.50 per day for days 21–100; all costs beyond the 100th day of stay. |
| | Home health care | Nothing for home health care services; 20 percent of the Medicare-approved amount for durable medical equipment. |

| | Hospice care | A co-payment of up to $5 for outpatient prescription drugs and 5 percent of the Medicare-approved payment amount for inpatient respite care (short-term care given to a hospice patient by another caregiver, so that the usual caregiver can rest). You also pay for room and board for inpatient care. |
|---|---|---|
| | Blood | For the first three pints, unless you or someone else donates blood to replace what you use. |
| Medicare Part B or medical insurance | Medical and other services | $100 deductible (once per calendar year); 20 percent of Medicare-approved amount after deductible, except in the outpatient setting; 20 percent for all outpatient physical, occupational, and speech-language therapy services; 50 percent for outpatient mental health care. |
| | Clinical lab service: blood tests, urinalysis, etc. | Nothing for Medicare-approved services. |
| | Home health care | Nothing for Medicare-approved services; 20 percent of Medicare-approved amount for durable medical equipment. |
| | Outpatient hospital services | A co-insurance or co-payment amount, which may vary depending on the service. |
| | Blood | For the first three pints of blood, then 20 percent of the Medicare-approved amount for additional pints of blood (after the deductible), unless you or someone else donates blood to replace what you use. |

*Source:* U.S. Department of Health and Human Services.

deductible and co-payment reimbursement, skilled nursing care, and prescription drugs. The difference between the two premiums is likely to be $1,500 a year.

The easiest way to sort through the clutter is by limiting your search to three types of policies: "A," if that's all you can afford; "J," if you're looking for comprehensive coverage; and "F," a good middle ground that offers a solid package of extras along with the basics, including medical expenses incurred while traveling abroad. The surprise here is that, once you've picked your type of policy, it's possible to shop by price. Despite the fact that they are all part of a federally funded program, premiums can vary greatly depending on your age, where you live, and the insurance company from which you buy the policy. One recent General Accounting Office survey found that premiums for "F" policies for a 65-year-old in Ohio ranged from $996 to $1,944 and in Illinois plan "J" premiums ranged from $2,247 to $3,502.

That's because insurance companies have three different ways of pricing policies based on your age: no-age-rated, issue-age-rated, and attained-age-rated. With no-age-rated policies (sometimes they're called community-rated), everyone gets charged the same amount no matter how old they are; for example, an elderly woman would pay the same rate (plus any premium hikes to adjust for inflation) whether she signs up at age 65, 75, or 85.

The monthly premium for issue-age-rated policies is based on your age when you first buy the policy. So if an elderly woman buys a policy at 65, she'll pay $130 (for example) for the rest of her life (plus any premium hikes to adjust for inflation). But buy the same policy at age 75, and she'll pay $165 for the rest of her life (plus those inflation-premium hikes).

Finally, the premiums on attained-age-rated policies go up as you get older. That's why at age 65 the premiums generally cost less than either of the first two scenarios, but their costs climb more every year. In general, according to the U.S. Department of Health and Human Services, the no-age-rated policies are the least expensive over your lifetime.

There's one problem with Medigap: Even after you've paid the annual premiums, there are still out-of-pocket costs, regardless of whether you opt for a plan that covers prescription drugs. According to the GAO report in 2001, out-of-pocket costs (excluding long-term facility costs) in 1998 amounted to over $1,300 on average with or without prescription drug coverage. That's significantly higher than the $1,056 average out-of-pocket costs for all Medicare beneficiaries, which is why some people consider Medicare+Choice, a program launched with the Balanced Budget Act of 1997. This is an alternative to getting a Medigap policy (in fact, it's illegal for anyone to sell you a Medigap policy if they know you are in a Medicare+Choice plan).

Medicare+Choice isn't available everywhere. To find out whether it's available in your state, look at www.medicare.gov on the Internet or call 800-633-4227. On the web site, you can compare different plans and even calculate estimated premiums online by clicking "Medicare Health Plan Compare."

# What Your Medicare + Choice Plan Won't Tell You

**SIDEBAR 13.3**

**1.   "We cost more than we let on."**

More than 39 million Americans have their health coverage provided by Medicare. But the vast majority of them—some 80 percent—must buy an additional source of health insurance to make up for Medicare's gap in coverage. Nearly 20 percent of them buy a so-called Medigap policy to fill coverage gaps such as prescriptions, deductibles, and co-payments. The problem with these policies, however, is that they're costly; a comprehensive one can run more than $3,000 a year.

But in 1997 the Balanced Budget Act initiated the Medicare+ Choice program, which allows Medicare beneficiaries to sign up with an HMO, which will in turn provide the same benefits as Medicare plus a few extra benefits—with a lower premium or even no premium.

But beware: When you factor in all the Medicare+Choice out-of-pocket costs, you may well find you're paying nearly as much as you would with traditional Medicare—while sacrificing the level of care you receive.

What many Medicare+Choice enrollees don't realize is that they still need to pay a $54 (in 2002) monthly Medicare premium for Part B, not to the insurer but to the federal government. Moreover, enrollees typically pay $10 to $15 each time they see a doctor and $5 to $25 each time they fill a prescription. Finally, 58 percent of all Medicare HMOs charge a premium (more than $1,000 a year in some cases), up from 38 percent in 1998, particularly if they are in rural areas that aren't well served by HMOs.

In fact, Medicare+Choice members spend an average of just over $1,700 a year out of pocket on health services, according to the AARP. When health insurance costs, such as the average annual HMO premium of $515, are included, Medicare+Choice enrollees spend a total of $2,215 out of pocket on average, just $435 less than the $2,650 spent by the typical fee-for-service enrollee.

**2.   "We'll dump you when it suits us. . . ."**

In 2001, almost one million older and disabled people were dropped by HMOs that left the Medicare program. And the number of plans has shrunk to just 196 from a peak of 346 in 1998, a 43 percent drop-off, according to the GAO. Surprised? You shouldn't be. After all, in 1997 Congress cut projected Medicare spending by $115 billion over five years, limiting most managed-care companies to only 2 percent annual increases. That's less than half the national medical-cost inflation rate. So even though premiums have doubled or even tripled in the past two years, many companies are cutting their losses by opting out of the Medicare program.

The reason for this, of course, is the high and ever-rising cost of health care. Congress earmarked $11 billion in Medicare funding in a late 2000 bill in order to, among other things, allow companies to keep the money in a reserve account for emergencies, as well as to lower premiums and provide more benefits. The idea was to shore up ailing plans and restore coverage to counties where insurers dropped out. But the money wasn't enough to do anything basically: Kaiser Permanente, the Cleveland area's largest Medicare HMO, expected to get an additional $1.6 million. But if 20 of its 28,544 seniors were hospitalized in any one-year period, that money would be gone, said a company spokeswoman.

What about those left stranded? There's always traditional Medicare coverage again. And federal law guarantees former enrollees the right to buy certain Medigap policies. But with weak federal oversight, warns Diane Archer, founder of the nonprofit Medicare Rights Center in New York City, "the question is whether insurance companies will honor that right." Or you can hunt around for another HMO to cover you in your area.

**3.   ". . . . if we're willing to cover you in the first place."**

If you live in Dade County, Florida, you have multiple Medicare HMOs to choose from. But what if you live in Vermont, South Carolina, Montana, Wyoming, Utah, Maine, or Alaska? Your choices are simple: You have none.

This lopsided coverage results from lopsided reimbursement plans (putting aside the high cost of health care). For each subscriber, the federal government pays HMOs roughly 12 percent more than the average amount the agency spends on each enrollee in the traditional Medicare program. But that rate varies widely by county, from the lowest floor rate of $475 a month in rural areas to $839 in Richmond County, New York. So even though there are nearly 200 HMOs contracting with Medicare, 31 percent of all Medicare beneficiaries have no managed-care option where they live, according to the AARP. Rural Medicare beneficiaries have it worst—in 2001, 86 percent had no managed-care option, according to the GAO.

**4.   "Our patients just don't understand us."**

Traditional Medicare—with its Plan A, Plan B, and 10 supplemental policies labeled "A" through "J"—is confusing enough. The Dr. Kildare generation is ill-prepared to navigate the additional bureaucratic maze of HMOs.

According to a report by the Health & Human Services Department, hundreds of current and former Medicare+Choice enrollees don't understand such basics as their primary physician's "gatekeeper" role. Even more alarming, Medicare beneficiaries enrolled in a Medicare+Choice program know *less* about managed care than do their fee-for-service counterparts, according to an AARP study. "The most vulnerable beneficiaries, those with lower incomes and education levels, are the ones enrolling in HMOs," says AARP's Joyce Dubow.

Government auditors—and members of Congress—have repeatedly called on the Centers for Medicare and Medicaid Services (CMS), formerly known as the Health Care Financing Administration, the federal agency that oversees Medicare, to provide more and better consumer information to seniors. The CMS has a web site for consumers (www.medicare.gov) and toll-free hot lines, and says it has numerous publications that it sends out annually describing the choices.

It hasn't helped.

According to the results of an AARP study in September 2000, which posed questions to 253 older Americans about Medicare and health insurance options, an estimated 56 percent of all Medicare beneficiaries have difficulty accurately using comparative information to make choices. "Many Medicare beneficiaries feel burdened by making choices. Those with less skill viewed Medicare decision-making as burdensome. Compared to those with higher comprehension skill, they more often preferred to delegate these decisions. Those with less skill are no more likely to seek help than those with higher skill. Those who are seeking assistance are not necessarily those who need the most help," the report concludes.

### 5. "We don't want you if you're sick. . . ."

Medicare HMOs are prohibited by law from rejecting applicants based on their health. But since most Medicare HMOs receive a set monthly fee from Medicare, which in 2001 was a base rate of $475 per enrollee (can be higher depending on the area; and the base rate is going up to $500 in 2002), regardless of the cost of delivering care, it's no surprise that they try to cherry-pick healthy clients.

Mutual of Omaha's Medicare HMO was fined $50,000 by the Health and Human Services inspector general's office in June 1998 for allegedly screening applicants for health problems. In March 1998, nearly a fifth of the 4,065 Medicare beneficiaries from 40 HMOs surveyed by the inspector general's office reported that they'd been asked on applications about their health problems. Dozens of them reported that an HMO required them to undergo a physical exam before they could join.

Often the screening tactics are indirect. A popular location for marketing seminars? Health clubs. And nearly a third of the 21 marketing seminars attended by researchers from the nonprofit Kaiser Family Foundation in Menlo Park, California, which specializes in health care policy, were held at sites that were not wheelchair accessible.

**6.    ". . . . but you probably won't want us, either."**

When Martha Bergren's father, Robert Dewey, signed up for United HealthCare Medicare HMO, she says, he never knew how his hands would be tied later. As he waited for more than a week in early 1998 at the University of Florida's Shands Transplant Center in Gainesville while the HMO tried to negotiate a lower fee for a liver transplant, his condition deteriorated significantly. Soon after the HMO flew him to another medical center in Miami—one it had a contract with—Robert Dewey, who was 67, died. Phil Soucheray, a spokesman for United HealthCare, says, "The effort was made to arrange a transplant, but Shands was unwilling to make any movement toward an agreement."

While there's evidence that HMO enrollees are more likely to be diagnosed at an early stage than are people in the traditional fee-for-service plans, several studies report that elderly HMO patients with chronic illnesses have poorer health outcomes than those with fee-for-service coverage. A study conducted by the New England Medical Center and published in the *Journal of the American Medical Association* reported that elderly patients with at least one of four chronic conditions, from high blood pressure to congestive heart failure, were more than twice as likely to decline in health in an HMO than in traditional fee-for-service Medicare.

As Dewey's case illustrates, one reason Medicare recipients fare worse in HMOs is because these plans limit access to medical services. According to a recent federal study, the sickest Medicare HMO members report having "significantly more problems assessing specialists, hospital care, and other Medicare-covered services" than do healthy enrollees. The same report also found that "a sizable group" reported having to wait from 13 to more than 20 days for scheduled appointments.

Says Bergren of her father, "He'd have been much better off with [traditional] Medicare."

### 7. "We'll say anything to get you to sign up."

No doubt you've heard of "slamming." That's when phone companies switch customers' long-distance providers without their permission. Well, some Medicare HMOs do it, too.

Consider the case of Helen Platt. The 80-something Arlington, Texas, resident received a letter from Humana welcoming her to its Medicare HMO. But there was only one problem: She'd never signed up for it. A call to what she thought was her current HMO, Harris Methodist, confirmed her fears: She'd been "disenrolled" and was now a Humana member—but her primary-care physician was not in her new plan.

Humana and CMS officials acknowledge Platt's case but call it extreme. A Humana spokesman says a rogue salesman who had worked for another plan had forged Platt's and other members' signatures and has since been terminated.

But a less egregious form of slamming is not so unusual, according to the Medicare Rights Center. What typically happens is that aggressive sales representatives sign up beneficiaries without explaining how HMOs differ from the traditional program—even though CMS requires them to do so. In one case, a Medicare HMO marketing agent signed up a Creole-speaking senior attending an English as a second language class. "He had no idea what he was getting into," says a Medicare Rights Center spokesman.

The problem, of course, is that a beneficiary's doctor may not be in the HMO's network, and the patient may get stuck paying for an expensive medical treatment on his or her own. This is what happened to 68-year-old Peter Rizzo of Schenectady, New York who found himself enrolled in a Medicare HMO after he returned an application for what he thought was a Medigap policy. Says Rizzo, who faces a bill for a surgical procedure performed by an out-of-network doctor, "If I had known [the application] was for an HMO, I never would have signed up."

8.  **"Our prescription drug policy will turn your
    stomach."**

One of the main reasons Mary Jane Lathrop enrolled in Pacifi-
Care Health Systems' "zero premium" Medicare HMO was because of the plan's generous prescription drug benefits.
Co-payments for each of her three medications were a mere $10,
allowing her to forgo a Medigap policy that would have cost her
over $1,000 a year. But then the plan switched her off her high
blood pressure medication and onto a generic substitute. Her
blood pressure shot up, and Lathrop left the HMO.

Such occurrences, known as "therapeutic interchanges" are
common, according to the International Patient Advocacy Association (IPAA), a Bellevue, Washington–based nonprofit that provides
legal support to individuals with chronic illnesses. To hold down
costs, HMOs are switching patients from brand-name to generic
drugs, from one generic version to another, or from one medication to a different drug entirely. After placing newspaper ads in five
different states offering assistance to patients who have been
switched or denied medications, IPAA received some 500 calls—
many of them from seniors, who account for more than a third of
all prescription drug sales.

In fact, during a nine-month period in 1997, doctors reported
more than 100 "adverse events" to the MedWatch program of the
Food and Drug Administration (FDA) after such substitutions. They
included hospitalization for liver toxicity, gastrointestinal bleeding,
and "profound nausea."

Not all generics have been recognized as equivalent by the
FDA. Ask your doctor or pharmacists whether a generic is listed in
the FDA's bible of drug equivalents, known as the "orange book."
The information is also available on the agency's web site
(www.fda.gov).

Meanwhile, prescription drug coverage at most Medicare+
Choice HMOs—a major reason why retirees sign up in the first
place—these days is laughable. First, fewer companies are willing
to offer it: In 2001, 67 percent of Medicare+Choice enrollees had
some kind of drug coverage. That's down from 84 percent in 1999.
Many of those (26 percent) now have to comply with a $500 or *less*

SIDEBAR 13.3

**SIDEBAR 13.3**

cap on the benefit. By contrast, in 1999, only 10 percent of Medicare+Choice beneficiaries had a benefit cap of $500 or less. (In 2000, all Medicare beneficiaries spent an average of $480 out of pocket on prescription drugs.)

**9.   "Our comparison data is a joke."**

Looking to compare different health plans? If you're shopping for cost, there's data available for you, but if you're shopping for quality, you're out of luck. CMS provides beneficiaries with information on each Medicare HMO in their areas (click on "Medicare Health Plan Compare" on www.medicare.gov), including items from plan costs and benefits to telephone numbers and web site addresses. In addition, the National Committee for Quality Assurance, the managed-care industry's leading accreditation group (http://hprc.ncqa.org) has a report card tool you can use to help you find the right health plan for you. Its measures include patient satisfaction and availability of doctors, as well as several process measures that have been linked to survival and quality of life, such as mammography screening rates.

Still, these data don't directly measure the quality of care, according to Families USA, a health care advocacy group. Instead, they measure the adequacy of the systems that plans have in place to deliver care. Want to know about outcomes, like survival rates after heart surgery, or how well patients function after treatment? Sorry, those aren't measured.

Says William Scanlon, director of health care issues for the General Accounting Office, "The development of reliable health outcome measures is a much more complicated task and remains a long-term goal."

There are two kinds of Medicare+Choice plans: managed care plans (like HMOs) and private fee-for-service plans. Signing up for one of these programs can cut your out-of-pocket expenses down even more—an average of $755 a year in a Medicare HMO, according to the GAO study—but also limits the kinds of services available as well as the places you can go to get them. A good source for advice on HMOs is the National Committee for Quality Assurance (NCQA), an organization that accredits these health organizations. The NCQA's "report cards" on well over 100 HMOs are available on its web site (www.ncqa.org).

If you decide to join an HMO or take a private fee-for-service policy, experts suggest holding on to your Medigap coverage for at least a few months until you are sure you are happy with your choice. If you drop your supplemental insurance and then become ill, your insurer is under no obligation to reinsure you at the same rates—or at all.

## Long-Term Care Insurance

We know. You feel vibrant and alive. What will you ever need to be in a nursing home for? People come up with all kinds of excuses about why they won't need home health care or won't ever end up in a nursing care facility: They have children who will care for them; they'll be dead before they'd consider a nursing home. The truth is, however, that two out of every five Americans will need to enter a long-term care (LTC) facility at some point in their lives. Deloitte & Touche says that everyone over 75 years old has a 60 percent chance. And those numbers are even higher if you're a woman (75 percent of all nursing home patients over 65 are female, and of those 63 percent are either disoriented or memory impaired).

That's the sad stuff.

Now for the truly depressing stuff: The average cost of one year in a nursing home is nearly $50,000. The average stay in one: two and a half years. And that's just the average. There are certainly states where the yearly cost is less—in Georgia, South Carolina, and Wyoming, for example, it's below $40,000. But it's also more expensive in others—in New York, and Connecticut it's a whopping $70,000; in Alaska it costs more than $110,000. (See Table 13.2.) And some averages for stays in nursing centers top three years.

Is this why you've been working so hard on your retirement investment strategy?

If you don't have long-term care insurance, the answer is yes. That's because Medicare won't cover it—unless you go to the nursing home after at least a three-day hospital stay. And in that case, only the first 20 days are fully covered; after that and up to the 100th day of your stay, you have to pay $101.50 of each day's cost. At day 101, you're on your own—unless, of

## TABLE 13.2   STATE-BY-STATE NURSING HOME CARE COSTS

| State | Cost per Day | Cost per Year |
|---|---|---|
| Alabama | $100 | $ 36,500 |
| Alaska | 313 | 114,245 |
| Arizona | 135 | 49,275 |
| Arkansas | 118 | 43,070 |
| California | 142 | 51,830 |
| Colorado | 119 | 43,435 |
| Connecticut | 195 | 71,175 |
| Delaware | 129 | 47,085 |
| Florida | 125 | 45,625 |
| Georgia | 100 | 36,500 |
| Hawaii | 185 | 67,525 |
| Idaho | 115 | 41,975 |
| Illinois | 130 | 47,450 |
| Indiana | 130 | 47,450 |
| Iowa | 100 | 36,500 |
| Kansas | 110 | 40,150 |
| Kentucky | 127 | 46,355 |
| Louisiana | 90 | 32,850 |
| Maine | 165 | 60,225 |
| Maryland | 150 | 54,750 |
| Massachusetts | 190 | 69,350 |
| Michigan | 125 | 45,625 |
| Minnesota | 130 | 47,450 |
| Mississippi | 100 | 36,500 |
| Missouri | 105 | 38,325 |
| Montana | 109 | 39,785 |
| Nebraska | 120 | 43,800 |
| Nevada | 136 | 49,640 |
| New Hampshire | 200 | 73,000 |
| New Jersey | 190 | 69,350 |
| New Mexico | 144 | 52,560 |
| New York | 192 | 70,080 |
| North Carolina | 121 | 44,165 |
| North Dakota | 113 | 41,245 |

TABLE 13.2    *(Continued)*

| State | Cost per Day | Cost per Year |
|---|---|---|
| Ohio | 135 | 49,275 |
| Oklahoma | 94 | 34,310 |
| Oregon | 136 | 49,640 |
| Pennsylvania | 145 | 52,925 |
| Rhode Island | 159 | 58,035 |
| South Carolina | 104 | 37,960 |
| South Dakota | 100 | 36,500 |
| Tennessee | 130 | 47,450 |
| Texas | 120 | 43,800 |
| Utah | 112 | 40,880 |
| Vermont | 135 | 49,275 |
| Virginia | 128 | 46,720 |
| Washington | 165 | 60,225 |
| West Virginia | 125 | 45,625 |
| Wisconsin | 166 | 60,590 |
| Wyoming | 100 | 36,500 |
| Average | $136 | $ 49,691 |

course, you have less than $2,000 of personal assets. Then Medicaid covers it. (Medicare's real hidden benefits are for home care. If you need the intermittent services of nurse or therapist and are under a doctor's care, Medicare pays for the nurse or therapist as well as for a part-time home health aide.)

Right now, only 3 percent of all national nursing care costs are covered by long-term care insurance. Medicaid covers the bulk of it, 69 percent. But up to 24 percent of the costs are covered by personal funds, and only 7 percent is covered by Medicare.

The message is simple: Be prepared to fork over your hard-earned, diligently saved and wisely invested cash for your care (and leave less to your children or to charity)—or buy a long-term care policy. Now.

Long-term care coverage, first introduced several years ago, has only recently become an attractive insurance option. Thanks to the Kennedy-Kassebaum Bill of 1996, LTC insurers must now conform to national standards. LTC premiums offer some tax perks as well: Individuals can deduct a percentage of their long-term care premiums as part of their total medical expenses (exceeding 7.5 percent of adjusted gross income). More importantly, LTC benefits themselves have been clarified as tax-free income (just like health insurance benefits have always been).

Who should consider purchasing one of these new and improved long-term care policies? David Theis, a fee-only financial planner in Palantine, Illinois, recommends long-term care insurance for anyone with less than $1 million in investment assets. "It's a good idea for anyone who has the financial means to do so," adds Madelyn Flanagan, consumer affairs advocate at the Independent Insurance Agents of America. "But it is expensive. If you're going to put yourself at a real financial disadvantage by buying it, don't."

If you decide you need LTC insurance, you'll need to do your research. The increase in LTC popularity has led to a greater variety of offerings from more insurance companies. Currently, more than 100 insurers offer some form of long-term care coverage. And annual LTC premiums can range from $200 to $6,000 a year, depending on the age at which you purchase the policy and the benefits that you choose, according to Flanagan.

Clearly it pays to shop around for the right policy from the right insurer. An easy way to compare rates and policy provisions is to call Long-Term Care Quote at 800-587-3279—or visit their web site at www.longtermcarequote.com to get an instant (well, Web-instant) quote online. This independent, Chandler, Arizona–based company will provide you with a free comparison of the three best policies based on the parameters you choose.

But first, check with your employer to find out if an LTC plan is offered. Employer plans are on the rise thanks to the tax deductions offered by the Kennedy-Kassebaum bill, according to Joseph Luchok, spokesman for the Health Insurance Association of America. And according to a May 2000 study by the Department of Health and Human Services, employee group plans are often better than you'll ever buy on your own. They often have less restrictive underwriting policies (like you don't need to hand over health information), and a majority offer extended coverage to parents, in-laws, spouses, and retired employees.

Some people may have problems getting policies because of preexisting medical conditions. If you can answer "yes" to any of the following three questions, for instance, according to Long-Term Care Quote, you may not qualify for one:

1. Have you ever been diagnosed as having any one of the following conditions: chronic memory loss, liver cirrhosis, muscular dystrophy, Parkinson's disease, Alzheimer's disease, senility, dementia, or multiple strokes?

2. Do you currently need a walker, a wheelchair, oxygen, or kidney dialysis?

3. Do you currently need ongoing assistance from or supervision by another person to get out of bed or up from a chair, take a bath, dress, go to the bathroom, control your bladder, or eat?

If you decide to get a long-term care policy, here's what to look for.

## Benefits

Long-term care policies are indemnity policies: They pay a fixed dollar amount for each day you receive specified care either in a nursing home or at home. According to the American Health Care Association, the average cost of a day in a nursing home is $136. But you'll want to check costs in your area and make sure you are covered for at least the average daily cost locally. (See the state-by-state of daily and annual costs in Table 13.2.) You will also want to be covered for home health care benefits, including intermediate and custodial care. Again, call around to determine the going rate. The daily home health care benefit you'll want usually amounts to about half of the nursing home daily benefit you select, according to Richard Coorsh. In other words, if you choose a policy that covers you for $100 a day in a nursing home, you'll probably want $50-a-day coverage for in-home care. You'll also want to ensure you're covered for cognitive impairments like Alzheimer's disease.

These days you can buy "integrated"—sometimes known as "comprehensive"—policies. These are policies that cover all kinds of care: nursing home care, home health care, assisted living care (those are the big three), as well as adult day care, respite care, and hospice care. They're more expensive, but if you can afford it, buy one. Policies that cover just home health care or just nursing-home care are 20 to 40 percent cheaper, according to Long-Term Care Quote.

Watch out, too, for benefit triggers in the policy, according to Long-Term Care Quote. These are the litmus tests, if you will, that you have to meet before your insurer will pay your claim. Typically, policies require that you meet at least one of the following two: an inability to perform basic daily living activities, and/or a cognitive impairment like memory loss. That's acceptable. But some of the policies slice and dice the requirements—like you have to have shown an inability to perform more than two daily living activities (and, according to Long-Term Care Quote, the policy may omit bathing as a day-to-day activity that qualifies). Avoid those. Some policies also require their own "care coordinators" or "personal care advisers" to certify your eligibility for benefits. A good plan will let *you* choose the doctor or nurse to do this.

## Length of Coverage

Statistics show that people who need long-term care need it for an average of two and a half years, so Robert Davis, president of Long-Term Care Quote, suggests starting with at least a three-year benefit period to see how the premiums fit into your financial picture. A lifetime benefit will obviously provide the most peace of mind, but can be an average of 70 percent more expensive than a three-year benefit period. Here's another tip from Davis: Make sure your policy pays you for 100 percent of "actual" (and not just "usual and customary" or even "pending" expenses) up to the daily maximum you've selected, regardless of where you receive care.

## Elimination Period

This is the length of time between when your long-term care needs begin and your LTC benefits become payable. The elimination period can be any length from zero days up to a year, on some policies. The longer an elimination period you can tolerate financially, the more affordable your premium will be.

## Age of the Insured

Although the average age of a person buying LTC insurance today is 61, according to Davis, the optimal age to purchase such a plan is actually between the ages of 50 and 55. When you're younger and in better health, the LTC rates are markedly cheaper and there are more choices of insurers and policies available. For example, a five-year LTC policy with a $100 daily benefit, 100 percent home health care benefit, and 90-day elimination period from Prudential is $1,165 a year for a 55-year-old. An identical policy jumps to $2,122 a year for a 65-year-old and skyrockets to $4,597 for a 75-year-old. And that's not even taking into account possible deteriorating health conditions in those later years that would up the ante still more. Davis advises considering the purchase of long-term care coverage while you're still planning your retirement, rather than once you've already entered it.

## Inflation Protection

Inflation protection usually comes in two forms, a 5 percent fixed annual increase or a 5 percent compounded annual increase. A fixed increase in benefits will add an average of 35 percent to your premium, while a compounded increase (which more closely approximates actual inflation) will add 70 percent. The younger you are when you purchase your policy, the more important inflation protection is. "You'll pay more money for it, but it is absolutely a must-have, especially when purchasing it at 50 or 55 years of age," says consumer affairs advocate Madelyn Flanagan of the Independent Insurance Agents of America.

## Insurer Rating

Finally, make sure the insurance company has received at least an A rating from Standard & Poor's Corporation and Moody's Investors Service. Seems like standard advice, but the long-term care sector of the industry went through a hairy phase in the mid-1990s, when the sales pitches were sleazy, the policies inconsistent, and the payoffs uncertain. So a little caution is always wise. Look for the "excellent" rating from credit bureaus. Also look for well-established companies—businesses with 50 years behind them and at least $500 million in assets with a low percentage being high-risk assets—that have been in the long-term care underwriting business for at least five years.

# Long-Term Care:
# Did You Know That . . .

- Two out of every three nursing home residents rely on Medicaid to pay for their care.
- Every eight seconds in the United States, a baby boomer turns 50.
- Americans aged 85 and older are the fastest growing segment of population and the heaviest users of long-term health care services. From 1990 to 1998, the 85 and older age group increased by 34 percent. Longevity is expected to rise for all ages.
- Two out five Americans will need long-term care at some point in their lives.
- In 2000, the average cost of a stay in a nursing facility was $50,000 per year.
- Only one in four Americans can afford private nursing home care for one year, yet the average length of a stay in 1997 was 2.4 years.
- Only 4 percent of current nursing home care costs are paid by long-term care insurance; 68 percent by Medicaid; 8 percent by Medicare; 20 percent by private pay or funding.
- Deloitte & Touche says that 60 percent of people over 75 will need some form of long-term care.
- The average age of a nursing home patient is 79; 75 percent of nursing home patients over 65 are women, and 63 percent are disoriented or memory impaired.

*Source:* American Health Care Association.

# GLOSSARY

**AARP**   Founded in 1958 as the American Association for Retired Persons, the AARP is the nation's leading organization for people age 50 or older. It services the needs and interests of more than 34 million members through information and education, advocacy, and community services.

**agency bonds**   Bonds issued by government-sponsored agencies and federally related institutions. All government agency bonds carry the highest credit ratings—AAA from Standard & Poor's and Aaa from Moody's Investors Service. The quality of agency bonds and the liquidity for certain agency issues are considered second only to Treasurys. Normally, agency bonds offer a slightly higher interest rate over comparable Treasury issues. Agency bonds are issued by institutions like the Federal Home Loan Mortgage Corporation and the Federal National Mortgage Association.

**aggressive growth funds**   Funds that seek rapid growth of capital and that may invest in emerging-market growth companies without specifying a market capitalization range. They often invest in small or emerging growth companies and are more likely than

other funds to invest in initial public offerings or in companies with high price-to-earnings and price-to-book ratios. They may use such investment techniques as heavy sector concentrations, leveraging, and short selling.

**alpha**   A measure of a fund's risk-adjusted return. Alpha can be used to directly measure the value added or subtracted by a fund's manager. It is calculated by measuring the difference between a fund's actual returns and its expected performance given its level of market risk as measured by beta. An alpha of 1.0 means the fund produced a return 1 percent higher than its beta would predict. An alpha of −1.0 means the fund produced a return 1 percent lower. The accuracy of an alpha rating depends on two factors: (1) the assumption that market risk, as measured by beta, is the only risk measure necessary; (2) the strength of the fund's correlation to a chosen benchmark such as the S&P 500. Correlation is measured by R-squared. An R-squared of less than 50 makes a fund's alpha rating virtually meaningless.

**American depositary receipts (ADRs)** Shares of non-U.S. companies that trade in the U.S. stock market.

American depositary receipts, or ADRs, offer distinct advantages to the U.S. investor. First, they require no complex currency transactions as they can be purchased in U.S. dollars. Also, most ADR companies are required to report financial details of their operations in accordance with generally accepted accounting principles. That makes their earnings more transparent and less subject to manipulation or fraud.

**American Stock Exchange (AMEX)** The third most active market in the United States, behind the New York Stock Exchange (NYSE) and the Nasdaq Stock Market. The exchange was founded in 1842 in New York City. Most stocks traded on it are those of small to midsize companies. Also called AMEX and the curb exchange.

**American-style option**   An option that may be exercised at any time prior to expiration.

**AMEX Market Value Index**   A stock index that measures the performance of more than 800 companies representing all major industry groups on the American Stock Exchange.

**analyst**   An employee of a brokerage or fund management firm who studies companies and makes buy and sell recommendations on stocks of these companies. Most specialize in a specific industry such as health care, semiconductors, or banks.

**annual effective yield**   The actual annual return on an account after interest is compounded.

**annualized return**   A way to calculate the return on an investment of more than one year. The annualized or average annual return is calculated by adding each year's return on investment and dividing that number by the number of years invested. The return takes into account the reinvestment of dividends (and distributed capital gains for mutual funds) as well as the change in the price of the investment over time. *Compare* **cumulative return**.

**annual report**   A record published every year by a publicly held corporation that details its financial condition. The report, which must be distributed to all shareholders, contains a description of the company's operations, its balance sheet, income statement, and other relevant information. The official SEC terminology for an annual report is a 10-K form.

**annuity**   A tax-deferred investment product sold by insurers, banks, brokerage firms, and mutual fund companies. Fixed annuities provide a rate of return that is fixed for a year or so but then can move up and down. Variable annuities allow investors to allocate their money among a basket of mutual fund-like subaccounts; the return depends on the performance of the funds selected. Watch out for high sales commissions, expense ratios, and penalties for early withdrawals.

**ask or asked price**   The price at which someone is willing to sell a security or an asset. In the stock market, the ask portion of a stock quote is the lowest price a seller is willing to accept at that time. The difference between the ask price and bid price is known as the spread.

**asset allocation**    An investment technique that diversifies a portfolio among different types of assets such as stocks, bonds, cash equivalents, precious metals, real estate, and collectibles. When it comes to risk and reward, different asset classes behave quite differently. Stocks, for instance, offer the highest return, but they also carry the highest risk of losses. Bonds aren't so lucrative, but they offer a lot more stability than stocks. Money-market returns are puny, but you'll never lose your initial investment. An asset allocation strategy allows you to achieve the optimal blend of risk and reward.

**asset-backed bonds**    Bonds backed by loans or accounts receivable. An asset-backed bond is created when a securities firm bundles some type of debt—such as car loans, credit card debt, or bank loans—and sells investors the right to receive the payments that consumers make on those loans.

**asset-backed securities**    Securities backed by loans or accounts receivable. For example, an asset-backed bond is created when a securities firm bundles some type of debt, like car loans, and sells investors the right to receive the payments that consumers make on those loans.

**asset-management accounts**    All-in-one accounts that allow customers of brokerage firms to buy and sell securi-

ties and store cash in one or more money-market mutual funds. Asset-management accounts generally offer check-writing privileges, credit or debit cards, and automatic transfers from one account to another. They often come with an annual fee of up to $100.

**assets**    Any item of economic value owned by an individual or corporation, especially that which could be converted to cash. Examples are cash, securities, accounts receivable, inventory, office equipment, a house, a car, and other property.

**assets under management**    The total market value of a mutual fund. The asset level can change, depending on the flow of money into and out of the fund, as well as the change in market valuation. Asset figures are useful in gauging a fund's size, agility, and popularity. They help determine whether a small-company fund, for example, can remain in its investment objective category if its asset base reaches an ungainly size.

**assisted living**    Group residential facilities (not nursing homes) that provide 24-hour personal care for people who need help performing daily living activities.

**auction market**    Trading securities on a stock exchange where buyers compete with other buyers and sellers compete with other sellers for the best stock price. Trading in individual stocks is managed and kept orderly by a specialist.

**auditor's report**    An independent accounting firm's opinion on whether a company's financial statements conform to generally accepted accounting principles (GAAP). The auditor's report is included in a company's annual report.

**average annual yield**    A way to calculate the return on investments of more than one year. It is calculated by adding each year's return on investment and dividing that number by the number of years invested.

**averages**    In the stock market, averages are indicators that measure price changes in representative stock prices. The most popular indicator is the Dow Jones Industrial Average, which measures the performance of 30 large-capitalization stocks.

**back-end load**    A sales charge that is imposed when investors redeem shares of a mutual fund. Also known as the contingent deferred sales charge (CDSC), a back-end load generally declines over time. For instance, if you sell the mutual fund shares after one year, you may owe a 5 percent charge, but if you hold for three years, the charge may decline to 2 percent. Unfortunately, the cumulative 12b-1 fee always compensates the fund company for any possible loss it might incur by long-term shareholders holding on to their shares until the stated load is 0 percent. Paying the front-end load is often the better deal.

**balanced fund**    A mutual fund that invests in a mixture of stocks, bonds, and cash. A balanced fund attempts to blend asset classes to produce a conservative growth and income portfolio. It is also known as a hybrid or asset allocation fund.

**balance sheet**    Financial statement that lists a company's assets and liabilities as of a specified date. The balance sheet presents a company's financial condition by listing what it owns (assets such as cash, inventory, factories, equipment, and accounts receivable) and what it owes (liabilities such as short-term and long-term debt and accounts payable). The difference between assets and liabilities is known as shareholders' equity or book value.

**bankruptcy**    A state of insolvency of an individual or an organization—in other words, an inability to pay debts. The U.S. bankruptcy code is divided into chapters that provide different types of relief from insolvency. Under Chapter 7 bankruptcy, you petition the court to be freed from all your debts following the liquidation of almost all your assets. Certain assets, like your house, are usually exempt from liquidation. Chapter 11 allows businesses to remain in possession of assets, but a repayment schedule must be negotiated with creditors. Chapter 13 is for individuals.

**basis point**    One-hundredth of one percentage point, or 0.01 percent. Basis points make for a handy way to state small differences in yield. For example, it's much easier to say one bond yields 10 basis points more than another than it is to say it yields one-tenth of one percentage point more. It is also used for interest rates. An interest rate of 5 percent is 50 basis points greater than an interest rate of 4.5 percent.

**bearer stock** Stock certificates that aren't registered in any name. They are negotiable without endorsement by any person.

**bear market** Any market in which stock prices decline for a prolonged period, usually falling by 20 percent or more.

**bellwether bond** For the U.S. market, it is the 10-year Treasury note, which replaced the 30-year Treasury bond as the benchmark for evaluating the bond market in general.

**beneficiary** A person you name in your will, life insurance policy, retirement plan, or other financial arrangement to receive a benefit at your death.

**best three-month return** A fund's highest three-month return measured in rolling three-month periods over the past five years.

**beta** A measure of an investment's volatility relative to a chosen benchmark. For stocks or stock funds, the benchmark is usually the S&P 500. For bonds or bond funds, it is typically the Lehman Brothers Aggregate Bond Index, which tracks the bond market. The beta of the benchmark is always 1.00. So a stock fund with a beta of 1.00 has experienced up and down movements of roughly the same magnitude as the S&P 500. Meanwhile, a fund with a beta of 1.25 is expected to do 25 percent better than the S&P in an up market and 25 percent worse in a down market. Generally speaking, the higher the beta, the more risky the

investment. But without a high R-squared, a beta statistic can be meaningless. R-squared determines how much an investment's return is correlated to its benchmark.

**bid** The price that someone is willing to pay for a security or an asset. In the stock market, the bid portion of a stock quote is the highest price anyone is willing to pay for a security at that time. The difference between the ask price and bid price is known as the spread.

**Big Board** Another name for the New York Stock Exchange (NYSE).

**blend fund** A mutual fund that is somewhere between a growth fund and a value fund. Applying both strategies, it might, for instance, invest in both high-growth Internet stocks and cheaply priced automotive companies. As such, blend funds are difficult to classify in terms of risk. The S&P 500 index funds invest in every company in the S&P 500 and could therefore qualify as blend funds. But other funds are more extreme in using both styles.

**block trade** Buying or selling 10,000 shares of stock or $200,000 or more worth of bonds.

**blue-chip stocks** Stocks of companies known for their long-established record of earning profits and paying dividends. Blue chips tend to be large, stable, and well known. Most of the top stocks in the S&P 500 are blue chips.

**bond** A debt instrument that pays a set amount of interest on a regular basis. The amount of debt is known as the principal, and the compensation given to lenders for making such money available is typically in the form of interest payments. There are three major types of bonds: corporate, government, and municipal. A corporate bond with a low credit rating is called a high-yield or junk bond.

**bond broker**   A bond broker acts as your agent, calling around to different bond dealers to find the best prices for the bonds you want. Brokers may charge fees for their services or simply make money by increasing the markup (the spread between the purchase price and sale price of a bond).

**Bond Buyer Municipal Bond Index**
An index based on 40 long-term municipal bonds that is often used to track the performance of tax-free municipal bonds. The index is compiled by *The Bond Buyer*, a trade publication that also has several other closely watched municipal bond indexes.

**bond dealers**   Dealers maintain their own inventories of bonds and make trades with either the general public or brokers. A dealer makes money from the difference between the bid price and ask price of a bond. Brokers who offer to act as dealers can sell you bonds from their own inventories. This is usually a better deal since it removes a layer of commissions that will be added if your broker has to go to another dealer to find you a particular bond.

**bond fund**   A bond mutual fund specializes in pooling the purchase of

bonds into a diversified, managed portfolio. Most bond fund portfolios pay income (which can be reinvested or distributed) on a monthly basis. Bond fund maturities can be as short as one year and as long as 30 years. The disadvantage of a bond fund is that it's not a bond. It has neither a fixed yield nor a contractual obligation to give the investor back the principal at some later maturity date—the two key characteristics of individual bonds. However, there are many varieties of bond funds, including government, corporate, and municipal. In the case of corporate bonds, which can be volatile, a diversified fund could be the better option than buying individual issues.

**bond rating**   An assessment of the likelihood that a bond issuer will pay the interest on its debt on time. Bond ratings are assigned by independent agencies, such as Moody's Investors Service and Standard & Poor's. Ratings range from AAA or Aaa (highest) to D (in default). Bonds rated below B are not investment grade and are called high-yield or junk bonds. Since the likelihood of default is greater on such bonds, issuers are forced to pay higher interest rates to attract investors.

**bond yield**   Stated simply, the yield on a bond is the interest you actually earn on your investment. If you buy a new issue, your yield is the same as the interest rate, but if you buy on the secondary market, your yield may be higher or lower. When its price has fallen the yield of a bond goes up. Conversely, if its market value has risen a bond's yield falls.

**book value**   The difference between a company's assets and its liabilities, usually expressed in per-share terms. Book value is what would be left over for shareholders if the company were sold and its debt retired. It takes into account all money invested in the company since its founding, as well as retained earnings. It is calculated by subtracting total liabilities from total assets and dividing the result by the number of shares outstanding. Examining the price-to-book (P/B) ratio of an industrial company with a lot of hard assets is a good way of telling if it's undervalued or overvalued.

**bottom fishing**   Buying stocks whose prices have fallen to low levels or bottomed out. Value investors favor this investment technique.

**bottom line**   Accounting term for the net profit or loss.

**break the buck**   When a money-market fund's share price falls below the $1-a-share value it is intended to maintain, the fund is said to "break the buck." Money funds are supposed to be safe investments and easily convertible into cash—thus the stable $1 share price. Cases of breaking the buck have been rare.

**broker**   A person who gives advice and handles orders to buy or sell stocks, bonds, commodities, and options. Brokers work for full-service and discount brokerage firms. The type of firm you use determines the amount of commissions you pay and advice you receive from your broker.

**brokerage firm**   When you buy or sell a security, you generally do so through a brokerage firm. Brokerage firms fall into two main camps: full-service brokers and discount brokers. Discount brokers charge far lower commissions than full-service brokers, and a growing number of deep discounters charge especially low commissions. But there is a trade-off. If you use a discount broker, you will get little or no investment advice, so you must be willing to make your own buy and sell decisions. A full-service broker will help you pick investments and devise a financial plan.

**bull market**   A bull market is a stretch of time, from several months to years, in which stock prices rise. Excluding a few nasty short-lived corrections, for the past 20 years U.S. stocks have experienced healthy returns, rising 12 percent a year. During the bull market of 1995 to 1999 stocks rose more than 250 percent.

**call**   The issuer's right to redeem a bond or preferred share before it matures. A bond will usually be called when interest rates fall so significantly that the issuer can save money by floating new bonds at lower rates. The first date when an issuer may call a bond is specified in the bond's prospectus.

**callable bond**   A bond that the issuer can decide to redeem before its stated maturity date. A call date and a call price are always given. You face a risk with a callable bond that it will be redeemed if its stated coupon is higher than prevailing rates at the time of its call date. If that happens, you won't be able to reinvest your capital in a comparable bond at as high a yield.

**call option** An agreement that gives an investor the right but not the obligation to buy a stock, bond, commodity, or other instrument at a specified price within a specific time period. *Compare* **put option**.

**capital gains** Profit realized from the sale of securities, property, or other assets. How much the IRS taxes gains depends on how long the security is held. Gains from stocks held for less than 12 months are considered short-term capital gains, which are taxed at the regular income-tax rate. That can be as high as 38.6 percent in 2002. But for stock purchased after January 1, 2001, and held for more than five years, the gains tax will be a maximum of 18 percent.

**capital gains distribution** The amount of capital gains a mutual fund distributes to its shareholders per share. Distributions usually occur once or twice per year and can be taxed as long-term or short-term gains, depending on how long the fund manager held securities in the portfolio. When purchasing a mutual fund, make sure it is not right before a distribution. Otherwise, you'll get slapped with a tax bill for money you didn't make. Also, pay attention to the fund's turnover ratio to see how tax-efficient it is.

**capital loss** Loss suffered from the sale of an asset for less than the price you paid for it. Capital losses can be used to your advantage come tax time. By balancing your capital losses with your capital gains, you can reduce your tax bill. This tactic is called harvesting losses.

**cash-equivalent** The proportion of a fund's assets held in cash or short-term, fixed-income securities. Too much cash in an equity fund's portfolio can be a drag on performance. At the same time, cash can also be used by cautious managers to preserve capital in a down market. It is also used to take advantage of buying opportunities and to meet shareholder redemptions.

**cash flow** Net earnings before depreciation, amortization, and noncash charges. It is useful for determining how solvent a company is.

**Centers for Medicare and Medicaid Services (CMS)** Formerly known as the Health Care Financing Administration, the CMS (a federal agency within the Department of Health and Human Services) has oversight over Medicare and Medicaid programs.

**certificate of deposit (CD)** A certificate of deposit or CD is a certificate issued by a bank or thrift that indicates a specified sum of money has been deposited. The certificate guarantees to repay your principal—the amount you deposited—with interest on a specific maturity date. The amount of interest you receive depends on prevailing interest rates, the length of maturity, and how much you deposited. There are often significant penalties for early withdrawal of your money. CDs are insured by the Federal Deposit Insurance Corporation (FDIC). That makes your investment safe from everything but inflation and a raging bull market.

**Certified Financial Planner (CFP)** The best-known financial planning designation, given to qualifying planners by the CFP Board of Standards in Denver.

**chartered financial consultant (ChFC)** Financial planning designation given to qualifying planners by the American College, Bryn Mawr, Pennsylvania.

**Chicago Board of Trade (CBOT)** A commodity-trading market.

**Chicago Board Options Exchange (CBOE)** An exchange set up by the Chicago Board of Trade to trade stock options, foreign currency options, and index options of the S&P 500 and other benchmarks.

**churning** To trade securities excessively. In taxable investment accounts, churning invariably leads to reduced returns because of the hefty short-term capital gains tax. But even in tax-deferred 401(k)s or IRAs, trading commissions can eat into your return. In fact, brokers who encourage churning to increase their commissions are committing a securities law violation. A fund manager churning the portfolio also will make you feel the tax bite.

**circuit breakers** Measures used by some major stock and commodities exchanges to restrict trading temporarily when markets rise or fall too far too fast. For example, the New York Stock Exchange employs a circuit breaker that will halt trading if the Dow Jones Industrial Average declines by more than 10 percent in one day.

**closed-end fund** A type of mutual fund that issues a set number of shares and typically trades on a stock exchange. Unlike more traditional open-end funds, transactions in shares of closed-end funds are based on their market price as determined by the forces of supply and demand in the marketplace. Interestingly, the market price of a closed-end may be above (at a premium) or below (at a discount) the value of its underlying portfolio (or net asset value). Investors in closed-ends will often try to capitalize on large discounts, hoping that eventually the gaps will narrow.

**closely held** Refers to a company that has a small group of controlling shareholders. In contrast, a widely held firm has many shareholders. It is difficult or impossible to wage a proxy fight for any closely held firm.

**closing price** The last trading price of a stock when the market closes.

**COBRA** The Consolidated Omnibus Budget Reconciliation Act of 1985 provides people the right to buy continuing health insurance through their former employers for a minimum of 18 months. COBRA offers up to 36 months of continuing coverage for those people insured through a spouse's work plan who lose that coverage due to divorce, separation, or death of the spouse.

**collateral**    Stock or other property that a borrower is obliged to turn over to a lender if unable to repay a loan. Collateral is important for companies that default on their debts. In such cases, hard assets such as plant, property, and equipment can be repossessed and liquidated.

**collateralized mortgage obligations (CMOs)**    Mortgage-backed securities that are carved into an array of bonds of varying maturity, coupon, and risk. The principal payments from the underlying pool of pass-through securities are used to retire the bonds on a priority basis as specified in the prospectus.

**commodities**    Bulk goods such as grains, metals, livestock, oil, cotton, coffee, sugar, and cocoa. They can be sold either on the spot market for immediate delivery or on the commodities exchanges for later delivery. Trade on the exchanges is in the form of futures contracts. Commodities are often viewed as a hedge against inflation because their prices rise with the consumer price index.

**common stock**    Represents part ownership of a company. Holders of common stock have voting rights but no guarantee of dividend payments. In the event that a corporation is liquidated, the claims of owners of bonds and preferred stock take precedence over those who own common stock. For the most part, however, common stock has more potential for appreciation.

**composite trading**    The total amount of trading across all markets in a share that is listed on the New York Stock Exchange or American Stock Exchange. This includes transactions on those exchanges, on regional exchanges, and on the Nasdaq Stock Market.

**compounding**    Financial advisers love to talk about the magic of compounding. What it this magic? If your investments make 10 percent a year for five years, you earn not 50 percent but 61.1 percent. Here's the reason: As time goes on, you make money not only on your original investment but also on your accumulated gains from earlier years.

**consumer price index (CPI)**    A gauge of inflation that measures changes in the prices of consumer goods. It is based on a list of specific goods and services purchased in urban areas, including food, transportation, shelter, utilities, clothing, medical care, and entertainment. Index data are released monthly by the U.S. Department of Labor.

**contingent deferred sales charge (CDSC)**    A back-end load that declines over time. For instance, if you sell your mutual fund shares after one year you may owe a 5 percent charge, but if you hold for three years the charge you owe may decline to 2 percent.

**contrarian**    An investor who does the opposite of what most investors are doing at any particular time. According to contrarian opinion, if everyone is certain that something is going to happen, it won't. This is because most people who say the market will go up are fully invested so they have no more purchasing power, which means the market is at its peak. When people predict decline they have already sold out, so the market can only go up. Contrarian investing shares many qualities with value investing. The difference is that contrarian stocks aren't just cheap, they are also actively disliked by investors. That can make them risky but potentially lucrative investments.

**convertible bond**   A bond that investors may exchange for stock at a future date under certain conditions. Convertibles are an intriguing hybrid investment, offering some of the upside potential of stocks but also the downside protection of bonds. On the upside, bonds offer a conversion ratio that dictates how many shares of stock you can receive if you trade in your bonds. Typically, you'll pay a premium for the exchange, but if the underlying stock is on fire, conversion is worthwhile. On the downside, bonds offer a guaranteed dividend yield, even if the underlying stock slides. Because of their complexity, the best way to invest in convertibles is through a convertible bond fund.

**corporate bonds**   A corporate bond is a debt instrument issued by a private or public corporation. Corporate bonds are rated by Standard & Poor's, Moody's, and other credit rating agen-

cies. They assign ratings based on a company's perceived ability to pay its debts over time. Those ratings—expressed as letters (AAA, AA, A, etc.)—help determine the interest rate that company or government has to pay. A bond with a rating below BBB or Baa is considered a high-yield or junk bond. Such bonds pay higher interest rates but have greater risk of default. Corporate bonds have historically been viewed as safer investments than stocks. The main reason for this is the prior claim corporate bondholders have on a company's earnings and assets.

**corporation**   A business entity treated as a person in the eyes of the law. A corporation is allowed to own assets, incur liabilities, and sell securities, among other things. It is also able to be sued.

**correction**   A downward movement in the price of an individual stock, bond, commodity, index, or the stock market as a whole.

**cost basis**   The original price of an asset, used in determining capital gains. It usually refers to the purchase price of a stock, bond, or other security.

**cost of living**   The level of prices of goods and services required for a reasonable standard of living.

**coupon**   The stated interest rate on a bond when it is first issued. A $1,000 bond with a coupon of 6 percent will pay you $60 a year until its maturity. Of course, not everyone holds bonds until maturity. The actual dividend yield you get from buying a bond on the secondary market can vary greatly from the coupon rate because the bond can sell above or below its face value.

**Coverdell Education Savings Account (ESA)** A tax-advantaged account for college savings: Money grows tax-free and once withdrawn is free from federal income tax as well, as long as it is used for qualified educational expenses (includes elementary, secondary, and college expenses). One account can be opened per beneficiary, and you (a parent, grandparent, or any other person) can make a nondeductible contribution of up to $2,000 for any other person. There are, however, income limitations: Contributors must have less than $190,000 in modified adjusted gross income ($95,000 for single filers) in order to qualify for a full $2,000 contribution. The $2,000 maximum is gradually phased out if your modified adjusted gross income falls between $190,000 and $220,000 ($95,000 and $110,000 for single filers). That means when a modified family annual gross income reaches $220,000, no contribution is allowed. You can contribute to both a Coverdell Education Savings Account (ESA) and a Section 529 college savings plan in the same year. Any bank, mutual fund company, or financial institution that can serve as a custodian for a traditional IRA can serve as a custodian for an ESA.

**credit ratings** Formal evaluation of a government body's or a company's credit history and ability to repay its debts. An AAA rating is the highest credit rating assigned by Standard & Poor's to a debt obligation. It indicates an extremely strong capacity to pay principal and interest. Bonds rated AA are just a notch below, then single A, then BBB, and so on. (A similar ratings system is available from Moody's Investors Service, with Aaa being the highest rating.) Some ratings show a + or − to further differentiate creditworthiness. Bonds rated BBB or Baa and above are considered investment grade, a category to which certain investors, including many pension funds, confine their bond holdings. Bonds rated BB, B, CCC, CC, and C are regarded as speculative. Such bonds are called high-yield or junk bonds. They offer higher interest rates but greater risk of default. A bond rating of D indicates payment default or the filing of a bankruptcy petition.

**cumulative return** The total return an investment earned over a specific period. Returns are added year by year instead of averaged as they are with an annualized return. The end result takes into account the reinvestment of dividends (and distributed capital gains for mutual funds) as well as the change in the price of the investment over time.

**currency** A country's official unit of monetary exchange. When investing overseas, currency risk can be problematic. Even when foreign economies are doing reasonably well, currency fluctuations can have a negative effect on stock prices. While stocks in the chosen country could be soaring, a decline in the value of the currency's exchange rate to the dollar could eliminate your stock gains.

**current assets**   Assets that can be converted to cash within 12 months. These include cash, marketable securities, accounts receivable, and inventory.

**current liabilities**   Obligations that must be paid within 12 months. These include accounts payable, short-term debt, and interest on long-term debt.

**current ratio**   A measure of a company's liquidity, or its ability to pay its short-term debts, calculated by dividing current assets by current liabilities. Having current assets at least twice current liabilities is considered a healthy condition for most businesses.

**current yield**   You might think the current yield would be the same as the coupon rate on a bond. But, unless you're buying a new issue of a bond trading at face value, it's not. Unlike the coupon rate, which doesn't change, the current yield of a bond fluctuates with a bond's price on the secondary market. To get the current yield, divide the coupon by the bond's current market price. For example, a bond with a $1,000 face value and a coupon of 6 percent (i.e., paying $60 per year) purchased at $900 has a current yield of 6.7 percent. When its market price declines the current yield of a bond rises. Conversely, when the price of the bond rises the current yield declines.

**CUSIP number**   An identification number for securities. CUSIP is an acronym for Committee on Uniform Securities Identifying Procedures.

**cyclical stocks**   Stocks that tend to rise quickly during an upturn in the economy and fall quickly during a downturn. Examples are housing, steel, automobiles, and paper. These economically sensitive stocks are the bread and butter of value investors, who pick them up during economic troughs and wait for the recovery.

**day order**   An investor's order to buy or sell stock that will be canceled by the end of the day if not filled.

**debenture**   A common kind of corporate bond, often issued by a firm during restructuring. Debentures are backed only by the credit quality or essentially the good name of the issuer. Since there is no collateral, these bonds may carry a higher risk, and therefore a higher rate of return, when compared to an asset-backed bond. However, debentures of solid companies may be very highly rated.

**debt**   Securities such as bonds, notes, mortgages, and other forms of paper that indicate the intent to repay an amount owed. A company that takes on too much debt can wind up in dire financial straits.

**debt-to-equity ratio**   A measure of financial leverage, the debt-to-equity ratio is calculated by dividing long-term debt by shareholders' equity. (Shareholders' equity is the same as book value.) The higher the ratio, the greater the chance a company won't be able to pay its debts in the future.

**debt-to-total-capital ratio**    This ratio indicates how much financial leverage a company has. It is calculated by dividing total debt by total invested capital. Total invested capital is a tally of all the outside investments a company's management has used to finance its business—everything from equity (the amount of stock sold) to long-term debt. The major difference between the debt-to-equity ratio and this ratio is that debt-to-capital includes long-term debt as part of the denominator. The higher the ratio, the greater the chance a company will not be able to pay its debts in the future.

**deductible**    Under an insurance policy, the amount of loss or expense that you must shoulder yourself before the insurance company begins paying.

**default**    Failure to pay principal or interest on a debt security. Owners of a bond that is in default can usually make claims against the assets of the issuer to recover their loss. A bond that is in default is rated D by Standard & Poor's. A default generally does not mean that the investor loses his or her entire investment. Sometimes the default will be the result of a temporary cash crunch and won't result in a bankruptcy filing. In other cases, a company will enter bankruptcy and either liquidate or reorganize its capital structure and business operations. In either case, the bond investor will generally recover some percentage of the bond's face value.

**defensive securities**    Stocks with investment returns that do not tend to decline as much as the market in gen-eral in times when stock prices are falling. These include companies with earnings that tend to grow despite the business cycle, such as food and drug firms, or companies that pay relatively high dividends like utilities.

**defined-benefit plan**    A traditional pension plan usually paid for by your employer. Upon retirement, you receive a fixed monthly check based on your age, salary, and length of service. Unlike a 401(k) or other defined-contribution plans, it does not necessarily require you to contribute any portion of your salary to receive a retirement benefit.

**defined-contribution plan**    A pension plan in which the level of contributions is fixed at a certain level, while benefits vary depending on the return from the investments. In some cases, such as 401(k), 403(b), and 457 plans, employees make voluntary contributions into tax-deferred accounts, which may or may not be matched by an employer. Defined-contribution plans, unlike defined-benefit plans, give the employee options on where to invest the account, usually among stock, bond, and money-market mutual funds.

**deflation**    A decline in the general price level of goods and services that results in increased purchasing power of money. The opposite of inflation. Deflation is not always good for an economy because companies have no pricing power.

**depression**    A severe downturn in an economy that is marked by falling prices, reduced purchasing power, and high unemployment. The Great Depression began in 1929 and continued through most of the 1930s. But even depressions haven't stopped the general upward trend of stock prices and earnings.

**derivative**   A security whose value is derived from the performance or movement of another financial security, index, or other investment. For example, derivatives may be futures, options, or mortgage-backed securities. Derivatives may be used to short sell a security or to hedge against downside risk.

**devaluation**   Lowering of the value of a country's currency relative to the currencies of other nations. When a nation devalues its currency, the goods it imports become more expensive, while its exports become less expensive abroad and thus more competitive.

**dip**   A slight decline in securities prices followed by a rise. Analysts often advise investors to buy on the dips, meaning buy when a price is momentarily weak.

**discount**   When the market price of a closed-end fund is less than its underlying net asset value (NAV), it is said to be trading at a discount. That discount allows you to buy a dollar's worth of securities for less than a dollar. So if a closed-end fund trading at a 10 percent discount owns a portfolio of stocks collectively worth $10 a share, you can buy that portfolio for $9 a share. Unlike open-end funds, closed-ends trade like

stocks on an exchange, so a fund's price is determined by investor demand for its shares. A lack of demand can cause the fund's market price to be less than its underlying portfolio value—the source of the discount.

**discount bond**   One that sells at a current market price that is less than its face value. Bonds sell at a discount when the coupon on the bond is lower than prevailing rates. For example, you might have to pay only $812 for a bond with a 6.5 percent coupon if new issues yielding 8 percent are available for $1,000.

**discount brokers**   Brokers who charge lower commissions than full-service brokers. Investors often give up the benefits of stock-picking advice, updates on news affecting their investments, and research services normally provided by full-service brokers. Increasingly, however, the line between discount and full-service brokers has begun to blur.

**discount rate**   The interest rate the Federal Reserve charges its member banks for loans. This rate influences the rates these financial institutions then charge to their customers. The Fed uses this rate as one method of influencing monetary policy. The rate is also very important to the bond and stock markets as it provides a clue to interest rate trends and future Federal Reserve policy.

**disinflation**   A slowdown in the rate of price increases. Disinflation occurs during a recession, when sales levels drop and retailers are unable to pass higher prices along to consumers.

**diversification**   When you diversify, you spread your money among a slew of different securities, thereby avoiding the risk that your portfolio will be badly bloodied because a single security or a particular market sector turns sour.

**dividends**   A portion of a company's net income paid to stockholders as a return on their investment. A stock's dividend yield is determined by dividing a company's annual dividend by its current share price. So a stock selling for $20 a share with an annual dividend of $1 a share yields the investor 5 percent. Dividends are declared or suspended at the discretion of the company's board of directors. A prime benefit of dividends is that once paid, they are money in the bank and provide your only return when stocks are weak. One disadvantage is that dividends are taxed as ordinary income, which, if you're in a high tax bracket, can ramp up your tax bill.

**dividend yield**   A company's annual dividend expressed as a percentage of its current stock price. As a stock's price declines, its dividend yield goes up. So a stock selling for $20 a share with an annual dividend of $1 a share yields an investor 5 percent. But if the same stock falls to $10 a share, its $1 annual dividend yields 10 percent. Value investors often see high dividend yields as a sign that a stock is cheaply priced. A high yield also acts as a cushion in a declining market, which is attractive to risk-averse investors. The

downside is that dividends are taxed as ordinary income. The greater the yield, the more taxes you will have to pay.

**dollar-cost averaging**   A strategy to invest fixed amounts of money in securities at regular intervals, regardless of the market's movements. Dollar-cost averaging is another form of diversification—only instead of spreading your money over a bunch of different stocks or bonds, it diversifies your investments over time. As a result, when the price is lower, more shares of the security are purchased than when prices are higher. Investing $300 into the same stock every month will get you a lot more shares when the stock is depressed than when it's flying high. This strategy causes your overall cost of investment to go down.

**Dow Jones averages**   There are four Dow Jones averages that track price changes in various sectors. The Dow Jones Industrial Average tracks the price changes of the stocks of 30 industrial companies. The Dow Jones Transportation Average monitors the price changes of the stocks of 20 airlines, railroads, and trucking companies. The Dow Jones Utility Average measures the performance of the stocks of 15 gas, electric, and power companies. The Dow Jones 65 Composite Average monitors the stocks of all 65 companies that make up the other three averages. One consistent criticism of the averages is that they're price weighted, not market-capitalization weighted like the S&P 500. Since each Dow Jones index calculates the average price of its participants, higher-priced stocks have a greater influence on index movements than lower-priced stocks do. But a stock's price is less significant to the broader market than its market capitalization.

**Dow Jones Equity Market Index** Index that measures price changes in more than 100 U.S. industry groups. The stocks in the index represent about 80 percent of U.S. market capitalization and trade on the New York Stock Exchange, the American Stock Exchange, and the Nasdaq Stock Market. The equity-market index is market-capitalization weighted, which means that a stock's influence on the index is proportionate to its size in the market.

**Dow Jones Global Indexes** More than 5,000 companies' stocks in 33 countries worldwide are tracked by Dow Jones Global Indexes. These indexes subdivide the companies by geographic region and industry group. Collectively, the indexes represent more than 95 percent of the equity capital on stock markets around the world. All of them are weighted by market capitalization, which is the product of price times shares outstanding. Thus, each country carries a weight proportionate to the relative value of its equities to all those in the world. The U.S. market is the world's biggest, and the U.S. component of the global indexes has the most stocks—more than 700.

**Dow Jones Industrial Average** Often referred to as the Dow or DJIA, the Dow Jones Industrial Average is the best known and most widely reported

indicator of the stock market's performance. The Dow tracks the price changes of 30 large blue-chip stocks. Their combined market value is equal to roughly 20 percent of the market value of all stocks listed on the New York Stock Exchange (NYSE). That said, the Dow is frequently criticized for lacking the breadth of the S&P 500, which accounts for more than 80 percent of NYSE's market value. It is also a price-weighted index, weighting higher-priced stocks more than lower-priced ones. The S&P 500 is a market-capitalization-weighted index, weighting the total market value of each stock's shares. Some financial analysts believe a market-cap-weighted index paints a more accurate picture of the stock market.

**Dow Jones World Stock Index** An index that measures the performance of more than 2,000 companies worldwide that represent more than 80 percent of the equity capital on 25 stock markets. It is a composite of the Dow Jones Global Indexes.

**downtick** A sale of a listed security that occurs at a lower price than the previous transaction.

**drag on returns (drag grade)** The negative impact on mutual fund returns of three factors—sales charges, annual expenses, and portfolio turnover. High-turnover funds can lead to large capital-gains distributions and tax inefficiency. If you aren't careful, management expenses and capital gains taxes can shave hundreds—if not thousands—of dollars from your returns over the years.

**duration**    A way to measure part of the risk in a bond or bond fund. Duration tells you how long it will take to recoup your principal. It's a complicated calculation, so you'll have to get the number from your fund company or bond dealer, but it makes for a handy way to judge interest rate risk. If a bond or a bond fund has a duration of seven years, a 1 percent drop in interest rates will raise its value by 7 percent, while a 1 percent rise in interest rates will lower its price by 7 percent. The greater the duration of a bond, the greater its percentage volatility. In general, duration rises with maturity and falls with the frequency of coupon payments.

**Dutch auction**    A procedure for buying and selling securities named for a system used for flower auctions in Holland. A seller seeks bids within a specified price range, usually for a large block of stock or bonds. After evaluating the range of bid prices received, the seller accepts the lowest price that will allow it to dispose of the entire block. U.S. Treasury bills are sold under this system.

**earnings**    The amount of profit a company realizes after all costs, expenses, and taxes have been paid. It is calculated by subtracting business, depreciation, interest, and tax costs from revenues. Earnings are the supreme measure of value as far as the market is concerned. The market rewards both fast earnings growth and stable earnings growth. Earnings are also called profit or net income.

**earnings growth**    The percentage change in a company's quarterly earnings per share versus the same period from the previous year. For example, a company that earned $1 a share in the second quarter of 2001 and then earned $1.25 in the second quarter of 2002 would have experienced a 25 percent growth in earnings. To gauge how successful a company is at growing its earnings, you should compare its earnings growth to other companies in its industry.

**earnings per share (EPS)**    The portion of the company's earnings allocated to each share outstanding. EPS is a company's net income divided by its number of outstanding shares. If a company earning $2 million in one year had 2 million shares of stock outstanding, its EPS would be $1 per share. In calculating EPS, the company often uses a weighted average of shares outstanding over the reporting term. EPS is the denominator in the price-to-earnings (P/E) ratio.

**earnings yield**    A company's per-share earnings expressed as a percentage of its stock price. This provides a yardstick for comparing stocks with bonds, as well as with other stocks.

**economic indicators**    Key statistics used to analyze business conditions and make forecasts. Among them are the unemployment rate, inflation rate, factory utilization rate, and balance of trade.

**Education IRA**    A tax-advantaged college savings account, renamed in 2002 the Coverdell Education Savings

Account (ESA). *See* **Coverdell Education Savings Account (ESA).**

**emerging markets** The financial markets of developing countries. Examples include Mexico, Malaysia, Chile, Thailand, and the Philippines. Emerging-market securities are the most volatile in the world. They have tremendous growth potential, but also pose significant risks: political upheaval, corruption, and currency collapse, to name just a few.

**Employee Benefit Research Institute (EBRI)** A group supported by private corporations, labor unions, insurers, financial institutions, and trade associations, among others, to advance the knowledge and understanding of employee benefits through research, policy forums, workshops, educational publications, and periodicals.

**Employee Retirement Income Security Act of 1974 (ERISA)** A law that governs most private pension and benefit plans. It sets minimum standards for employee pension and welfare plans in the private sector that employers must meet to qualify for tax-favored status. It does not require employers to establish a plan. But those that do must meet certain standards as to vesting, participation, nondiscrimination, investing, and funding.

**employee stock ownership plan (ESOP)** A program encouraging employees to buy stock in their company and thereby have a greater stake in its financial performance.

**entitlements** Government benefits such as Social Security and Medicare that must be paid to anyone meeting specific eligibility requirements.

**equity** Ownership interest possessed by shareholders in a corporation— stocks as opposed to bonds. It is the part of a company's net worth that belongs to shareholders.

**equity-income funds** Funds that seek current income by investing a minimum of 65 percent of their assets in dividend-paying securities. Equity-income funds are most akin to value funds in their investment philosophy because stocks with high dividend yields tend to be the cheapest stocks. Since dividends are the primary criterion by which these funds select stocks, they often lose out on capital appreciation. This means that as the market rallies, these funds will often lag. Conversely, when the market declines, the income generated by the stocks held in equity-income funds provides a buffer against losses.

**ERISA** *See* **Employee Retirement Income Security Act of 1974.**

**estate planning** Planning for the disposition and administration of an estate when the owner dies. Estate planning includes drawing up a will, setting up trusts, and minimizing estate taxes, perhaps by passing property to heirs before death.

**estate taxes** Taxes levied by the federal and state governments on the transfer of assets after someone dies. Uncle Sam levies estate taxes on the worldwide assets of both U.S. citizens and U.S. residents. Under the Economic Recovery Act of 1981, there is no estate tax on transfers of property between spouses.

**exchange**   A centralized place for trading securities and commodities, usually involving an auction process. Examples include the New York Stock Exchange (NYSE) and the American Stock Exchange (AMEX).

**exchange-traded fund (ETF)**   A basket of stocks that can be traded like a single stock. Unlike traditional mutual funds, which are priced once per day after the market closes, an ETF can be bought or sold at the market price anytime the exchanges are open. Investors can choose from many different ETFs, including SPDRS (Standard & Poor's Depository Receipts), which track the Standard & Poor's 500; Diamonds, which track the 30 stocks in the Dow Jones Industrial Average; and Qubes, which track the Nasdaq 100.

**ex-dividend**   A period of time immediately before a dividend is paid, during which new investors in the stock are not entitled to receive the dividend. A stock's price is revised lower to reflect the dividend value on the first day of this period. On that day, a stock is said to "go ex-dividend." Usually indicated in newspapers with an "x" next to the stock's or mutual fund's name.

**expense ratio**   The percentage of mutual fund assets deducted each year for expenses, which include management fees, operating costs, administrative fees, 12b-1 fees, and all other costs incurred by the fund. Recently, the average expense ratio for domestic equity funds was 1.4 percent. For fixed-income funds it was 1.1 percent. International funds have higher expense ratios, averaging around 1.8 percent. There is no reason to buy funds with expense ratios higher than that. Sometimes the fund's management may elect to waive part of the expenses charged to shareholders in order to boost returns. But this is usually a temporary waiver, so be careful because such funds often raise their expenses once the waiver period ends.

**face value**   Just like it sounds: The value a bond has printed on its face, usually $1,000. Also known as par value, it represents the amount of principal owed at maturity. The bond's actual market value may be higher or lower. When a bond's market price fluctuates, there is an impact on its yield. If the price drops below the bond's face value, its yield goes up. If the price rises above face value, the yield goes down.

**federal budget deficit**   The amount of money the federal government owes because it spent more than it received in revenue for the past year. To cover the shortfall, the government usually borrows from the public by floating long- and short-term bonds. Federal deficits, which started to rise in the 1970s, exploded to hundreds of billions of dollars per year in the 1980s and 1990s. Some economists think massive federal deficits can lead to high interest rates and inflation, since they compete with private borrowing from consumers and businesses, but such was not the case during the 1980s and 1990s. The *cumulative* unpaid debt of all past deficits is called the federal debt or national debt.

**federal debt**    The total amount the federal government owes because of past deficits. The federal debt is made up of such debt obligations as Treasury bills, Treasury notes, and Treasury bonds. Congress imposes a ceiling on federal debt, which has been increased on occasion when accumulated deficits have neared the ceiling. In the mid-1990s, the federal debt was more than $5 trillion. The interest due on the federal debt is one of the major expenses of the federal government. The federal debt, which is the total debt accumulated by the government over many years, should not be confused with the federal budget deficit, which is the excess of spending over income by the federal government in one fiscal year.

**federal funds**    Funds deposited by commercial banks at Federal Reserve district banks. Designed to enable banks temporarily short of their reserve requirement to borrow reserves from banks having excess reserves.

**federal funds rate**    The interest rate that banks charge each other for the use of federal funds. This rate is used for overnight loans to banks that need more cash to meet bank reserve requirements. It changes daily and is the most sensitive indicator of general interest rate trends. The rate is not set directly by the Federal Reserve, but fluctuates in response to changes in supply and demand for funds. It is reported daily in the business section of most newspapers.

**Federal Reserve (the Fed)**    The central bank of the United States that sets monetary policy. The Federal Reserve oversees money supply, interest rates, and credit with the goal of keeping the U.S. economy and currency stable. Governed by a seven-member board, the system includes 12 regional Federal Reserve Banks, 25 branches, and all national and state banks that are part of the system.

**Financial Accounting Standards Board (FASB)**    An independent board responsible for establishing and interpreting generally accepted accounting principles (GAAP). U.S. companies that adhere to GAAP are said to be more transparent and easier to analyze financially than companies in many foreign countries. In fact, the differences in accounting standards make it difficult to compare the earnings of companies in different countries.

**financial planner**    A type of financial adviser, ideally with broad knowledge of all areas of personal finance. Fee-only planners are paid solely by their clients—that is, they do not receive sales commissions or compensation from other sources. Fee-plus-commission planners charge fees for advice and other services, and also receive commissions on the sale of investment and insurance products. When choosing a financial planner, be aware that no particular training or credentials are required, so incompetents and even some outright crooks can call themselves financial planners. Instead, look for a Certified Financial Planner (CFP) designation. It is the best-known financial planning designation, requiring that the adviser be certified by the CFP Board of Standards.

**Financial Times–Stock Exchange 100-Share Index (FTSE 100)**    Index of 100 large companies, on a capitalization basis, on the London Stock Exchange. (The FTSE 250 is an index of the next largest 250 companies after the top 100.)

**fiscal year (FY)**    The 12-month period that a corporation or government uses for bookkeeping purposes. A company's fiscal year is often, but not necessarily, the same as the calendar year. A seasonal business will frequently select a fiscal rather than a calendar year so that its year-end figures will show it in its most liquid condition, which also means having less inventory to verify physically. The fiscal year of the U.S. government ends September 30.

**fixed-income security**    A security that pays a fixed rate of return. This usually refers to government, corporate, or municipal bonds, which pay a fixed rate of interest until the bonds mature, and to preferred stock, paying a fixed dividend. Since fixed-income investments guarantee you an annual payout, they are inherently less risky than stocks, which do not.

**float**    The number of outstanding shares in a corporation available for trading by the public. A small float

means the stock will be more volatile, since a large order to buy or sell shares can influence the stock's price dramatically. A large float will mean a stock is less volatile. Since small-capitalization stocks tend to have less shares outstanding than larger companies, their float is smaller and they tend to be more volatile. The same is true for closely-held companies.

**floating an issue**    Offering stocks or bonds to the public. It can be an initial public offering or an offering of new issues by companies that are already public.

**401(k) plan**    An employer-sponsored retirement savings plan funded by employees with contributions that are deducted from pretax pay. Employers frequently add matching contributions up to a set limit. Employees are responsible for managing the money themselves, allocating the funds among a selection of stock, bond, and cash investment funds. Investment gains aren't taxed until the money is withdrawn.

**403(b) plan**    A retirement savings plan for employees of colleges, hospitals, school districts, and nonprofit organizations. The plan, which is similar to the 401(k) plan offered to many corporate employees, is funded by employees with contributions that are deducted from pretax pay. Employees manage the money themselves, selecting from fixed and variable annuities and from mutual funds. Investment gains aren't taxed until the money is withdrawn.

**FTSE 100** *See* **Financial Times–Stock Exchange 100-Share Index**.

**full-service brokers**    Brokers who execute buy and sell orders, research investments, help investors develop and meet investment goals, and give advice to investors. They charge commissions for their work. During a bull market, when stocks are going up consistently, good ideas are a dime a dozen. But when the markets turn choppy, solid advice can save you. Some full-service firms offer a range of good mutual funds, estate-planning services, and tax advice. A full-service broker will set up a financial profile for you—based on your assets, income, and goals—and advise you appropriately. All of this, of course, will cost you a lot more than using a bare-bones discount broker.

**fundamental analysis**    Asserting that a stock's price is determined by the future course of its earnings and dividends, the fundamental analyst tries to determine what the intrinsic value of a stock's underlying business is by looking at its financial statements and its competitive position within its industry. If this intrinsic value is greater than the market price of the stock, the stock is said to be undervalued. In other words, the company has greater earning potential than its stock price would indicate. Fundamental analysis is the antithesis of technical analysis, which focuses on stock price movements instead of underlying earnings potential.

**fund company or fund family**    A business entity that manages, sells, and markets mutual funds to the public. Fund companies typically offer a wide variety of funds, investing in both the equity and fixed-income markets. They also perform administrative tasks, such as fund accounting and customer service, although these responsibilities are sometimes contracted out. Some of the larger fund companies are Fidelity, Vanguard, Franklin Templeton, and T. Rowe Price. In many cases, investors may move their assets from one fund to another within a fund company at little or no cost.

**futures**    An agreement to buy or sell a set amount of a commodity or security in a designated future month at a price agreed upon today by the buyer and seller. A futures contract differs from an option because an option is the right to buy or sell, whereas a futures contract is the promise to actually make a transaction. A futures contract is part of a class of securities called derivatives, so named because such securities derive their value from the worth of an underlying investment.

**generally accepted accounting principles (GAAP)**    Guidelines that explain what should be done in specific accounting situations as determined by the Financial Accounting Standards Board. U.S. companies that adhere to GAAP are said to be more transparent and easier to analyze financially than companies in many foreign countries. In fact, the differences in accounting standards make it difficult to compare the earnings of companies in different countries.

**general-obligation bond**    A government bond that is approved either by the voters or their legislature. The government's promise to repay the principal and pay the interest is constitutionally guaranteed, based on its ability to tax the population. Also called a full-faith-and-credit bond.

**global funds**    A fund that invests in stocks located throughout the world while maintaining a percentage of assets (normally 25 percent to 50 percent) in the United States. Global funds tend to be the safest foreign-stock investments because they typically lean on better-known U.S. stocks. Also called World funds.

**Great Depression**    The worldwide economic hard times that began after the stock market collapse on October 28, 1929, and continued through most of the 1930s. Even the Great Depression didn't stop the long-term upward trend of stock prices and earnings. If in 1929 you had invested $800 in the market, you would be sitting on $83,369 in 2002 (assuming you reinvested all the dividends).

**gross domestic product (GDP)**    The total value of goods and services produced by a nation. The GDP is made up of consumer and government purchases, private domestic investments, and net exports of goods and services. In the United States it is calculated by the Commerce Department every quarter, and it is the main measure of economic output. Because GDP measures national output, and strong output is indicative of a healthy economy, bond prices react negatively to strong GDP data. A strong economy ignites inflationary fears, which is a negative for bond prices. Equities, conversely, tend to perform well when GDP is rising since earnings-growth prospects are better during economic expansions.

**gross margin**    A company's profitability after the costs of production have been paid. Gross margin is calculated by dividing gross income (revenue after production costs are subtracted) by revenue and then multiplying by 100. The result is expressed as a percentage. Gross margin shows you how profitable the basic business of a company is before administrative costs, taxes, and depreciation have been taken out. Operating margin may paint a truer picture of a company's profitability. *Compare* **operating margin**.

**growth**    An investment style that looks for companies with above-average current and projected earnings growth. Growth investors believe in buying stocks with superior earnings growth regardless of price. Thus, growth stocks tend to have very high earnings-growth rates but very low dividend yields. These firms all trade at high valuation levels, meaning they usually have high price-to-book (P/B), price-to-earnings (P/E), and price-to-sales (P/S) ratios. Because of their high prices and low yields, growth stocks tend to have less downside protection and more volatility than cheaper companies. They are particularly sensitive to rising interest rates, which can put a damper on their rapid earnings growth. *Compare* **value investing**.

**growth and income fund**    A mutual fund that seeks long-term growth of capital as its primary objective. Current income is a secondary objective. Growth and income funds typically buy shares of large companies that have good prospects for future earnings growth and solid dividend payment histories. They are generally more value oriented than growth oriented in style, since value stocks produce more dividend income than growth stocks. From a risk perspective, growth and income funds tend to move in tandem with the broad market averages, such as the S&P 500. The upside is that growth and income funds tend to be less volatile than the overall market. The downside is that such funds aren't generally the leaders on a total-return basis.

**growth fund**    As its name implies, this type of fund tends to look for the fastest-growing companies on the market. Growth managers are willing to take more risk and pay a premium for their stocks in an effort to build a portfolio of companies with above-average earnings momentum or price appreciation. Growth stock funds usually have higher return volatility than most other funds. This means that if the market declines, a growth fund's return will tend to decline more than the overall market. On the upside, if the market rallies, growth funds typically outperform most market measures such as the S&P 500. A growth fund invests in stocks of all market capitalization ranges—small, medium, and large.

**guaranteed investment contract (GIC)**    An investment offered by an insurance company that promises preservation of principal and a fixed rate of return. Many defined-contribution plans, such as 401(k) and 403(b) plans, offer GICs as retirement options to employees. Although the insurance company takes all market, credit, and interest rate risks on the investment portfolio, it can profit if its returns exceed the guaranteed amount. Only the insurance company backs the guarantee, not any government agency, so if the insurer fails it is possible there could be a default on the contract. But overall GICs offer a stable way to achieve a fixed rate of return.

**Health Care Financing Administration (HCFA)**    HCFA, established in 1977, is now known as the Centers for Medicare and Medicaid Services (CMS). It is a federal agency within the Division of Health and Human Services and has oversight over Medicare and Medicaid.

**health maintenance organization (HMO)**    The most common form of a managed care plan. It typically restricts patients to the HMO's own stable of doctors. Premiums are lower than for traditional fee-for-service health care plans, and the charge for each doctor visit is modest.

**hedge fund**    A private investment partnership, owned by wealthy individuals and institutions, which is allowed to use aggressive strategies that are unavailable to mutual funds, including short selling, leverage, program trading, swaps, arbitrage, and derivatives. Since hedge funds are restricted by law to less than 100 investors, the minimum hedge-fund investment is typically $1 million.

**hedging**    A strategy designed to reduce investment risk using call options, put options, short selling, or futures contracts. A hedge can help lock in existing profits. Examples include a position in a futures market to offset the position held in a cash market, holding a security and selling that security short, and a call option against a shorted stock. A perfect hedge eliminates the possibility of a future gain or loss. An imperfect hedge insures against a portion of the loss.

**high-yield bond**    These are the lowest-quality bonds in terms of default risk. Bonds with credit ratings below BBB from Standard & Poor's or Baa from Moody's Investors Service are considered speculative because they have a greater chance of default than investment-grade bonds. High-yield bonds, also called junk bonds, are usually issued by smaller companies without long track records or by companies with questionable credit ratings. To compensate for the additional risk, issuers offer higher yields than those of investment-grade bonds. In recent years, however, junk-bond yields have declined as their popularity has increased and default rates have slowed.

**holding company**    A company whose principal assets are the securities it owns in companies that actually provide goods or services. A holding company enables one corporation and its directors to control several companies by holding large stakes in the companies.

**illiquid**    Refers to an asset not readily convertible into cash. Illiquid investments include antique cars, paintings, and stamp collections. An illiquid security is one without an active secondary market, making it difficult for an owner of the security to sell it. Small-capitalization stocks tend to be somewhat illiquid because they have fewer shares outstanding and lower trading volumes. That can make them more volatile to own.

**income bond fund**    A mutual fund that seeks a high level of steady income by investing in a mix of corporate and government bonds.

**income fund**    A mutual fund that seeks a high level of current income by investing in income-producing securities, including both stocks and bonds.

**index**    A composite of stocks, bonds, or other securities selected to represent a specific market, industry, or asset class. Examples include the S&P 500, which represents large U.S. stocks; the Russell 2000, which represents smaller U.S. stocks; the Morgan Stanley Capital International EAFE index, a foreign stock index that represents Europe, Australasia, and the Far East; and the Lehman Brothers Aggregate Bond index, which represents the total U.S. bond market. Investors use these composites to measure the overall health of specific markets and as benchmarks of comparison. For example, if you own a large-cap mutual fund, you can compare its total return to the S&P 500 to see whether it is performing well.

**index fund** A mutual fund that seeks to produce the same return that investors would get if they owned all the securities in a particular index. The most common variety is an S&P 500 index fund, which tries to mirror the return of the Standard & Poor's 500-stock index. Index funds have the lowest expense ratios in the fund universe and are also very tax-efficient because of their low turnover ratios. They are good funds for novice investors.

**indexing** A passive investment strategy that tracks the total return of a securities index, such as the S&P 500. Robotic indexing offers some unique advantages over active portfolio management. Discipline and style consistency are first and foremost. If you buy an S&P 500 index fund, it will never invest in anything but stocks in the S&P 500. That kind of consistency is necessary if you want the asset allocation in your portfolio to be precise. An active fund manager could be guilty of style drift, investing in parts of the market that don't suit your asset allocation scheme. Other advantages of indexing are low expenses and tax efficiency.

**individual retirement account (IRA)** A tax-deferred retirement plan that can help build a nest egg. Individuals whose income is less than a certain amount or who aren't active participants in an employer's retirement plan—such as a 401(k) or 403(b)—generally can deduct some or all of their annual IRA contributions when figuring their income taxes. Others can make non-deductible IRA contributions (to a Roth IRA, for example). A single person can contribute up to $3,000 (in 2002) and a married couple up to $6,000 annually. The contributions grow tax-deferred until withdrawn. (In contrast, a Roth IRA's contributions are tax-free upon withdrawal.) Withdrawals before age $59^1/_2$ are subject to a 10 percent penalty charge.

**inflation** The rate at which the general level of prices for goods and services is rising. Inflation has an uncanny ability to erode the value of securities that don't grow fast enough. That's why investing only in a money-market fund can be more risky than it appears on the surface. If inflation is rising at 3 percent a year and your money market is growing at 5 percent or 6 percent, you won't have much money left over for your retirement. Measures of inflation include the consumer price index (CPI) and the producer price index (PPI).

**inflation-indexed securities** These Treasury notes and bonds are designed to keep pace with inflation. The principal is adjusted to match changes in the consumer price index (CPI), while the interest rate remains fixed. In this way, inflation cannot erode the value of your principal.

**initial public offering**   The first time a company issues stock to the public. This process often is called going public. Securities offered in an IPO are often, but not always, those of young, small companies seeking outside equity capital and a public market for their stock. Investors purchasing stock in IPOs generally must be prepared to accept very large risks for the possibility of large gains.

**insider**   A person, such as an executive or a director, who has information about a company before the information is available to the public. An insider also is someone who owns more than 10 percent of the voting shares of a company. All insider trades must be disclosed to the Securities and Exchange Commission. However, it is illegal for insiders to trade on corporate information that hasn't yet been released to the public.

**insider trading**   In one respect, the term refers to the legal trading of securities by corporate officers based on information available to the public. In another respect, it refers to the illegal trading of securities by any investor based on information not available to the public. Many professional investors watch insider activity closely for clues to a company's future.

**interest rate**   The rate of interest charged for the use of money, usually expressed as an annual rate. The rate is derived by dividing the amount of interest by the amount of principal borrowed. For example, if a bank charges $50 a year to borrow $1,000, the interest rate would be 5 percent. Interest rates are quoted on bills, notes, bonds, credit cards, and many kinds of consumer and business loans. Rates in general tend to rise with inflation and in response to the Federal Reserve raising key short-term rates. A rise in interest rates has a negative effect on the stock market because investors can get more competitive returns from buying newly issued bonds instead of stocks. It also hurts the secondary market for bonds because rates look less attractive compared to newer issues.

**interest rate risk**   The danger that prevailing interest rates will rise significantly higher than the rate paid on bonds you are holding. This drives down the price of your bonds on the secondary market, so if you sell you'll lose money. This is a serious risk for anyone investing in long-term bonds, including Treasurys, because the longer the maturity, the higher the interest rate risk.

**intermediate-term bonds**   Treasury notes that mature in 2 to 10 years, or corporate bonds that mature in 5 to 15 years.

**internal rate of return**   An accounting term for the rate of return on an asset. It is the discount rate on an investment that equates the present value of its cash outflows to the present value of its cash inflows.

**international funds**   Mutual funds that invest primarily in stocks located outside the United States. While having international exposure adds diversification to your portfolio, there are some risk factors to note: currency risk, political risk, and economic risk. In particular, currency risk can cause investment returns to vary considerably. Also, because of the high cost of investing abroad, most international funds have higher expense ratios than their domestic peers.

**International Monetary Fund (IMF)** An organization that makes loans and provides other services intended to stabilize world currencies and promote orderly and balanced trade. Member nations may obtain foreign currency when needed, making it possible to adjust in their balance of payments without currency depreciation.

**intrinsic value**    The underlying value of a business separate from its market value or stock price. In fundamental analysis, the analyst will take into account both the quantitative and qualitative aspects of a company's performance. The quantitative aspect is the use of financial ratios such as earnings, revenue, and so on, while the qualitative perspective involves consideration of the company's management strength. Based on such analysis, the fundamental analyst will make a forecast of future earnings and prospects for the company to arrive at an intrinsic value of its shares. The intrinsic value of a share can be at odds with its stock market price, indicating that the company is either overvalued or undervalued by the market.

**investment bank**    A securities firm, financial company, or brokerage house that helps companies take new issues to market. An investment bank purchases new securities from the issuer, then distributes them to dealers and investors, profiting on the spread between the purchase price and the offering price. Additionally, an investment bank handles the sales of large blocks of previously issued securities and private placements. Most investment banks also maintain brokerage operations and other financial services.

**investment grade**    An assessment of a bond by a credit-rating firm that indicates whether investors are expected to receive principal and interest payments in full and on time. A grade of BBB or higher from Standard & Poor's or Baa or higher from Moody's Investors Service is considered investment grade. Lower grades (BB, Ba, B, etc.) are considered speculative. Investment-grade bonds have less risk of default but lower yields than speculative bonds (also called high-yield or junk bonds).

**junk bond**    *See* **high-yield bond**.

**Keogh plan**    A tax-deferred retirement savings plan for small business owners or self-employed people who have earned income from their trades or businesses. Contributions to the Keogh plan are tax-deductible.

**kiddie tax**    Special tax treatment for investment earnings of children under the age of 14. The child's investment income is reported by parents on IRS Form 8615 if it is greater than $1,500.

Such income is taxed at the parents' top tax rate.

**knock-in option**   An option activated only when the price of the option's underlying instrument or market reaches a certain level above or below an agreed-upon range.

**knock-out option**   An option that becomes worthless when the price of the option's underlying instrument or market reaches a previously agreed-upon point.

**ladder**   A portfolio strategy where investors stagger the maturities of their bond holdings in order to provide regular income as the bonds come due and smooth out the effects of interest rate fluctuations. For those with enough assets allocated to bonds, we recommend putting equal amounts of money into Treasurys due to mature in one-, three-, five-, seven-, and nine-year periods. That gives your portfolio an average maturity of five years. As the principal comes due every two years, you can reinvest that amount in bonds due to mature in 10 years. That way, you keep your portfolio's average maturity at five years or so.

**lagging economic indicators**
Economic indicators that lag behind the overall pace of economic activity. The Conference Board publishes the Index of Lagging Indicators monthly along with the Index of Leading Indicators and Index of Coincident Indicators. The seven components of the lagging indicators are the unemployment rate, business

spending, unit-labor costs, bank loans outstanding, bank interest rates, ratio of credit to income, and book value of manufacturing and trade inventories.

**large-capitalization stock**   A share of a large publicly traded corporation, typically with a total market capitalization of greater than $5 billion. (Also called large-cap stocks, large caps, and blue chips.) These companies play an especially significant role in driving the economy. The two most watched indexes—the Dow Jones Industrial Average and the S&P 500—are both composed of large-cap stocks. The Dow tracks 30 of the biggest stocks. The S&P tracks 500 companies with an average market value of $20.2 billion. Because of their sheer size, large caps tend to grow slower than small-capitalization stocks, but they also tend to be much more stable.

**leading economic indicators**   A composite of 10 economic measurements developed to help forecast likely changes in the economy as a whole. It is compiled by the Conference Board. The components are: average work week, unemployment claims, orders for consumer goods, vendor performance, plant and equipment orders, building permits, interest rate spread, stock prices, M2 money supply (liquid forms of money such as traveler's checks, currency, deposits against which checks can be written, savings accounts, and balances in money market funds), and consumer expectations.

**limit order** An order to buy or sell a stock at a specific price or better. The broker will execute the trade only within the price restriction. This type of trade provides more investment control than a market order, which will buy or sell the security at any price.

**liquidity** The ease with which financial assets can be converted to cash without creating a substantial change in price or value. Liquidity is influenced by the amount of float in the security, investor interest, and size of the investment being converted to cash. A blue-chip stock like Microsoft is liquid because it is actively traded so its share price won't be dramatically affected by a few buy or sell orders. Money-market funds and checking accounts provide instant liquidity because you can write a check on the assets.

**load** A sales charge for buying or selling a mutual fund. For initial, or front-end, loads, this figure is expressed as a percentage of the initial investment and is incurred upon purchase of fund shares. For back-end loads, the amount charged is based on the lesser of the initial or final value of the shares sold.

**load fund** A mutual fund that charges a sales commission, as opposed to a no-load fund, which doesn't levy a fee when you buy or sell. To compensate brokers, load funds usually charge either a front-end sales commission when you buy the fund or a back-end sales commission when you sell. In addition, many broker-sold funds charge an annual 12b-1 fee, which is also used to compensate brokers. The 12b-1 fee is included in the fund's expense ratio. The supposed advantage of a load fund is that the broker/salesperson will provide you with financial advice, telling you when it is appropriate to sell the fund or buy more shares.

**loan-participation fund** A fund that invests in loans that are made by banks to companies with low credit ratings. The loans are not investment grade, but they are secured by assets, which means they are the first to be paid off in the case of a bankruptcy. (And that makes them higher-quality than junk bonds.) Because of the nature of their portfolio, the funds are able to offer higher yields than investment-grade and government-bond funds. Also, since the rates on these loans are reset every 30, 60, or 90 days to reflect changes in current interest rates, these funds have little interest-rate risk. That makes them fairly stable investment vehicles. Also called floating-rate funds.

**long** The opposite of short selling, establishing a long position means to own a security with the expectation that it will appreciate. One would say, "I'm long bank stocks but short semiconductor companies."

**long-term bonds** Treasury bonds with maturities of more than 10 years; corporate bonds with maturities of more than 15 years. Long-term bonds pay higher yields but have greater inflation and credit risk.

**long-term-care insurance** Insurance that provides some coverage for nursing-home stays and home health care for people with disabling conditions.

**Major Market Index** This stock index encompasses 20 blue-chip stocks, including 17 that are also in the Dow Jones Industrial Average. Options and futures are based on this index.

**managed care** Medical plans in which access to health care services is managed to hold down unnecessary costs. The most common form of managed care is the health maintenance organization, or HMO, which restricts patients to the HMO's own stable of doctors. Premiums are lower than for traditional fee-for-service health care plans, and the charge for each doctor visit is modest. Some newer arrangements are the point-of-service and preferred-provider plans, which may charge the low per-visit price of an HMO for treatment by doctors in the plan's network and allow out-of-network treatment with reimbursement at about 70 percent of eligible costs. *See* **traditional health care**.

**margin** To buy on margin means to borrow money from a broker to buy securities. The margin is the amount you must deposit with the broker in order to borrow. The minimum is 50 percent of the purchase, or short sale price, in cash. So if you want to buy $10,000 in stock on margin, you have to put up at least $5,000 to make the purchase. Buying on margin poses the threat of not only losing your own money but the money you borrowed as well.

**margin account** A brokerage account allowing customers to buy securities with money borrowed from the brokerage.

**margin call** A demand from a broker for additional cash or securities to bring a margin account back within minimum maintenance limits. The National Association of Securities Dealers (NASD) requires that a margin be maintained equal to 25 percent of the market value of securities in established margin accounts. Brokerage firm requirements are typically a more conservative 30 percent. If an investor fails to meet the minimum, securities in the account may be liquidated.

**market capitalization** The total market value of a company or stock. Market capitalization is calculated by multiplying the number of outstanding shares by their current market price. Investors generally divide the U.S. market into three basic market caps: large-cap, mid-cap and small-cap. Large-cap stocks typically have market capitalizations upwards of $5 billion. Because they are more liquid, large caps tend to be less volatile than small caps, which have capitalizations less than $1 billion.

**market maker** In the over-the-counter market, a trader responsible for maintaining an orderly market in an individual stock by standing ready to buy or sell shares. The market maker's job is to maintain a firm bid and ask price for the assigned security. If a broker wants to buy a stock but there are no offers to sell it, the market maker fills the order himself by selling shares from his own account. And vice versa—if a broker wants to sell but no one wants to buy, the market maker buys the shares. On a stock exchange like AMEX or NYSE, a market maker is known as a specialist.

**market order**   An order to execute a buy or sell order for a security at whatever price is available when the order reaches the exchange floor. Unlike a limit order, a market order gives you no control over the price at which you buy the security. But it does guarantee you will get the security if it's available.

**market timing**   Shifting money in and out of investment markets in an effort to take advantage of rising prices and avoid being stung by downturns. For example, investors in mutual funds will shift from an equity fund to a money-market fund if the stock market outlook turns ugly. Unfortunately, few, if any, investors manage to be consistently successful in timing markets.

**maturity date**   When a bond expires and the principal must be paid back in full. The later the bond's maturity date, the greater the risk of it defaulting or being negatively impacted by a rise in inflation or interest rates.

**Medicaid**   The government program that provides health-care assistance to the poor.

**Medicare**   A U.S. government program that provides medical expense coverage to people aged 65 and older.

Medicare is comprised of two major programs: hospital insurance (Part A) and supplementary medical insurance (Part B). The Medicare coverage for Part A has no premium and will pay 100 percent of your hospital costs for the first 60 days after you have paid a deductible of about $800. Medicare Part B pays up to 80 percent of your doctor's bills for a monthly premium of about $50.

**Medicare HMO**   An HMO that has contracted with the federal government under the Medicare+ Choice program to provide health benefits to people eligible for Medicare who choose to enroll in an HMO instead of receiving their benefits and care through the traditional fee-for-service Medicare program.

**Medicare+Choice**   A program initiated in 1997 through the Balanced Budget Act, which allows Medicare beneficiaries to sign up with an HMO instead of the traditional fee-for-service Medicare program, that in turn provides the same benefits as Medicare as well as a few extra benefits, without, in most cases, the premium.

**Medigap insurance**   Health care insurance that pays certain costs not covered by Medicare and that meets minimum standards set by state and federal law.

**merger**   The formation of one company from two or more previously existing companies through pooling of common stock, cash payment, or a combination of both. Mergers where common stock is exchanged for common stock are nontaxable and are called tax-free mergers.

**micro-cap fund**   Fund that invests primarily in equity securities issued by companies with very small market capitalizations; they typically have median market caps of approximately $250 million or less. With stocks this small, the volatility is always extremely high, but the growth potential is exceptional.

**mid-cap stock**   Shares of medium-sized publicly traded corporations, typically with a total market capital-ization between $1 billion and $5 billion. (Also called mid-cap stocks or mid-caps.) Mid-caps are established companies that haven't quite become household names yet. They make excellent diversifiers, hav-ing both the growth characteristics of small-cap stocks and the stability of larger companies. One of the most watched mid-cap indexes is the S&P MidCap 400, which has an average market capitalization of $2.1 billion.

**monetary policy**   The regulation of the money supply and interest rates by a central bank, such as the U.S. Federal Reserve, in order to control inflation and stabilize currency. If the economy is heating up, the Fed can withdraw money from the banking system, raise the reserve requirement, or raise the discount rate to make it cool down. If growth is slowing, the Fed can reverse the process—increase the money supply, lower the reserve requirement, and decrease the discount rate.

**money-market account**   A federally insured account available at many banks, credit unions, and savings and loan associations. Money-market accounts are liquid (because you can usually write three checks against the account per month) and are very stable (because they invest only in short-term debt instruments with maturities of less than a year). Accounts are also insured by the Federal Deposit Insurance Corporation (FDIC), unlike money-market funds. But since the interest rates on money-market accounts are so low, if you're not care-ful the value of your investment can be eroded by inflation.

**money-market fund**   A type of mutual fund that invests in stable, short-term securities. Money-market funds are easily convertible into cash and usually maintain an unchanged value of $1 a share, but aren't insured by the federal government. There are various types of money-market funds based on the types of securities they buy, but the most important distinction is whether your dividends are taxable or tax-free.

**MSCI EAFE index**   A widely accepted benchmark of foreign stocks (EAFE refers to Europe, Australasia, and the Far East). The index, which is compiled by Morgan Stanley Capital International, is an aggregate of 21 individual country indexes that collec-tively represent many of the major markets of the world. Most international mutual funds measure their performance against this index. It is market-capitalization weighted.

**municipal bond**   Bond issued by local government authorities, including states, cities, and their agencies.

**municipal bond fund**   Mutual fund that invests in municipal bonds. There are two main types of municipal bond funds: national tax-free funds and state tax-free funds. National tax-free funds invest in municipalities across the United States and are exempt from federal income taxes. State tax-free funds invest in specific states and are exempt from federal and state taxes if you live in the state of issue. National funds offer more diversification and less risk but also fewer tax benefits.

**mutual fund**   An investment company that pools the money of many individual investors to purchase stocks, bonds, or other financial instruments. Professional management and diversification are the two primary benefits of mutual fund investing. A management fee is charged for these services, typically 1 percent or 2 percent a year. Funds also levy other fees and charge a sales commission (or load) if purchased from a financial adviser. Funds are either open-end or closed-end. An open-end fund will issue new shares when investors put in money and redeem shares when investors withdraw money. The price of a share is determined by dividing the total net assets of the fund by the number of shares outstanding. Closed-end funds issue a fixed number of shares in an initial public offering, trading thereafter in the open market. Open-end funds are the most common type of mutual fund.

**Nasdaq**   An electronic stock market where brokers get price quotes through a computer network and trade via telephone or computer network. The index that covers all the stocks that trade on this market is called the Nasdaq Composite index. Since there is no centralized exchange, Nasdaq is sometimes referred to as an over-the-counter market, or a negotiated marketplace. Many of the stocks traded through Nasdaq are in the technology sector.

**Nasdaq Composite index**   An index that covers the price movements of all stocks traded on the Nasdaq Stock Market.

**Nasdaq National Market**   A subdivision of the Nasdaq Stock Market that contains the largest and most actively traded stocks on Nasdaq. Companies must meet more stringent standards to be included in this section than they do to be included in the other major subdivision, the Nasdaq SmallCap Market.

**National Association of Securities Dealers (NASD)**   A self-regulating securities industry organization responsible for the regulation of the Nasdaq Stock market and other over-the-counter markets. NASD members include almost all investment banking houses and firms dealing in the over-the-counter market. The organization sets guidelines for ethics and standardized industry practices, and has a disciplinary structure for looking into allegations of rules violations.

**net assets**   The total assets (net of liabilities) held in a fund. Pay close attention to this statistic when investing in small-cap or aggressive equity funds. Because of the illiquidity and volatility of the companies they buy, such funds need to be able to move quickly in and out of positions. Having more than $1 billion in assets can be a real detriment to their performance.

**net asset value (NAV)** Also known as price per share, NAV is the value of a fund's assets divided by the number of its outstanding shares, and is calculated daily at the close of the markets. Open-end funds always trade at NAV, but closed-end funds often trade at a premium or discount to their asset values.

**net income** Also known as the bottom line, this is the profit a company realizes after all costs, expenses, and taxes have been paid. It is calculated by subtracting business, depreciation, interest, and tax costs from revenues. Investors often pay too much attention to net income, the calculation of which can be easily manipulated by accountants. A better measure of corporate growth, some analysts say, is cash flow. Net income is also called earnings or profit.

**net margin** A company's profitability after all costs, expenses, and taxes have been paid. The net margin is calculated by dividing net earnings by revenue and then multiplying by 100. The result is expressed as a percentage. Net margin is used to measure operating efficiency at a company. It is the one profit margin investors watch most closely because it takes into account all

expenses of running the company. But operating margin may paint a truer picture of a company's profitability.

**net worth** The amount by which total assets exceed total liabilities. Also known as shareholders' equity or book value, net worth is what would be left over for shareholders if the company were sold and its debt retired. It takes into account all money invested in the company since its founding, as well as retained earnings.

**New York Stock Exchange (NYSE)** The oldest and largest stock exchange in the United States, the New York Stock Exchange is located on Wall Street in New York City. The total market value of the roughly 2,700 companies whose shares are listed on the NYSE is about $10 trillion. It was founded in 1792. Also called the Big Board.

**Nikkei** A price-weighted index of 225 large-capitalization stocks on the Tokyo Stock Exchange. This is the Japanese equivalent of the Dow Jones Industrial Average. In fact, it was called the Nikkei Dow Jones Stock Average until 1985. Like the Dow, it is composed of representative blue chips and moves on price, not market capitalization.

**no-load mutual fund** A mutual fund that sells its shares without a sales charge or commission. Investors buy shares of no-load funds directly from the fund companies or brokerages. Buying a no-load fund is a good way to cut costs. The listing of the price of a no-load fund in the newspaper is accompanied with the designation NL.

**note**    A bond with a maturity greater than one year and less than 10 years.

**NYSE Composite index**    An index that covers the price movements of all stocks listed on the New York Stock Exchange (NYSE). It is market-capitalization weighted.

**OASDI**    Federal Old-Age, Survivors, and Disability Insurance, more popularly referred to as Social Security, was enacted in 1935 and is designed to replace a portion of earned income lost as a result of retirement, disability, or death. Monthly benefits are paid as a matter of earned right (based on income you earned in your lifetime) to workers who gain insured status and to their eligible spouses, children, and survivors.

**odd lot**    Purchase or sale of securities in any amount less than 100 shares. An investor buying or selling an odd lot often pays a higher commission rate than someone making a round lot trade. This odd-lot differential varies between brokers.

**open-end mutual fund**    A type of fund that issues as many shares as investors demand. This contrasts with a closed-end fund, which has a fixed number of shares that trade over the counter or on a stock exchange. The share price of an open-end fund is determined by dividing the total net assets of the fund by the number of shares outstanding. This figure is called the fund's net asset value (NAV). The net asset value of an open-end fund is calculated at the end of each trading day. Most mutual funds are open-end funds.

**operating income**    A measure of a company's earning power from ongoing operations, equal to earnings before deduction of interest payments and income taxes. Operating income is calculated by subtracting costs of sales and operating expenses from revenues. It is often used to gauge the financial performance of companies with high levels of debt and interest expenses. Also called operating profit or EBIT (earnings before interest and taxes).

**operating margin**    A company's profitability after all operating costs have been paid. Operating margin is calculated by dividing cash flow by revenue and then multiplying by 100. The result is expressed as a percentage. Operating margin shows you how profitable a company is before interest expenses on debt and depreciation costs have been deducted. Since accountants often manipulate depreciation and amortization costs on income statements, many analysts feel operating margin paints a truer picture of a company's profitability than does gross margin.

**option**    An agreement that gives an investor the right, but not the obligation, to buy or sell a stock, bond, or commodity at a specified price within a specific time period. A call option is an option to buy the security; a put option is an option to sell. Even if the option is not exercised before the expiration date, the money paid for the option is not returnable. Options are traded on several exchanges, including the Chicago Board Options Exchange, the American Stock Exchange, the

Philadelphia Stock Exchange, the Pacific Stock Exchange, and the New York Stock Exchange.

**over-the-counter (OTC) market**   A market in which securities transactions are conducted by dealers through a telephone and computer network connecting dealers in stocks and bonds.

**over-the-counter securities**   Securities that aren't listed and traded on an organized exchange. Over-the-counter securities are traded via a telephone and computerized network linking OTC security dealers. The National Association of Securities Dealers (NASD) oversees over-the-counter transactions and regulations. Nasdaq is the best-known market for trading OTC securities.

**par**   A bond that is trading at par is selling for the same amount as its face value (par value).

**par value**   The nominal dollar amount assigned to a bond by its issuer. Par value represents the amount of principal you are owed at a bond's maturity. The bond's actual market value may be higher or lower. When a bond's market price fluctuates, there is an impact on its yield. If the price drops below the bond's par value, its yield goes up. If the price rises above par value, the yield goes down. Also called face value.

**payment date**   The date when a stock's dividend or a bond's interest payment is scheduled to be paid.

**penny stocks**   Many penny stocks do indeed have a share price of less than

$1, but this informal designation now often includes stocks that are priced at $5 and below. While many legitimate companies have share prices that low, the term "penny stocks" usually refers to speculative companies with little or no real business that are heavily promoted by unscrupulous, hard-selling brokerage firms.

**pension**   Income received upon retirement. There are two basic types of benefits: a defined-benefit plan and a defined-contribution plan. A defined-benefit plan is a traditional pension plan usually paid for by your employer. Upon retirement, you receive a fixed monthly check based on your age, salary, and length of service. A defined-contribution plan puts the onus on you to contribute a percentage of your current income to the plan, whereupon your employer will match part or all of your contribution—the combined sum to be received upon your retirement. The typical defined-contribution plan is a 401(k) or 403(b) plan.

**pension maximization**   A controversial strategy, often espoused by life insurance agents, of using insurance to augment a company benefit plan. Under this arrangement, a retiree takes pension payments for his or her own life only and buys life insurance to provide for a surviving spouse. Also known as pension max.

**percent in top five holdings** Proportion of total assets in a mutual fund's largest five positions. Funds that have too much money invested in their top five holdings may not be properly diversified.

**personal financial specialist**
Financial planning designation given to qualifying accountants by the American Institute of CPAs, based in New York.

**pink sheets**    The printed quotations of the bid and ask prices of over-the-counter stocks, published by Pink Sheets, formerly called the National Quotation Bureau.

**portfolio**    A collection of securities held by an investor. Portfolios tend to consist of a variety of securities in order to minimize investment risk.

**portfolio insurance**    A method of hedging, or protecting, the value of a stock portfolio by selling stock-index futures contracts when the stock market declines. The practice was a major contributor to the October 1987 stock market crash.

**portfolio manager**    The manager of a mutual fund or an investment trust.

**precious metals**    Commodities such as gold, silver, and platinum that are used as investment instruments. Investors can buy physical metal in bullion or jewelry or can purchase precious metals futures and options contracts or mining stocks. A precious metals investment is often considered a hedge against inflation.

**preferred stock**    A stock that pays dividends at a specified rate and that has preference over common stock in the payment of dividends and the liquidation of assets. Preferred stock

enjoys prior claim to company assets over common stock in the case of a bankruptcy but does not usually carry voting rights.

**premium**    When a closed-end fund's market price is more than its underlying net asset value (NAV), it is said to be trading at a premium. So if a fund trading at a 10 percent premium owns a portfolio of stocks collectively worth $10 a share, the market price for the fund is actually $11 a share. Unlike open-end funds, closed-ends trade like stocks on an exchange, so a fund's price is determined by investor demand for its shares. An excess of demand can cause the fund's market price to be more than its underlying portfolio value—the source of the premium.

**premium bond**    Bond selling at a current market price that is more than its face value. Bonds sell at a premium when the coupon on the bond is higher than prevailing rates. For example, you might have to pay $1,090 for a bond with a 6 percent coupon if new issues yielding 5.5 percent are available for $1,000.

**price-to-book (P/B) ratio**    A company's stock price divided by its per-share book value. Examining the P/B of an industrial company with a lot of hard assets is a good way of telling if it's undervalued or overvalued.

**price-to-cash flow (P/C) ratio**    A ratio that shows how much investors are paying for a company's cash flow. There are various calculations because there are various definitions of cash flow. But the one used most often divides a company's price per share by its EBITDA per share. (EBITDA stands for earnings before interest expense, taxes, depreciation, and amortization.) Many stock analysts think cash flow paints a better picture of a company's true growth potential than net earnings do because company accountants can use crafty write-offs to alter earnings numbers. Cash flow is harder to manipulate.

**price-to-earnings-growth (PEG) ratio** Ratio calculated by dividing a stock's forward P/E by its projected three- to five-year annual earnings-per-share growth rate. It is used to find companies that are trading at a discount to their projected growth. A PEG ratio of less than 1 is considered a sign that a stock is a good value. Generally speaking, the higher the PEG, the pricier the stock.

**price-to-earnings (P/E) ratio** A ratio to evaluate a stock's worth. It is calculated by dividing the stock's price by an earnings-per-share figure. If calculated with the past year's earnings, it is called the trailing P/E. If calculated with an analyst's forecast for next year's earnings, it is called a forward P/E. The biggest weakness with either type of P/E is that companies sometimes "manage" their earnings with accounting wizardry to make them look better than they really are. That's why some analysts prefer to focus on the price-to-cash-flow measure instead.

**price-to-sales (P/S) ratio** The ratio of a stock's latest closing price divided by revenue per share. (Sales are the same thing as revenues.) Revenue per share is determined by dividing revenue for the past 12 months by the number of shares outstanding. This ratio is particularly useful for companies that have little or no earnings.

**principal** The face value or par value of a bond. It represents the amount of money you are owed when a bond reaches its maturity. So if you buy a 10-year Treasury note with a 5 percent coupon rate and a $1,000 face value, $1,000 is the principal owed to you in 10 years.

**private placement** The sale of stocks or other investments directly to an investor. The securities in a private placement don't have to be registered with the Securities and Exchange Commission.

**producer price index (PPI)** Index that measures inflation in wholesale goods. The PPI tracks the prices of food, metals, lumber, oil, and gas, as well as many other commodities, but does not measure the prices of services. It is reported monthly by the Bureau of Labor Statistics. Economists look at trends in the PPI as an accurate precursor to changes in the consumer price index (CPI) because upward or downward pressure on wholesale prices is usually passed through to the consumer over time. Bond prices are perhaps the most responsive to PPI data. This is because inflation undercuts the value of the future interest and principal payments that bonds yield. With the consumer price index coming only days after this release, the stock market's reaction is usually delayed until the CPI either confirms or refutes what the PPI trend is indicating.

**profit**   The earnings a company realizes after all costs, expenses, and taxes have been paid. It is calculated by subtracting business, depreciation, interest, and tax costs from revenues. Profit is the supreme measure of value as far as the market is concerned. Profit is also called earnings or net income.

**profit margin**   A measure of a company's profitability, cost structure, and efficiency, calculated by dividing earnings or cash flow by revenue. There are four basic types of profit margin: gross, operating, pretax, and net. Net margin is the one investors pay the most attention to. It shows a company's profitability after all costs, expenses, and taxes have been paid. Margins are particularly helpful since they can be used both to compare profitability among many companies and to look for financial trouble at a single outfit.

**profit-taking**   Selling securities after a recent, often rapid price increase. This is often the action of short-term traders cashing in on gains from the rise. Profit-taking pushes down prices, but only temporarily; the term implies an upward market trend.

**pro forma results**   A projection of a financial statement that shows how the actual statement would look under certain conditions. For example, pro forma results are used to show the earnings that newly merged companies would have achieved had they been combined throughout the entire period.

**program trading**   Stock trades involving the purchase or sale of a basket including 15 or more stocks with a total market value of $1 million or more. Most program trades are executed on the New York Stock Exchange, using computerized trading systems. Index arbitrage is the most prominently reported type of program trading.

**prospectus**   A formal, written offer to sell securities that sets forth the plan for a proposed or existing business. The prospectus must be filed with the Securities and Exchange Commission and given to prospective buyers. A prospectus includes information on a company's finances, risks, products, services, and management. Prospectuses are also used by mutual funds to describe the fund objectives, risks, fees, and other essential information.

**proxy**   A proxy is the authorization or power of attorney, signed by a stockholder assigning the right to vote his or her shares to another party. A company's management mails proxy statements to registered stockholders prior to the annual shareholder meetings. The statement contains a brief explanation of proposed management-sponsored voting items, along with the opportunity to vote for or against each individual issue or transfer the right to vote to company management or another party.

**proxy fight**    A contest for control of a company in which one or more companies, groups, or individuals seek proxies from a company's shareholders to back a takeover attempt. The acquirer tries to persuade the shareholders of the target company that the present management of the firm should be ousted in favor of a slate of directors favorable to the acquirer. If the shareholders, through their proxy votes, agree, the acquiring company can gain control without paying a premium price for the firm.

**proxy statement**    Information that the Securities and Exchange Commission (SEC) requires must be provided to shareholders before they vote by proxy on company matters. The statement contains proposed members of the board of directors, inside directors' salaries, and any resolutions of minority stockholders or management.

**public company**    A company that sells shares of its stock to the public. Public companies are regulated by the Securities and Exchange Commission (SEC). Also called a publicly held company.

**put option**    An agreement that gives an investor the right, but not the obligation, to sell a stock, bond, commodity, or other instrument at a specified price within a specific time period.

**qualified education expenses**    In general, tuition and fees required for enrollment or attendance at an eligible educational institution. Student activ-ity fees and fees for course-related books, supplies, and equipment are included in qualified expenses only if the fees must be paid to the institution as a condition of enrollment or attendance.

**qualitative analysis**    Security analysis that uses subjective judgment in evaluating securities based on nonfinancial information such as management expertise, cyclicality of industry, strength of research and development, and labor relations. *Compare* **quantitative analysis.**

**quant**    Slang reference to an analyst who uses quantitative analysis techniques.

**quantitative analysis**    A research technique that deals with measurable values as distinguished from such qualitative factors as the character of management or labor relations. Quantitative analysis uses financial information derived from company balance sheets and income statements to make investment decisions. Examples of quantitative analysis include a review of company financial ratios, the cost of capital, asset valuation, and sales and earnings trends. Although quantitative and qualitative analysis are distinct, they must be used together to arrive at sound financial judgments.

**quote or quotation**    The highest bid price and lowest ask price currently available for a security in a given market. The difference between the bid and ask is called the price spread. *See* **spread.**

**real estate investment trust (REIT)**
A publicly traded company that manages a portfolio of real estate to earn profits for shareholders. Patterned after mutual funds, REITs hold a diverse portfolio of real estate such as apartment buildings, offices, industrial warehouses, shopping centers, hotels, and nursing homes. Shareholders receive income in the form of dividends from the rents generated by the property. To avoid taxation at the corporate level, 75 percent or more of a REIT's income must come from real property and 90 percent of its taxable net income must be distributed to shareholders annually. Because REITs must distribute most of their earnings, REITs pay high yields of 5 percent to 10 percent or more.

**recession**　A downturn in economic activity, broadly defined by many economists as at least two consecutive quarters of decline in a nation's gross domestic product (GDP).

**record date**　The date on which a shareholder must own a company's stock to be entitled to receive a dividend. For example, a company's board of directors might declare a dividend on October 1, payable on November 1 to stockholders of record on October 15. Investors who buy after October 15 wouldn't be entitled to the dividend. After the date of record, the stock is said to be ex-dividend.

**recovery**　In a business cycle, the period after a downturn or recession when economic activity picks up and the gross domestic product (GDP) increases.

**redemption fee**　A fee charged when money is withdrawn from a mutual fund. Unlike a back-end load, this fee doesn't go back into the pockets of the fund company, but rather into the fund itself, and doesn't represent a net cost to shareholders. Also, redemption fees typically operate only in short, specific time frames, commonly 30, 180, or 365 days. Charges aren't imposed after the stated time has passed. These fees are usually imposed to discourage market timers, whose quick movements into and out of funds can be disruptive. The typical redemption fee is 1 percent or 2 percent of withdrawn assets.

**regional exchange**　Securities exchanges located outside of New York City. They include the Boston, Philadelphia, Chicago, Cincinnati, and Pacific stock exchanges. Stocks listed on the New York Stock Exchange or the American Stock Exchange also may trade on regional exchanges. These exchanges usually list only securities traded within their regions.

**return on assets (ROA)**　The rate of investment return a company earns on its assets. An indicator of profitability, ROA is determined by dividing net income from the past 12 months by total assets and then multiplying by 100. Within a specific industry, ROA can be used to compare how efficient a company is relative to its competitors. Unlike return on equity, ROA ignores a company's liabilities.

**return on equity (ROE)**　The rate of investment return a company earns on shareholders' equity. An indicator of profitability, ROE is determined by dividing net income from the past 12 months by net worth (or book value). This statistic shows how effectively a company is using its investors' money. Within a specific industry, it can be used to compare how efficient a company is relative to its competitors. *Compare* **return on assets**.

**return on investment (ROI)** A measure of how much the company earns on the money the company itself has invested. It is calculated by dividing the company's net income by its net assets.

**revenue** The earnings of a company before any costs or expenses are deducted. Revenue includes all net sales of the company plus any other revenue associated with the main operations of the business (or those labeled as operating revenues). It does not include dividends, interest income, or nonoperating income. Also called sales.

**revenue bond** A municipal bond issued to finance public works such as bridges, tunnels, or sewer systems and supported directly by the revenues of the project. For instance, if a municipal revenue bond is issued to build a bridge, the tolls collected from motorists using the bridge are committed for paying off the bond. Holders of these bonds have no claims on the issuer's other resources.

**rights offering** Offering of additional shares, usually at a discount, to existing shareholders who have rights to those shares. The shares can be actively traded.

**risk** Risk is the financial uncertainty that the actual return on an investment will be different from the expected return. Factors of risk that can affect an investment include inflation or deflation, currency exchange rates, liquidity, default by borrower, and interest rate fluctuation.

**Roth IRA** A type of IRA established in the Taxpayer Relief Act of 1997 that allows taxpayers, subject to certain income limits, to save for retirement while allowing the savings to grow tax-free. Taxes are paid on contributions, but withdrawals, subject to certain rules, aren't taxed at all. A single person can contribute up to $3,000 and a married couple up to $6,000 annually to this type of individual retirement account in 2002.

**R-squared** A measure of a fund's correlation to the market calculated by comparing monthly returns over the past three years to those of a benchmark. The benchmark for equity funds is the S&P 500. For fixed-income funds, it is the T-bill. The R-squared number ranges from 0 to 100. A score of 100 means a perfect correlation with the benchmark. A score of 85 means an 85 percent correlation. Generally, a higher R-squared will indicate a more useful beta figure. For instance, if a fund is earning a return near its most closely related index (indicated by an R-squared near 100), yet has a beta below 1, it is probably offering higher risk-adjusted returns than the benchmark. If the R-squared is lower, then the beta is less relevant to the fund's performance.

**Russell 2000 index**    Index that is the best-known benchmark of small-cap stocks. It is market-capitalization weighted and measures the 2,000 smallest companies in the U.S. market. These stocks represent only about 8 percent of the total market's capitalization (as represented by the broader Russell 3000 index). As of the latest reconstitution, the average market capitalization of the Russell 2000 was approximately $530 million. The largest company in the index had an approximate market capitalization of $1.4 billion. There are a number of index funds that track the Russell 2000.

**sales**    Money a company receives from the goods and services it sells. In some cases, the amount includes receipts from rents and royalties. Also called revenue.

**sales charge**    Also referred to as a load. This is the fee investors must pay to buy shares in a mutual fund. There are front-end loads that are charged upon the initial investment and back-end loads (deferred sales charges) that are assessed upon withdrawal.

**savings bond**    Similar to zero-coupon bonds, savings bonds are sold at a discount to their face value, which is fully paid at maturity. They are exempt from state and local taxes and you can defer paying federal taxes until maturity. They can be purchased for as little as $50 or up to $10,000. The cost and the maturity depend on the series (E, EE, and HH) and the interest rate being paid. They can be bought or redeemed (after six months) at your local bank, the Federal Reserve, or the Bureau of the Public Debt. Call 304-480-6112 or go to www.savingsbond.gov to get more information and current rates.

**secondary market**    The market where previously issued securities are traded. Most trading is done in the secondary market. The New York Stock Exchange, AMEX, Nasdaq, the bond markets, and so on, are secondary markets.

**secondary offering**    The sale of already issued stock. It is usually a large block of stock that is owned by an institution. As with a primary offering (or IPO), secondary distributions are usually handled by an investment banker who purchases the shares from the seller at an agreed-upon price, then resells them at a higher public offering price, making a profit off the spread.

**Section 529**    The section of the IRS tax code that allows families and individuals to prepare for the future costs of a college education. There are two kinds of 529 plans: college savings plans and prepaid tuition plans. Plan participants contribute to an account or purchase tuition credits or certificates on behalf of a beneficiary—a parent for a child or grandparent for grandchild, for example. The plans are administered through the states, so some states offer tax advantages, like deductions on state tax returns for contributions or state tax exemption on withdrawals. All 50 states have passed legislation authorizing 529 plans, and most states have one in operation.

**Section 529 college savings plan**
State programs that offer families and individuals (in most cases you do not have to be a resident to participate) a way to save for college in federal-tax-free accounts managed by professionals. (Withdrawals from the accounts are exempt from any federal tax as long as the money pays for qualified college costs.) Any withdrawals made that do not cover qualified education expenses will be subject to income tax and a penalty tax of 10 percent. In addition, some states offer deductions from state income tax returns for annual contributions and/or state income-tax exemption for qualified education withdrawals. *See* **qualified education expenses.**

**Section 529 prepaid tuition plans**
State programs that offer residents a way to lock in future tuition rates at today's prices at a specified list of schools (many times the public colleges and universities located in the state sponsoring the program). Contributions made now purchase a certain amount of tuition at a later date. For this reason, Section 529 prepaid programs are a very different type of vehicle than a 529 savings plan. Prepaids essentially offer a hedge against tuition inflation, and savings programs seek to offer a market return. Some states will allow you to transfer the value of your prepaid contract to private and out-of-state schools. However, there may be penalties if the beneficiary in a prepaid program does not attend one of the colleges under the plan.

**sector fund**    Mutual fund that invests in a single-industry sector, such as biotechnology, gold, or regional banks. Sector funds tend to generate erratic performance, and they often dominate both the top and bottom of the annual mutual fund performance charts.

**secular**    Long-term as opposed to seasonal or cyclical.

**Securities and Exchange Commission (SEC)**    The federal agency that enforces securities laws and sets standards for disclosure about publicly traded securities, including mutual funds. It was created in 1934 and consists of five commissioners appointed by the U.S. president and confirmed by the Senate to staggered five-year terms. To ensure its independence, no more than three members of the commission may be of the same political party.

**Securities Investor Protection Corporation (SIPC)**    The nonprofit corporation that insures the securities and cash in the customer accounts of brokerage firms up to $500,000 in the event a firm fails. All brokers and dealers registered with the Securities and Exchange Commission are required to be members.

**security**    Generally, a stock or a bond. Specifically, a piece of paper that indicates the holder owns a share or shares of a company (stock) or has loaned money to a company or government organization (bond).

**sell-off**    A period of intensified selling in a market that pushes stock or bond prices sharply lower.

**senior security**   A security with claims on income and assets that ranks higher than certain other securities. Debt, including notes, bonds, and debentures, is senior to stock. In the event of bankruptcy, senior securities have first claim on corporate assets.

**share**   A unit of ownership in an equity or a mutual fund. This ownership is represented by a certificate, which names the share owner and the company or fund. The number of shares a company is authorized to issue is detailed in its corporate charter. Open-end mutual funds can issue unlimited shares.

**shareholders' equity**   The amount by which a company's total assets exceed total liabilities. Also known as net worth or book value, shareholders' equity is what would be left over for shareholders if the company were sold and its debt retired. It takes into account all money invested in the company since its founding, as well as retained earnings.

**short selling**   A trading strategy that anticipates a drop in a share's price. Stock or another financial instrument is borrowed from a broker and then sold, creating a short position. That position is reversed, or covered, when the stock is repurchased to repay the loan. If the stock price falls, the short seller will profit by replacing the borrowed shares at a lower cost.

**short-term bonds**   Treasury bills that mature in 90 days to one year. Or, corporate bonds that mature in one to five years. Because of their short maturities,

these bonds are particularly safe from default and interest-rate risk, but they also pay lower yields.

**short-term gain or loss**   For tax purposes, the profit or loss from selling capital assets or securities held 12 months or less. Short-term gains are taxed at your regular income-tax rate, which can be as high as 38.6 percent in 2002. It pays not to trade. At the moment, the maximum federal tax rate on long-term capital gains is only 20 percent.

**simplified employee pension (SEP)** A retirement plan for the self-employed that is also referred to as a SEP-IRA. A SEP plan allows you to shelter a lot more money than a traditional IRA and is cheaper and less complicated to administer than other retirement plans. The contributions are tax-deductible to the company, and grow tax-deferred until the proceeds are withdrawn.

**small-capitalization stocks**   Shares of relatively small publicly traded corporations, typically with a total market capitalization of less than $1 billion. (Also called small-cap stocks or small caps.) Small-cap stocks tend to grow faster than larger-capitalization companies, but they also tend to be more volatile. Because they have fewer shares outstanding, their price movement is necessarily more erratic. When good news hits the tape, investors clamoring to get in will drive the price up quickly. When bad news hits, the opposite is true. The Russell 2000 is the most widely known small-cap index.

**Social Security Act**    Enacted in 1935 to provide for the general welfare of individuals and families by establishing a wide range of programs. The best known, of course, are the insurance for retired and disabled workers and their survivors (Federal Old-Age, Survivors, and Disability Insurance, or OASDI), as well as hospital and medical insurance for aged, disabled, and low-income people (Medicare and Medicaid). *See* **Medicaid**; **Medicare**; and **OASDI**.

**Social Security Administration (SSA)** The SSA administers Social Security, the national program of contributory social insurance. Employees, employers, and the self-employed pay Federal Insurance Contributions Act (FICA) taxes, which are used to pay current beneficiaries. Money not used is deposited into the Social Security Trust to pay future beneficiaries.

**specialist**    A stock exchange member who is designated to maintain a fair and orderly market in a specific stock. The specialist's job is to prevent imbalances in supply and demand for the assigned security. If a broker wants to buy a stock but there are no offers to sell it, the specialist fills the order himself by selling shares from his own account. And vice versa—if a broker wants to sell but no one wants to buy, the specialist buys the shares. A specialist is also known as a market maker (in the over-the-counter market).

**spin-off**    A form of corporate divestiture that results in a subsidiary or division becoming an independent company. In a traditional spin-off, shares of the new company are distributed to the parent corporation's shareholders. Spin-offs can also be accomplished through a leveraged buyout by the subsidiary's or division's management.

**spread**    In stocks, the difference between the bid price and ask price. In bonds, the difference between the yields on securities of the same credit rating but different maturities or the difference between the yields on securities of the same maturity but of different ratings. The term also represents the difference between the public offering price of a new issue and the proceeds the issuer receives.

**stagflation**    A combination of high inflation and slow economic growth. A term coined in the 1970s, stagflation described the previously unprecedented combination of high unemployment (stagnation) with rising prices (inflation). The principal factor was the fourfold increase in oil prices imposed by OPEC in 1973, which raised prices throughout the economy while slowing economic growth. Traditional fiscal and monetary policies aimed at reducing unemployment only exacerbated the inflationary effects.

**standard deviation**    A measure of a fund's volatility derived by looking at its range of historical returns. The higher the standard deviation, the greater the potential for volatility. Say a fund has an average annual return of 12 percent and a standard deviation of 20. By adding and subtracting 20 from

12, you can figure what the fund's high and low returns have been in two-thirds of the time periods over the past three years. In this case, the high would have been +32 percent (12 + 20). By multiplying the standard deviation by 2 and doing the same calculations, you can figure the fund's high and low returns for 95 percent of its history.

**Standard & Poor's 500 index (S&P 500)** An index of 500 stocks chosen for their market size, liquidity, and industry group representation. Experts use the S&P 500 as a benchmark for overall market performance. Representing the largest U.S. companies in 11 diversified sectors of the market, it is a broader, more comprehensive index than the Dow Jones Industrial Average. It is also a capitalization-weighted benchmark, with each stock's weight in the index proportionate to its market value. So price fluctuations in big companies in the index count proportionately more than fluctuations in little ones. In contrast, the Dow is a price-weighted index, which weights price movements for all its stocks equally, regardless of their size.

**stock** An investment that represents part ownership of a company's assets and earnings. There are two different types of stock: common and preferred. Common stocks provide voting rights but no guarantee of dividend payments. Preferred stocks provide no voting rights but have a set, guaranteed dividend payment. Preferred stock also enjoys prior claim to company assets over common stock in the case of a bankruptcy. *Compare* **bond**.

**stock fund** A mutual fund that invests in stocks. Stock funds have different investment strategies—growth, blend, and value—and invest in companies of different market capitalizations—small-cap, mid-cap, and large-cap. There are also index funds that track specific stock benchmarks such as the S&P 500 and sector funds that invest in specific industries such as technology and health care. One of the key advantages of owning a stock fund is diversification and active portfolio management.

**stock-index future** A contract to buy or sell the cash value of a stock index by a specified date. Investors can speculate on general market performance, short selling an index with a futures contract; or they can buy a contract to hedge a long position against a decline in value. Among the most popular indexes traded are the New York Stock Exchange Composite index on the New York Futures Exchange (NYFE) and the S&P 500 index on the Chicago Mercantile Exchange (CME).

**stock-index option** A call or put option based on a stock market index. Index options allow investors to trade in a particular market or industry group without having to buy all the stocks individually. For instance, someone who thought technology stocks were going to fall could buy a put on a technology index instead of short selling a dozen tech companies.

**stock option**   An option in which the underlying security is the common stock of a corporation, giving the holder the right to buy or sell its stock at a specified price by a specific date. Also, it is a method of employee compensation that gives workers the right to buy the company's stock during a specified period of time at a stipulated exercise price. In recent years, offering top executives stock options as compensation has become increasingly popular.

**stock split**   A change in a company's number of shares outstanding that doesn't change a company's total market value or each shareholder's percentage stake in the company. Additional shares are issued to existing shareholders, at a rate expressed as a ratio. A 2-for-1 stock split, for instance, doubles the number of shares outstanding. So an investor holding 100 shares of a $60 stock would have 200 shares of a $30 stock following a 2-for-1 split, but the percentage of equity in the company remains the same. Typically, management will split a stock to make the shares more affordable to a greater number of investors.

**stop order**   An order to buy or sell a security when a definite price is reached, either above (on a buy) or below (on a sell) the price that prevailed when the order was given. This type of trade provides more investment control than a market order, which will buy or sell the security at any price. A stop order to buy, always at a higher price than the current market price, is usually designed to limit a loss on a short sale. A stop order to sell, always at a lower price than the current market price, is usually designed to protect a profit, or to limit a loss on a security already purchased at a higher price.

**strike price**   A specified price at which an investor can buy or sell an option's underlying security. For example, a call option may allow the buyer to purchase 100 shares of a company in the next three months at a strike price of $50 a share. If the stock is currently trading at $75 a share and that's as high as you think it will go, you can exercise the call option at $50 and earn $25 a share less commissions. Also called exercise price.

**STRIPS**   A bond, usually issued by the U.S. Treasury, whose two components, interest and repayment of principal, are separated and sold individually as zero-coupon bonds. STRIPS generally have a slightly higher return than regular Treasury bonds, but they don't pay regular interest payments. Instead the buyer receives the return by the gradual appreciation of the security, which is redeemed at face value on a specified maturity date. STRIPS is an acronym for separate trading of registered interest and principal of securities.

**subsidiary**   A company of which more than 50 percent of its voting shares are owned by another corporation, called the parent company.

**technical analysis**   The study of all factors related to the supply and demand of stocks. Unlike fundamental analysis, technical analysis doesn't look at underlying earnings potential of a company when evaluating a stock. Rather, the technical analyst uses charts and computer programs to study the stock's trading volume and price movements in hopes of identifying a trend. Technical analysts don't care about a business's intrinsic value, only the movements of its stock. Most technical analysis is used for short-term investing.

**tender offer** A formal offer by a company to buy a certain amount of its own securities or another company's securities at a stated price within a specified time limit. The offer price is usually at a premium above the current market price. When the offer is for another company's shares, it usually involves a takeover attempt. The Securities and Exchange Commission requires any corporate suitor that acquires more than 5 percent of a company to disclose its position.

**10-year Treasury note** Debt obligation of the U.S. Treasury that has a maturity of 10 years. The 10-year Treasury note replaced the 30-year Treasury bond as the benchmark bond in determining interest rate trends. As a group, Treasurys are regarded as the safest bond investments, because they are backed by the "full faith and credit" of the U.S. government.

**30-year Treasury bond** Debt obligation of the U.S. Treasury that has a maturity of 30 years. Before being replaced as a bellwether by the 10-year Treasury note, the 30-year Treasury bond was considered the benchmark

bond in determining interest rate trends. (It was also known as the long bond.) It typically has a higher interest rate than other Treasurys, but more inflation and credit risk. But as a group, Treasurys are regarded as the safest bond investments, because they are backed by the "full faith and credit" of the U.S. government. Treasury bonds pay interest semiannually. The 30-year bond is no longer issued.

**ticker symbol** Letters that identify a security for trading purposes. Trades are reported on the consolidated tape and on quote machines by the company's symbol. For example, MSFT is Microsoft's ticker. Also called a stock symbol.

**total return** The full amount an investment earns over a specific period of time. When dealing with mutual funds or securities, total return takes into consideration three factors: changes in the NAV or price; the accumulation/reinvestment of dividends; the compounding factor over time. The return is presented as a percentage and is usually associated with a specific time period such as six months, one year, or five years. Total return can be cumulative for the specific period or annualized. If it is cumulative, it describes how much your investment grew in total for the entire period. If it is annualized, it describes the average annual return over the period of years described.

**traders** An individual who buys and sells securities for his or her own account as a dealer or principal, not as an intermediary (i.e., a broker). A secondary meaning is a short-term investor who buys or sells frequently in anticipation of a quick profit.

**traditional health care**    Also known as traditional fee-for-service health care. It is most identified, relative to managed care, with freedom of choice for patients and physicians. Patients can choose whatever doctor they want to see, and doctors can choose to order whatever service they feel is necessary. After medical services are rendered, the health plan is billed, and the patient must pay the difference between what the doctor charges and what the health plan pays.

**Treasury bills (T-bills)**    Debt obligations of the U.S. Treasury that have maturities of one year or less. Maturities for T-bills are usually 91 days, 182 days, or 52 weeks. Unlike Treasury bonds and notes, which pay interest semiannually, Treasury bills are issued at a discount from their face value. Interest income from a Treasury bill is the difference between the purchase price and the Treasury bill's face value. Bills are issued in denominations of $1000.

**Treasury bonds (T-bonds)**    Debt obligations of the U.S. Treasury that have maturities of more than 10 years. Treasury bonds pay interest semiannually and can be purchased in minimum denominations of $1,000 or multiples thereof. For many years the 30-year Treasury bond was considered the benchmark bond in determining trends in interest rates. (It was replaced by the 10-year Treasury note.) It typically has a higher interest rate than

other Treasurys, but more inflation and credit risk.

**Treasury notes (T-notes)**    Debt obligations of the U.S. Treasury that have maturities of more than one year to 10 years. Treasury notes pay interest semiannually and can be purchased in minimum denominations of $1,000 or multiples thereof. Treasury note yields typically are lower than Treasury bonds, which have longer maturities, but notes typically are about half as volatile as long bonds. The 10-year note now is considered the benchmark for determining interest rates.

**Treasurys**    Debt securities issued by the U.S. Department of the Treasury. Because principal and interest are backed by the "full faith and credit" of the U.S. government, Treasurys are viewed as having no credit risk. They are issued as bills, which have maturities of one year or less; notes, which have maturities of 2 to 10 years; and bonds, which have maturities of 10 years. Because Treasury issues have low liquidity risk and are considered to have no credit risk, required yields are typically lower than those of all other debt issues at any given maturity. Many other bonds, including corporate, municipal, and mortgage-backed bonds, are evaluated on a spread basis to Treasurys.

**triple witching hour**    Slang for the quarterly expiration of stock-index futures, stock-index options, and options on individual stocks. Trading associated with the expirations inflates stock market volume and can cause volatility in prices. Occurs on the third Friday of March, June, September, and December.

**turnover ratio** A measure of a fund's trading history that is expressed as a percentage. A fund with a 100 percent turnover generally changes the composition of its entire portfolio each year. A low turnover figure (20 percent to 30 percent) would indicate a buy-and-hold strategy. High turnover (more than 100 percent) would indicate an investment strategy involving considerable buying and selling of securities. Funds with higher turnover incur greater brokerage fees for effecting the trades. They also tend to distribute more capital gains than low-turnover funds, because high-turnover funds are constantly realizing the gains. A change in a fund's general turnover pattern can indicate changing market conditions, a new management style, or a modification of the fund's investment objective.

**12b-1 fees** These are fees the fund charges for marketing and distribution expenses. They are included in the expense ratio, but often are talked about separately. These fees are charged in addition to a front- or back-end load, and you'll find that many no-load funds charge them, too. If a 12b-1 fee puts a fund's expense ratio above the average for that class of fund, think twice before buying.

**underwriter** An investment banker who purchases shares of a company that is going public, then resells them to investors for a higher price. When an underwriter brings shares of a new company to market it is called an initial public offering (IPO). Investment banks can also underwrite secondary offerings of existing public companies.

**unemployment rate** The percentage of people in the workforce who aren't working and are looking for jobs. The numbers are compiled monthly by the Department of Labor and are adjusted for seasonal variations. The unemployment report is one of the most closely watched of all government reports, because it gives the clearest indication of the direction of the economy. A rising unemployment rate will be seen by analysts and the Federal Reserve as a sign of a weakening economy, which might call for an easing of monetary policy by the Fed. Conversely, a decline in the unemployment rate shows that the economy is growing, which may spark fears of higher inflation on the part of the Fed, which may raise interest rates as a result. When interest rates rise, the stock and bond markets tend to take a dive.

**Uniform Gifts to Minors Act (UGMA) and Uniform Transfers to Minors Act (UTMA)** Accounts governed by these acts allow a minor child to own property. The account is managed by a custodian until the child reaches the age of maturity. State law determines both the type of account and the age when the child gains control of the assets.

**value funds** These funds like to invest in companies that the market has overlooked. Companies favored by value funds may have an undistinguished track record because they are cyclical companies in industries such as steel or auto manufacturing, which are tied to the ups and downs of the business cycle. Value funds try to buy such stocks when they are near the bottom of a down cycle. The big risk is that the "undiscovered gems" they try to spot sometimes remain undiscovered. Still, because these fund managers tend to buy stocks and hold them until they turn around, expenses and turnover are low. That makes value funds suitable for conservative, tax-averse investors.

**value investing**   Value investors are the stock market's bargain hunters. They often lean toward beaten-down companies whose shares appear cheap when compared to current earnings or corporate assets. Value investors typically buy stocks with high dividend yields, or ones that trade at a low price-to-earnings (P/E) ratio or low price-to-book (P/B) ratio. The value investment style often is contrasted with the growth style. The two styles tend to take turns being popular on Wall Street. One year growth stocks will be all the rage; the next year value stocks may dominate.

**volatility**   The characteristic of a security or market to fall or rise sharply in price in a short-term period. A measure of the relative volatility of a security or mutual fund compared to the overall market is beta. A stock may be volatile because the outlook for the company is particularly uncertain; because there are only a few shares outstanding (i.e., it's illiquid); or for various other reasons. While beta can apply to both stocks and funds, standard deviation is more widely used to measure the volatility of mutual funds. Standard deviation examines a fund's range of historical returns, thus determining a portfolio's potential to swing between high and low returns.

**volume**   Number of shares traded in a company or an entire market during a given period. Days with unusually high volume typically correspond with the announcement of company news, either positive or negative. In the absence of news, high volume can indicate institutional (or professional) buying and selling. Technical analysis places a great emphasis on the amount of volume that occurs in the trading of a security. A sharp rise in volume is believed to signify future sharp rises or falls in price because it reflects increased investor interest in a security or a market.

**warrant**   A security entitling the holder to buy a proportionate amount of stock at some specified future date at a specified price, usually one higher than the current market price. Warrants are issued by corporations and often used as sweeteners bundled with bonds or preferred stock to enhance their marketability. They are like call options, but with much longer time spans that can stretch into years. In addition, warrants are offered by corporations, whereas exchange-traded options are not.

**Wilshire 5000 stock index**   An index of approximately 6,500 U.S.-based equities traded on the New York Stock

Exchange, American Stock Exchange, and Nasdaq. The Wilshire 5000 is the best measure of the entire U.S. stock market. It is market-capitalization weighted. *Compare* **Dow Jones Industrial Average; Standard & Poor's 500 index (S&P 500).**

**window dressing**   Trading activity near the end of a quarter or fiscal year that is designed to improve the appearance of a portfolio to be presented to clients or shareholders. For example, a mutual fund manager may sell losing positions in the portfolio right before the semiannual report is released in order to display only positions that have gained in value.

**wrap account**   An investment plan that wraps together money management and brokerage services. Wrap plans are popular for their simplicity. For one all-inclusive annual fee, an investment firm provides the services of a professional money manager, who creates a portfolio of stocks and bonds (or mutual funds), and takes care of all the trading.

**yield**   The annual rate of return on an investment, as paid in dividends or interest. It is expressed as a percentage, generally obtained by dividing the current market price for a stock or bond into the annual dividend or interest payment. As the price of a stock or bond declines, its yield rises. So a stock selling for $20 a share with an annual dividend of $1 a share yields an investor 5 percent. But if the same stock falls to $10 a share, its $1 annual dividend represents a yield of 10 percent.

**yield curve**   A graph showing the yields for different bond maturities. It can be used not only to show where the best values in bonds are, but also as an economic indicator. A normal yield curve is upward sloping, with short-term rates lower than long-term rates. An inverted yield curve is downward sloping, with short-term rates higher than long-term rates. A steep upward-sloping yield curve indicates the bond market anticipates an economic expansion. An inverted yield curve anticipates an economic decline.

**yield spread**   The difference in the yield between various securities. Yield spreads are often used to compare bonds of different maturities or credit ratings. Bonds with lower credit ratings and longer maturities tend to have higher yields than those with good ratings and shorter maturities. In evaluating a lower-quality bond, you must decide whether the yield spread to better-rated issues is worth the extra risk of default.

**yield to call**   The yield on a bond assuming the bond is redeemed by the issuer at the first call date. A bond's call provision is detailed in its prospectus. Yield to call differs from yield to maturity in that yield to call uses a bond's call date as the final maturity date. The price at which an issuer can call a bond is the call price. The call price generally includes a call premium that is greater than the bond's face value. Conservative investors calculate both a bond's yield to call and its yield to maturity, selecting the lower of the two as a measure of potential return.

**yield to maturity**    Yield to maturity is similar to current yield on a bond, but it also takes into account any gain or loss of principal at maturity. For example, if a $1,000 par bond was bought at a discount of $900, at maturity there would be a $100 gain. Likewise, if a $1,000 par bond is purchased for $1090, there will be a $90 loss in principal at maturity. Yield to maturity is a precise measure that allows you to compare bonds with different maturities that sell for more or less than par. The trouble is, it is a complex calculation that isn't printed in the newspaper, so you'll have to get it from your broker or bond dealer.

**zero-coupon bond**    A bond sold at a deep discount to its face value. It doesn't pay periodic interest payments to investors; instead, investors receive their return on investment at maturity. The return is equal to the difference between the bond's price at issuance and its face value.

**zeros**    Zero-coupon bonds (the Treasury's version of zeros are known as STRIPS) don't pay out interest annually. Rather, they are purchased at a discount, and at maturity all compound interest is paid and the bondholder collects the face value of the bond. However, since interest is technically earned and compounded semiannually, holders of zeros are obliged to pay taxes each year on the interest as it accrues. Many investors like to time the maturity of their zero-coupon bonds to coincide with certain anticipated expenses, such as college tuition.

# INDEX